BUXTON THE LIBERATOR

THE STATUE IN WESTMINSTER ABBEY.

BUXTON THE LIBERATOR

by

R. H. MOTTRAM

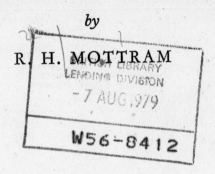
HUTCHINSON & CO. (Publishers) LTD.
LONDON : NEW YORK : MELBOURNE : SYDNEY

MADE AND PRINTED IN GREAT BRITAIN AT
THE FLEET STREET PRESS
EAST HARDING STREET, E.C.4

CONTENTS

LIST OF ILLUSTRATIONS

ACKNOWLEDGEMENTS

THE MAIN SOURCE OF KNOWLEDGE ABOUT THOMAS FOWELL BUXTON MUST ALWAYS be the *Memoirs* by his son, first published in 1848 and reprinted more than once, and still available in Dent's Everyman Library. There are two other main sources, necessary to qualify the picture. One is *Hansard*, for Buxton's parliamentary career, the other the intimate view of his early private life contained in the too little known *Gurneys of Earlham*, by Augustus Hare, from which Messrs. Allen & Unwin have kindly allowed me to quote. For sidelights on the liberation of the slaves, which was his life's work, I have consulted Barnes's *Duty of Empire ;* Macmillan's *Cape Colour Question ;* Mathieson's *The Slave of* 1807-1830 and biographies of Canning, Wilberforce and Dr. John Philip.

I have also to express my grateful thanks to the Anti-Slavery and Aborigines Protection Society of London and to many members of the Buxton and related families, for access to private papers, from which they have allowed me to quote hitherto unpublished information, and to reproduce illustrations. Those of the House of Commons of 1833 and the Anti-Slavery Convention were kindly supplied by the National Portrait Gallery. That of Earlham Hall is by courtesy of the Lord Mayor and Corporation of Norwich.

INTRODUCTION

SIR THOMAS FOWELL BUXTON, COUNTRY GENTLEMAN, SEVERAL TIMES MEMBER OF Parliament, finally a Baronet, above all prime mover in the campaign that liberated the slaves working in the British Colonies, died on the 19th February, 1845. Within three years, his younger son, Charles Buxton had compiled and published a volume of *Memoirs*. An enlarged edition was called for in 1848, and was dedicated to the elder daughter. As recently as 1925, this volume was republished in Dent's Everyman Library, with the addition of an essay entitled, *An Inquiry into the Results of Emancipation*, which Charles Buxton contributed originally to the *Edinburgh Review* for April, 1859, and an introduction by Earl Buxton, son of Charles, grandson of the subject of this book, and a prominent, if not dominating, member of the Liberal Party and administration from 1906 onwards. This work, of unchallenged accuracy and admirable filial devotion, nowadays suffers from the utter change in the political and world outlook. To the author and his eminent son, the Reform Bill of 1831, in home affairs, and the Bill for the Total Abolition of Colonial Slavery, which received the royal assent on 28th August, 1833, were victories in their several spheres as final and lasting as Waterloo, which just preceded these, was in the military one. Nor can they be blamed. Charles Buxton, at least, could as little have foreseen that the centenary of the Reform Bill would be one of the darkest in our history, as that the centenary of Waterloo would see us in danger of invasion, or that of the Abolition Bill would confront us with the rise of a state of slavery in Europe, far more murderous than anything against which his father had toiled. He had every justification for his view of the solidity of his father's achievement, in the half century of peace and progress, both at home and overseas, which immediately succeeded the death of Buxton the Liberator. We, to-day, are a wiser, in the grim sense of being a sadder, generation. Listen to this:

"With regard to the use of the whip, some official statistics remain, which show it to have been no imaginary evil. But it may be well to observe that the lash was, after all, but one of the many hardships which the slave endured. His scanty supply of food and clothing was a source of constant and bitter suffering; all his domestic ties were utterly dissolved; every hindrance was thrown in the way of his education; his religious teachers were persecuted, his day of rest encroached on; every prospect of attaining civil rights was taken away; however grievous the injury inflicted, to obtain redress was extremely difficult, if not impossible."

Those words were written in 1845. Were they not true early in 1945, of supposedly civilised nations?

Yes, with this difference. The tyranny with which Thomas Fowell Buxton wrestled and of which his son wrote the above paragraph was economic and historic. That which confronts us is recent and based on political theory and military expediency. Yet both are suicidal to the human society in which they have occurred on grounds of humanity and of productivity. Both still require a wide measure of racial, political and cultural regulation for resettlement if they are to be permanently overcome. Both are surrounded by clouds of sentiment, some deep-rooted, some irrelevant, both have been caused by wholesale displacement of population, both will need complicated legislative enactment for final cure. That was Buxton's great achievement in his day. It may be well worth while to follow up the course of his life, particularly the ten years of his extreme activity, with its subsidiary campaigns, and to see how the social structure, of which he was a part, equipped him for the work by which he is known.

Perhaps no one person will ever bestride the nineteen-forties as he did the eighteen-thirties. For one thing, the immense levelling that has since taken place no longer leaves such responsibilities on one pair of shoulders. For another, the modern conflict is so much greater in extent that it dwarfs any but the most colossal individual figure. The world which used to be dominated by one Napoleon is now confronted with half a dozen figures of international importance. Buxton was the forerunner rather of the social reformers than of any diplomat or soldier. It was his effect on the domestic administration of what is now the British Commonwealth that gained him so much success and recognition as the Liberator.

There are signs of a revival of interest not merely in formal Abolition, but also in the kind of social and political change which it involved. During the last twenty years several volumes have been published which deal more or less directly with all that great development of which the shortest name is the Abolition of Slavery, and in which the most conspicuous figure is that of Thomas Fowell Buxton, 1786-1845. No new life of him has appeared and, in view of the immense task of resettlement that now confronts the world, it may be worth while retracing the course he followed.

CHAPTER I

THE NURSERY OF HEROES, 1786—1807

THE NAME OF BUXTON ASTONISHES NO ONE IN THESE ISLANDS. IT IS THE AVERAGE English rather than British place name, of the kind which furnishes, in competition with those drawn from occupation, the majority of the surnames south of the Forth and east of the Severn. No member of the family seems to have pursued it into remote antiquity, it obviously is not one of those mono-syllables that are generally held to indicate a very primitive origin, though it may incorporate such in its first three letters. There need not be much doubt that, at any time after our basic island character had been fixed by vaguely Scandinavian influence, a family which had shifted its domicile came to be known as the people who had come from the ——ton or village of Bux, by much the same process as Walter de Bixton came to be Burgess for Norwich in the Parliament under Richard II.

The particular family with which we have to deal is traced by Charles Buxton in the *Memoirs*, to Sudbury, Suffolk, then a textile town of national importance such as that of Bradford to-day, in the middle of the sixteenth century, that is to say, at the time at which some sort of register was kept in most parishes, with fair regularity and some chance of preservation. This family moved to the equally busy, but already decaying, weaving town of Coggeshall, nine miles west of Colchester, where they seem to have inhabited the property known as "Paycocks," now safe in the hands of the National Trust through the generosity of Lord Noel Buxton, "A richly ornamental example of a merchant's house dating from about 1500 . . . the panelling and wood carving are exceptionally fine," says the Trust Report.

Here died, in 1624, William Buxton, whose son Thomas, ten years later, felt himself to be in a position to claim (successfully) from the Heralds' College, the arms borne by the Buxtons of Tibenham, Norfolk.

Here, then, we have the cradle of the family tradition, in the very centre of the squirearchy. There is nothing like it in any other nation. These small landowners, mostly innocent of title, manned the local administration, supplied members to the national one, occasionally rose into prominence in a Hampden, a Cromwell, or a Washington, but never deserted their lands for the Court, and never became an unwanted, dog-in-the-manger class as they have in so many continental countries. It may have been just good fortune, ostensible in the fact that their major political revolution was behind them. Or it may have been that they had never been divorced from trade, as some landed classes have been, but were still described often as merchants and had been so since the days of Sir Thomas Erpingham and Sir John Fastolf, who, known to history as soldiers, were far more remarkable to their contemporaries as wool staplers. Or it may have been farther back, in the fact that the population of these fortunate islands has never recovered from its original shake-up, its hazardous voyage in little boats, its complete severance from its one-time racial connection with some other land. Nothing less perhaps will explain the difference between the sort of people the Buxtons were, and the nearest equivalent in Poland, Spain, or even Ireland.

Four generations after Thomas, with his armorial bearings, came Isaac, described as a "merchant" who married Sarah Fowell of Fowelscombe, Devon, described as an heiress, but, we may think, roughly of the same social level, small landowning helped out with the wool trade, through which they probably met. It is not clear if it was something in her character, or the property she brought with her, which caused her name to be perpetuated by successive generations of Buxtons well into the twentieth century. The eldest son of this marriage, and first to be called Fowell, took what is for us a far more important step. He married Anna, daughter of Osgood Hanbury, the Quaker brewer of Holfield Grange, in Essex. This brings us to what may have been a decisive influence on their eldest son, Thomas Fowell Buxton, who was born, not at the home they made, at Earl's Colne, but at Castle Hedingham. The point is that it brought the Buxtons into the vital Quaker circle. It may even have influenced his father, who appears to have risen in importance in local affairs, either as the result of Fowell legacies or of property that came with his wife, for he served as High Sheriff of the County, entertained largely, was prominent in field sports. A significant hint is given in the *Memoirs* that "he availed himself of the authority of his office to relieve the miseries of the prisoners under his superintendence, visiting them sedulously, notwithstanding the prevalence of jail fever." So thought Charles Buxton. We may well wonder, when we find that he died when young Thomas was only six years old, the infant head of a family of two brothers and two sisters. This loss, again, may have emphasized the influence of the Quaker mother. It may be only coincidence that Rachel Hanbury, Mrs. Buxton's sister, married Richard Gurney of Keswick, whose step-daughter Agatha married Sampson Hanbury. Quaker families often intermarry closely without apparent detriment to their high vitality. What is more evident is the frame of mind of the Quaker widow, bringing up her eldest son, who wrote in later life:

". . . . I became at ten years old almost as much the master of the family, as I am of this family at the present moment. My mother, a woman of great talents and energy, perpetually inculcated on my brothers and sisters that they were to obey me, and I was rather encouraged to play the little tyrant. She treated me as an equal, conversed with me and led me to form and express my opinions without reserve. This system has obvious and great disadvantages, but it was followed by some few incidental benefits. Throughout life I have acted and thought for myself, and to this kind of habitual decision I am indebted for all the success I have met with."

We need only add to this self portrait, certain features of the boy's background, of which he was probably rendered unconscious by familiarity. He can only have known want and servitude objectively, growing up as he did in a home in which there was always enough and to spare, not merely for friends and local society, but for the needy and social outcast. It is not difficult to "form and express" opinions if one is already the young master. But more than that, behind him lay generations of land-owning on one side, and deep-rooted spiritual independence on the other. If, as a High Sheriff's son, he felt that his father represented the King, so as Anna Hanbury's son he early began to feel that he understood what God intended. This is probably the greatest difficulty we shall have to overcome in our consideration of Thomas Fowell Buxton. But it was real enough, and immensely potent, not only in the home of young Thomas, but in all those equally spacious, comfortable, and well-supplied ones which he visited. Nor had it, at its source, any taint of insincerity or self-righteousness. These may have come later, in less assured and scrupulous men; the first well-known evidence of such perversion is to be found in the works of Dickens and Barham, essentially caricaturists. All such comedy must have a basis of fact, but a heavy superstructure of satire. We must school ourselves to accept the conditions of that time, when young Thomas grew up, accustomed to hear his elders speak directly to the Almighty, as to one who was a mixture of King and Father, omnipotent but deeply concerned with his children's personal affairs, How widespread it became amid the social equals of the Buxtons can be seen by Besant's quotation that at the beginning of the century only two country gentlemen in Staffordshire read family prayers daily. By 1850 only two did not. We can measure our own difficulties in appreciating this statement by asking ourselves how many do to-day ?

In contrast to this strong element in the surroundings of young Thomas stands yet another, the (to us) incomprehensible attitude towards children and their education. Clearly neither money nor affection were in short supply in the Buxton home. Nor can there have been much doubt that the boy would profit by any chance that was given him. Yet "at the age of four and a half he was sent to a school at Kingston where he suffered severely from ill-treatment, and, his health giving way (chiefly from the want of sufficient food), he was removed, shortly after his father's death, to the school of Dr. Charles Burney at Greenwich." (This was the son of the more famous Dr. Burney).

What did parents then think about education ? It is not clear if this early misadventure made them think harder, or if the father's untimely death caused some heart-searching. All we know is that the second choice, taken just after the family bereavement, was more fortunate. Dr. Burney's school at Greenwich seems to have served not only Thomas but his brothers. If he did not show any remarkable aptitude as a scholar, he seems to have left the impression of a "character." When accused of talking in class by the usher he was punished by being "desired to learn the collect, epistle and gospel" (presumably the readings for the day). When Dr. Burney entered the school, young Buxton appealed to him, stoutly denying the charge. The usher as strongly asserted it; but Dr. Burney stopped him, saying, "I never found the boy tell a lie, and will not disbelieve him now." The usher's reactions are not recorded.

In his schooldays, therefore, Thomas was evidently already impressing his elders by what may have seemed nothing more than unusual pertinacity. That he certainly possessed, for in infancy it had been remarked. "When walking with his uncle, Mr. Hanbury, he was desired to give a message to a pig-driver who had passed along the road. He set off in pursuit and, although one of his shoes was soon lost in the mud, he pushed on through lonely and intricate lanes, tracking the driver by the footmarks of his pigs, for nearly three miles, into the town of Coggeshall; nor did he stop until he had overtaken the man and delivered his message."

What a picture of juvenile training! The limping infant following pig marks through wildest Essex, and defying the usher with his cane! Small wonder that the grown man pursued Peel, driving an assembly only slightly less Gadarene, and "delivered his message," fearless of what the planting interest could do.

Apparently such a character is accounted for largely by his mother's training. He at least thought so :

"I constantly feel, especially in action or exertion for others," he wrote to her long afterwards, "the effects of principles early planted by you in my mind!"

What these were we can gather from the fact that although, out of loyalty to her husband's Anglicanism, she had the boys baptised, at heart she remained a member of the Society of Friends. Another worried parent seemed to have asked if the revolutionary principles of the day were not making way among her boys. She replied, "I know nothing about revolutionary principles, my rule is that imposed on the people of Boston—implicit obedience, unconditional submission" (. . . to Divine Will, understood). She must have felt she had been successful, for when she was told that he was "of a daring, violent, domineering temper," she answered:

"Never mind, he is self-willed now—you will see it turn out well in the end!"

Nothing that she said, however, is as impressive as what she did. Instead of attaching the growing boy to her apron strings, as the phrase used to be, she seems to have let him run about with a character, local even to his name, Abraham Plastow, whom young Thomas of those days called, years later, "my guide, philosopher and friend . . . a man for whom I have ever felt, and still feel, very great affection. He was a singular character; in the first place, this tutor of mine could neither read nor write, but his memory was stored with various rustic knowledge. He had more of natural good sense, and what is called mother-wit, than almost any person I have met since; a knack which he had of putting everything into new and singular lights made him, and still makes him, a most entertaining, and even intellectual, companion. He was the most undaunted of men: I remember my youthful admiration of his exploits on horseback. For a time he hunted my uncle's hounds, and his fearlessness was proverbial. But what made him particularly valuable, were his principles of integrity and honour. He never said or did a thing in the absence of my mother, of which she would have disapproved. He always held up the highest standard of integrity, and filled our youthful minds with sentiments as pure and as generous as could be found in the writings of Seneca or Cicero. . . . He was our playfellow and tutor; he rode with us, fished with us, shot with us upon all occasions."

The figure of Abraham Plastow forms an important feature of the background against which we see the young Thomas. He was obviously more widely employed than anyone we should call a gamekeeper, who nowadays is not often entrusted with the duty of hunting the local pack of hounds. Still less would he be expected to check a youthful petulance which found vent in bad language. Yet the record continues:

"The young Buxtons had been sent out hunting, and, as usual, under Abraham's care. As they were approaching the scene of the sport, Fowell made use of an improper expression, upon which the gamekeeper insisted upon his returning home at once, and carried his point."

We cannot but be reminded of a similar relationship which existed between John Crome, whose formal status was that of a drawing-master to Fowell's Gurney cousins at Earlham, and who was, it appears, also treated much more as a friend of the family would be nowadays, and was left in charge of the bevy of nine pretty and vivacious girls, not only for long periods in the park, at his natural occupation, but once at least, on a prolonged holiday journey across the kingdom.

Perhaps we shall not be far out if we assume that in the simplicity and directness of human commerce as conducted by Quaker and semi-Quaker families, any dependent (for that is what both Plastow and Crome actually were) if found worthy was, in fact treated as a member of the family. Nor would there, at that time, have been anything unusual in such a mentor being unable to read and write. Crome, again, could little more than sign his name. Plastow lived until 1836, to see his young protégé a national and even a world figure, and died with the tears running down his face, at the memory of the rides they had taken together. He himself left sufficient mark upon the opinion of his neighbours to cause them to erect jointly a mural tablet in the churchyard of Earl's Colne:

"To the memory of Abraham Plastow, who lived for
more than half a century,
servant and gamekeeper,
in the families of Thomas Fowell Buxton and Osgood Gee Esquires.

Of humble station, yet of sterling worth;
Awaiting Heaven, but yet content on earth;
Quaint, honest, simple-hearted, kind, sincere:
Such was the man, to all our village dear!
He lived in peace, in hope resigned his breath.
Go—learn a lesson from his life and death."

One, at least, of all the boys and girls who rode and shot with him, learned it.
Thus, as young Tom emerges from childhood, and begins to be called "Fowell" we can begin to form a portrait of a big boy, not very clever in the bookish sense, spending his "quarters" at Dr. Burney's school at Greenwich without much profit; in his holidays rather inclined to domineer over his brothers and sisters, kept in check by a model senior servant of the family, he is not easily distinguishable from the average squire's son, from which class were still drawn at that date the executive personnel of the Services and the Royal administration, on the ground of social competence and inherent ability to give orders, long before any systematic training by examination had been thought of. From the same social group came most Members of Parliament of that date.
But Fowell Buxton was not destined to remain a typical member of that tough, capable, clear-headed set of people, of whom the younger Pitt was the most famous, and the rank and file often hard-drinking, hard-riding placemen if not nonentities. He fell, in these years, under the influence of two homes, that more than supplied whatever he may have missed from the lack of a father to guide him.
The first, and perhaps less important, was Bellfield near Weymouth. This property was discovered by Fowell's grandfather, Isaac, and his young wife the Fowell heiress, while visiting the district shortly after their marriage. She remarked to him then, what a beautiful spot it would be for a country seat. Next year, returning to the site, she was astonished to find an elegant country house had been built, surrounded by lawns and gardens, where before had been only fields and hedges. She long occupied this property, and it became known to her grandchildren as one of their childhood's resorts, vastly preferred to her London house in which she lived with a good deal of formality. There, Sunday discipline was strict, and only on one Sunday in the year did she give her grandchildren a drive in the park. At Bellfield, however, she seems to have felt able to relax, and from the house, commanding fine views of Weymouth Bay and the Island of Portland, they were able to escape to all the occupations

dear to country-bred, open-air children. Among others, Fowell related the following incident:

"In passing with my brother Edward, in a very small boat from Weymouth to Poxwell, a sudden storm came on and the boat filled. We turned to the shore; he could not swim. I could. I placed him in the front of the boat and rowed with all my force through the surf; the boat overturned, threw him on shore, but I went down. I swam to the boat, and after considerable difficulty was also thrown on shore by the surf."

Yet another memory of Bellfield were the visits of King George III and his family, whose favourite resort was Weymouth, to the Fowell grandmother. As in so many other instances, the obstinate autocrat who alienated his subjects at home, and drove English-speaking North America into revolt, showed in private life all the most charming family traits. He and his children mixed freely enough with the untitled Buxtons, as with their linen-draper Barclay connections in London. There seems to have been a total absence of condescension on one side, as of subservience on the other, little as it might appear probable to readers of the merely political history of the time.

Tom's other home was Earlham, the seat of the Gurneys, on the outskirts of Norwich, immortalised by Percy Lubbock, who, as the little grandchild, remembered it kept in much the state in which the younger Fowell saw it, by a younger family of Gurney relatives. Fortunately, when, in the present century, the property came into the market, the City Council of Norwich had the remarkable foresight to buy it, and to-day it remains preserved for us, perhaps the best specimen of the world-renowned English Home that can be found anywhere.

The very road that leads from St. Giles' Gates, Norwich, is not called after any of the market towns to which it leads, but is always known as "Earlham Road." Pursuing this for nearly two miles we come to the highest point at which a low (but for Norfolk, well marked) contour separates the valley of the Yare from that of the Wensum. Here, south of the road, lies a pleasant, but not enormous, park, and through the well-grown trees is visible the northern elevation of Earlham Hall.

The parish is a hamlet of the ancient county borough of Norwich, and at the foot of the gentle slope that falls westward from the house to where the Yare turns south to encircle the city, can be seen the parish church and rectory, the old white bridge and a farm amid the trees that make up practically the whole of the "agglomeration." In the foreground is a charming brick dovecote summer house, repaired by members of the Gurney family and now the dressing-room of those who play football in the park. The northern front of the house presents porch and pediment in walls of local flint such as are common enough in the district, but the design has spacious dignity, not destroyed by more modern wings built in sympathy with the style. When we pass round by the western end, however, we can see, between more recent accretions, that the core of the building is a Caroline semi-defensible block with the date 1643 in iron figures on the massive chimney stacks. Characteristically, when we come to the wide south lawn, we find an ample Queen Anne front has been built on, completely masking a rather grim original dwelling, while to the east, a wide courtyard gives upon the offices necessary for such a place, well and laundry, stables and kitchen garden, a peacock strutting beneath a cherry tree. In a word, a perfect English home, belonging to the time when a well-to-do family had long forgotten to keep its windows small and its doors inaccessible in case of attack, and long before there seemed anything unnatural in such people having the service of a score of domestics of either sex, ranging from butler and house-keeper, down to scullery maid and garden boy.

Twin influences were thus brought to bear on young Fowell's doubtless unconscious mind. Probably the house in which he had been born and brought up differed in no great degree from that of his cousins at Earlham. It can hardly have been more perfect as a specimen of domesticity of the more fortunate classes of Britain, as the eighteenth century passed into the nineteenth, but it happens to be less documented than the more celebrated Earlham, and we can learn more about the young man by studying him at his cousins' home than elsewhere.

The direct connection was not very close. Fowell's aunt, Rachel Hanbury, had married Richard, elder brother of John Gurney of Earlham. It was through the younger John, of his own generation, that Fowell first was invited to the house. The inhabitants of Earlham were far more important to young Fowell's development than its plan or materials, beautiful though both were.

It was in the autumn of 1801 that he first saw them. The occasion is related in Hare's *Gurneys of Earlham*, on the faith of a reminiscence of Hannah Gurney, the fifth daughter, destined, little as she may have been able to realise it, to be Lady Buxton and Fowell's wife:

". . . the Earlham family gathered on the steps of the hall door to watch a travelling carriage approaching, up the avenue. It contained Rachel (second daughter), Hannah and "Betsy" (Elizabeth Fry) with the darling baby, little Katherine Fry. Eager to display the treasure, no sooner was the carriage door opened, than Hannah sprang out with the baby in her arms, and wondered who was the tall, and to her unknown, boy, standing among the group. That boy was Thomas Fowell Buxton, her future husband, who looked on her then for the first time, and said at once in his large, strong heart: 'She shall be my wife'."

The group among which he then found himself consisted first of all, of the father, John Gurney of Earlham, second son of the Magdalen Street branch of the Gurneys with their country house at Keswick, then occupied by his elder brother Richard.

Born in 1749, John Gurney had been brought up to the family wool-stapling business in the house still visible in Gurney Court, Magdalen Street, Norwich, where his six elder children (one of whom did not survive infancy) were born. Quaker as he was, his portrait by Opie shows a man of strikingly handsome face and dignified figure. It is said of him that as a boy he had red hair. Being "cheeked" by Norwich boys in the rough street in which he grew up, he cut it off and appeared in a wig. Such childish petulances were far behind him when he welcomed Fowell Buxton to Earlham. Though he was only then about to become a partner in the Bank, into which the business of his cousin, Bartlett Gurney, had resolved itself, in 1775, on account of its wide connections and the character of its founders, he had prospered, and for fifteen years had left the old city merchant's dwelling to become the master of Earlham Hall.

A "wide" rather than "strict" Friend, while welcoming and keeping open house for all members of the Society, he mixed much with people of other beliefs, and perhaps influenced by his wife, with Unitarians, whose Octagon Chapel in Colegate his cousin Bartlett attended. He made no bones therefore over young Fowell's Anglican upbringing.

Up to ten years before Fowell's visit, John Gurney was a brilliant example of good fortune richly deserved. His worldly estate prospered on a basis of hard work and honest dealing. His lovely home was full of bright, healthy children. His tragedy was described eighty years after by the very Hannah who jumped out of the carriage with the little Fry baby and saw Fowell Buxton standing among her brothers and sisters (the date of the following incident is 9th March, 1791):

"We the younger girls, were spending the morning at the further end of the kitchen garden, old Nurse with us. Becky came to say a boy was born, and I remember the party of children allowed to go in to see the baby, holding on to each other's frocks in an orderly line. Not two years after, I remember them in a similar line walking past their dying mother."

That was why, during his autumn visit, Fowell found the chatelaine of Earlham was the eldest daughter, Catherine, by that time twenty-four years old, to whom, on her deathbed, their mother had confided the little ones, down to baby Daniel. True to her trust, Catherine never married, devoting herself to the welfare of the others for half a century.

Next in order came the beautiful and musical Rachel, who also never married.

Omitting the first boy to be called "John," who had died an infant, the next was Fowell's friend, also called John, who, luckier than his infant elder, was to live another fourteen years. Next came "Betsy" and then Hannah.

What sort of a girl was it to whom young Fowell attached himself at the age of sixteen and a half? She was two and a half years his senior, and if not the prettiest, was the middle one of the family of seven pretty sisters. Elizabeth, the stateliest, and perhaps even then marked out to be the most celebrated in the social history of her country, was already married to Joseph Fry. It is amusing to note that, eighty years after, Catherine described Betsy as "timid."

Younger than Hannah were Richenda, who married the Rev. Francis Cunningham, Louisa, who was to marry Samuel Hoare before Hannah herself married, Priscilla, who remained single, and three boys of nearly his own age, Samuel, some day to be a London banker, Joseph John, the sharer of Betsy's prison reform exploits, and Daniel, who became a great country gentleman and lived until 1880.

Fowell thus found himself amid a family of eleven cousins with no mother, who ranged from the eldest girl and foster mother, Catherine, ten years older than he, through his particular friend, John, five years his senior, down to Joseph John, with whom he was to be much associated, and young Daniel, respectively two and five years his junior. In the centre stood Hannah with whom he fell instantly in love, with a passion that was to last forty-four years, and to be the treasured memory by her for nearly another thirty that she survived him. At the date of that first meeting, only one, "Betsy" Fry, was married. The whole family was teeming with good fortune, good looks and high spirits, and they were admirably united.

"I do hope and believe," Betsy Fry wrote from her new home in St. Mildred's Court, London, to Hannah on 1st January, 1803, "that through all we shall feel the interest of our own family one of the first interests we have. I often, very often, think of you all, and love you with fresh warmth, and dream of you a-night. . . ."

What his place in such a family immediately became can be seen by a letter from Richenda to Betsy in that same year from Cromer, within a mile of which he was to find his own home:

"Our party is now complete, as John continues with us, and the Buxtons . . . (this means Fowell and his sister Anna and brother Charles) . . . arrived yesterday. It is extremely pleasant to us, seeing them both again, particularly Fowell; their being here will add very much to our pleasure, as there is a suitability between us and the Buxtons, which always makes it pleasant for us to be together. Our time here is spent in a way that exactly suits the place and the party. All are left in perfect liberty to do as they like all day, or to form any engagement. Yet the party is so connected that hardly a day passes but some plan is fixed for us all to meet. When all are met it is an uncommonly pretty sight, such a number of young women, and so many, if not pretty, very nice-looking. I wish thee could have seen us the other afternoon. Sally gave a grand entertainment at the Hall, where everybody met —the ladies almost all dressed in white gowns and blue sashes, with nothing on their heads; after dinner, we all stood on a wall, eighteen of us, and it really was one of the prettiest sights I ever saw.

"To give thee an idea how we are going on, I will tell thee how we generally pass the day. The weather since we came has on the whole been very fine, so imagine us before breakfast, with our troutbecks (hats) on and coloured gowns, running in all directions on the sands, jetty, etc. After breakfast we receive callers from the other houses, and fix with them the plans for the day; after this we now and then get an hour's quiet for reading and writing, though my mind has been so much taken up with other things, that I have found it almost impossible to apply to anything seriously. At eleven we go down in numbers to bathe and enjoy the sands, which about that time look beautiful: most of our party and the rest of Cromer company come down, and bring a number of different carriages, which have a very pretty effect. After bathing, we either ride on horseback or take some pleasant excursion or other. I never remember enjoying the sea so much, and never liked Cromer a quarter so well. Some of us continually dine out, whilst the others receive company at home. We always dine in the kitchen; Nurse is our cook, and makes a very good one. We have short afternoons, and spend the evening with music, or something of that sort: with all these and other delightful amusements, and this pleasant party, it would be very odd if we did not enjoy ourselves."

It was about this time, in his sixteenth year, that young Tom, as he was then called, must have left the care of Dr. Burney, for during this Earlham visit he wrote to his mother:

"I was very much pleased with all your last, excepting the part in which you mention the (to me at least) hateful subject of St. Andrew's.

"It gives me pain to write, because it will you to read, that my aversion is, ever was, and ever will be invincible, nevertheless, if you command, I will obey. You will exclaim—'How ungrateful, after all the pleasure he has had!' Pleasure, great pleasure, I certainly have had, but not sufficient to counterbalance the unhappiness the pursuance of your plan would occasion me, but, as I said before, I will obey.

"If you think fit I shall return to Cromer on Wednesday. Northrepps is perfectly delightful. . . ."

Here we get a glimpse of a strong-minded, self-willed, but not undutiful son, knowing well enough what he did not like, some of the things, but not enough, of what he did want. What was his mother's object in placing him at a Scottish University is not clear, unless it was that, as a Quaker, she resented the exclusion of her creed from the ancient universities of England. However, Fowell was spared both the immediate separation from the object of his young affections and her delightful family, and also the remoter and grimmer prospect of what must have seemed to him exile in Scotland.

There seems to have been an idea that he would inherit property in Ireland, and it says much for his mother's general outlook that this led her to determine that he should conclude his education in that country. Not all owners of Irish land have had so much imagination.

Accordingly we find him by the end of 1802, "placed in the family of Mr. Moore of Donnybrook who prepared pupils for the university . . . (we know subsequently that it was Dublin) . . . he found himself inferior to every one of his companions in classical acquirements; but he spent his (Christmas) vacation in such close study, that, on the return of the other pupils, he stood as the first among them."

In fact, the open-air athletic boy was developing mentally and setting his feet upon the path he was to tread. He had long been conscious of his lack of scholarly attainment. Before he left Earlham he had remarked in a letter to his mother:

". . . . Whilst I was at Northrepps (the Gurneys' house on the low hills just inland of Cromer) . . . I did little else but read books of entertainment, (except now and then a few hours Latin and Greek), ride and play chess. But since I have been at Earlham, I have been very industrious. . . ."

". . . . My visit here has completely answered, I have spent two months as happily as possible; I have learned as much, though in a different manner, as I should at Colne, and have got thoroughly acquainted with the most delight-ful family in the world."

This is proof, if any were needed, of the part Earlham played in his maturing. Many years after, he himself set down "first in an enumeration of the blessings of his life——"

"I know no blessing of a temporal nature (and it is not only temporal) for which I ought to render so many thanks as my connection with the Earlham family. It has given colour to my life. Its influence was most positive and pregnant with good, at that critical period between school and manhood. They . . . (the Earlham cousins) . . . were eager for inprovement—I caught the infection. I was resolved to please them, and in the College of Dublin, at a distance from all my friends, and all control, their influence, and the desire to please them, kept me hard at my books, and sweetened the toil they gave. The distinctions I gained at College (little valuable as distinctions, but valuable because habits of industry, perseverance, and reflection were necessary to obtain them) these boyish distinctions were exclusively the result of the animating passion in my mind, to carry back to them the prizes which they prompted and enabled me to win."

We know that courtship takes young men in all sorts of odd ways. This is how it took Fowell.

In a more generalised view, he wrote in later years to one of his own sons:

"I am sure that a young man may be very much what he pleases. In my own case it was so. I left school when I had learnt little or nothing, at about the age of fourteen. I spent the next year at home learning to hunt and shoot. Then it was that the prospect of going to College opened upon me, and such thoughts . . . occurred to my mind. I made resolutions and I acted up to them; I gave up desultory reading—I never looked into a novel or newspaper —I gave up shooting. During the five years I was in Ireland, I had the liberty of going when I pleased to a capital shooting place. I never went but twice.

In short, I considered every hour as precious, and I made everything bend to my determination not to be behind any of my companions—and thus I speedily passed from one species of character to another. I had been a boy fond of pleasure and idleness, reading only books of unprofitable entertainment—I became speedily a youth of steady habits of application and irresistible resolution. I soon gained the ground I had lost, and I found those things which were difficult, and almost impossible to my idleness, easy enough to my industry; and much of my happiness and all my prosperity in life have resulted from the change I made. . . ."

In 1802, however, when he prepared for his entry into Trinity College, Dublin, which he achieved in October, 1803, as a commoner, he little foresaw that the only important result of his Irish university would be his friendship with John Henry North, one of his "tremendous antagonists," destined to be a distinguished member of the Irish Bar and the House of Commons, and to leave the name of North to be borne by several generations of the Buxton family.

The immediate experiences of his life in Ireland in 1803 were totally un-connected with his personal affairs. He was a witness of Robert Emmett's "Kilwarden Rebellion." It had many striking resemblances to the events of 1916. The Lord Lieutenant, although well warned of what was afoot, only set 2,500 men in motion "to take care of his house and family in the Park." They had no ammunition, every officer in the Castle was on leave. Lord Kilwarden, Colonel Brown and many soldiers were caught and killed.

"Isaac and I watched last night at Donnybrook, with our pistols loaded," wrote Lieutenant Fowell Buxton of the Volunteer Corps, "it was expected they would attack . . . however they did not come . . . the gardener and workmen say there were 500 rebels at Mr. North's gate that night. The military soon mastered the situation, 10,000 pikes were taken, the prisons of Dublin were filled with rebels, 200 to 300 were supposed to be killed." By 7th August, he was able to write, "Dublin is in appearance perfectly normal again, but the minds of the people are in rebellion."

So ended another unhappy Irish incident. How near it came to affecting materially his career and this account of it may be judged by the following:

"A companion of mine, not knowing it was loaded, presented a pistol at me, and pulled the trigger. It had often missed fire before, and did so then; immediately afterwards, I pulled the trigger, it went off, and sent the ball into the wall."

During 1805 it became clear that the expectations his mother had entertained of his becoming an Irish landowner would not be fulfilled. Members of the Yorke family came forward to contest the claim, and in spite of the heavy expense of a lawsuit, it became obvious she would not succeed. This does not seem to have deterred him from completing his college career.

"The examinations are over," he wrote in April, 1805 . . . "my utmost examination hopes are realised—I have the certificate and *Valde bene in omnibus* and, what is better, that I can ascribe my success to nothing but my Earlham visit."

He was very preoccupied with his progress:

"I went yesterday to a schoolmaster who gives lectures on reading . . . (chiefly in English poetry) . . . . I felt a difficulty in that most useful qualifica-tion, especially when last at Earlham—I expect to gain two very material advantages by this plan; the first is that it may afford you pleasure, and secondly

that, as I go immediately after dinner, it will furnish an opportunity for avoiding
. . . a party of collegians, into whose society I have lately got, and whose habits
of drinking made me determine to retreat from them."

What a salutary resolve for the future brewer!

In that year, also, he made his first speech, all unconscious of the hundreds
that were to follow it. He and North had joined the Historical Society, a
very select body which chose its members with great circumspection from among
third year men, and gave medals for eloquence and history. We may regard
this speech, which seems to have caused something like a college sensation,
though its subject is not recorded, as his début. How far these decorous exercises
in English poetry and undergraduate dialectic seem from the figure to which
he was to attain.

How Fowell's courtship prospered may be judged by the report made by
Catherine, the eldest Gurney, and foster-mother to young Joseph John, who,
although he was not allowed, as a professed Quaker, to become a member of the
University of Oxford, was living in that town studying with a tutor. She wrote
often, prompted by that same feeling of unity in the family that we have already
noted in the words of the other absent member, Betsy Fry:

(Catherine to Joseph John Gurney:)

"Earlham, April, 1805—Hannah is in excellent spirits, much happier than
before Fowell's last visit; they correspond constantly, and he writes charming
letters. How very pleasant it will be to have thee at home with us. Having
one brother there, adds a cheerfulness and a sort of stimulus to a family. I
often think how blessed we are in our external circumstances, so much leisure
and liberty, and various other things that greatly contribute to the enjoyment
of life. Almost the first blessing is the pleasure that we have in each other's
society. Rachel and I find all the girls, according to their different characters,
such delightful companions. Chenda soothing and engaging, and more pleasing
than ever; Hannah full of life and spirit and acuteness; Louisa noble and strong,
and brimming with generous sympathy; and Priscilla most amiable, with all
that feminine sweetness which adorns a woman's character. Does not thee
think this is very much what they all are, only that in so small a compass one
cannot half do them justice ?"

Here is the view of another member of the family.

(Rachel Gurney to Elizabeth Fry:)

"Earlham, 16th March, 1805—Had thee been with us, thee would have felt
the same interest about Fowell and Hannah which has prevailed amongst
us sisters. I had told Fowell how great a satisfaction openness would be to us
all; for considering the situation that both himself and Hannah had for some
time been placed in, it had become a serious anxiety to us, expecially to my
father. So on Thursday, as soon as the family was dispersed, Kitty and I
settled them together in the dressing-room. They both looked a little miserable
on the occasion, but we stayed with them a minute or two, and laughed at the
extreme difficulty they both seemed to feel in speaking, and then shut the door
upon them.

"Great was our anxiety, but we recovered our composure when we found
an hour and a half had elapsed, and no effort made by either to disengage themselves, and we were almost surprised as well as comforted to see them walk
off into the garden arm in arm, off into the park, and into the meadows beyond

the pond, as if they wished to get out of everybody's way. I should think they walked at least an hour. The weather was beautiful, calm and sunshiny, and truly symbolical of the happy events of the morning. They at length joined the others, and I heartily wish thee could have seen the sunshine that prevailed on every countenance when they came in. Fowell looked like a person who had been condemned to be hanged and had gained a reprieve. Hannah quite easy and cheerful, as if her mind had cast off all its burdens. Anna cried for joy. All the others looked almost as relieved as Hannah. Fowell and Anna went off together, and then we all sat with Hannah on the sofa in Chenda's room to hear her history.

"She said that after they were left alone, almost all the difficulty vanished, and they felt at once at ease with each other, and by degrees very much unfolded the state of each other's minds. Fowell fully expressed to her the strength of attachment to her, which by his own account has long been the principal object of his heart. He also particularly told her what a preservation it had been to him against all the excesses common in a college life, and how afraid he had felt of being unable to gain her affection. She told him, in her turn, how much she had of late felt upon the subject, and those doubts that have arisen from his youth, but also told him what confidence and comfort his virtuous principles had afforded her. She says that when they had once broken down these barriers, they felt really happy together, and even enjoyed being alone, both when they spoke and when they were silent.

"On their return, we all assembled again in the music-room, and continued reading the *Life of Hooker* most peacefully and pleasantly. There did not seem to be one painful drawback in the mind of any individual, and yet there was nothing like enthusiastic pleasure or violent feeling on the part of any one concerned. They had before fixed to dance in the evening, and as it happened, it turned out very pleasantly. Several gentlemen, Mr. Pitchford, Ives, a Mr. Turner, and Miss Day dined here. We had quite a quiet and pleasant company day, and in the evening a remarkably pleasant dance, in which, though I know it cannot quite excite thy sympathy, it will be a satisfaction to thee to know that neither Fowell, nor Hannah, nor the girls seemed to be the least thrown off their centre; while as a divert from the cares of the morning, it was of use to the whole party. We could not help looking with feelings of great pleasure on Fowell and Hannah, both appearing to no small advantage in our eyes, who could read the expression of their countenances. Hannah was by no means merry, but seemed to be softened in feeling by her circumstances being so particularly interesting.

"We have not yet unfolded the present state of things to my father, but Kitty and I are to tell him everything, that Fowell may afterwards speak with more ease. . . . They both seem to feel it essential to be a good deal alone, that they may more fully enter into the state of each other's minds, and every interview of this kind has hitherto been attended by very satisfactory results. Instead of making Hannah uncomfortable, it more and more confirms her confidence in him. This morning she sat at work, and he by her side, and they looked as calm and comfortable as an old married pair: to me surprisingly so, for I had no idea that the course of Hannah's mind on the subject could have been so remarkably smooth. Personally, I am so free from any misgiving, that I have felt it to be an essential blessing that the way is so far opened for a continuance of their attachment."

There seems to have been the warmest feeling between Fowell and his pretty sister-in-law.

(Rachel Gurney to Fowell Buxton, at College:)
"14th May, 1805—I cannot easily tell you how heartily we all rejoice in your successes at college, and it is delightful to know how much value you set on our approbation. You have it, my dear brother, in full measure, and, with it, the heartfelt love of our family circle. You and Anna have so much increased the happiness of our family, and are become so like members of it, that I do not know how we should bear the loss of either of you. I love you partly for Hannah's sake, but I can truly say that I now love her also for yours, as well as so dearly for her own. I hope that, from your wish to marry, you may not do anything prematurely. I heartily wish you may stay at college till you are of age, and then, if there should be any opening in your circumstances, we should none of us be sorry to let you take Hannah away from us, though I can assure you we do not undervalue her at home."
This is how the "little mother" saw it.

(Catherine Gurney to Elizabeth Fry:)
". . . . Fowell and Hannah go on delightfully; they are just what thee would wish to see, so much true intimacy and love, without the least flirting or vanity excited. How much thee would admire them together. In their usual manner, they are most like a very affectionate brother and sister, but she is getting so dependent upon him, that it would not at all do to have him here very long, and this they both think: so I suppose he will leave us in about a week. He is on the most happy terms with all the rest of the family, very attentive to my father, and quite a brother to us. A real friend and valuable adviser I believe he will prove to Sam and Joseph. . . ."
She rallied him with the licence of a much loved sister.

(Catherine Gurney to T. Fowell Buxton:)
"Earlham, 15th December, 1805—I must tell thee what perhaps will amuse thee—that I have just left a pleasant party in the anteroom, consisting of Rachel, Chenda, Hannah, and Dan, employed in music and drawing, to come and sit in the dressing-room with Joseph, who is studying by the sofa while I am writing to thee.
"Now I daresay thee wishes me to tell thee about Hannah. She is, in the first place, quite well and in very good spirits. It seems to me that her attachment to thee is of the strongest, and consequently most durable, nature. One of the strongest proofs of this is its effect on her character, which has, in my opinion, been highly beneficial; so that if thee has derived advantages from her influence, thee may also have the satisfaction of knowing that thy influence over her has had a similar tendency.
"Thee knows without my repeating it here the great satisfaction and pleasure thee has hitherto afforded us all, and how much thee art, dear Fowell, after our own heart, and exactly what pleases both our judgment and taste. I like and love everything thee says and does. However, 1 do not like to give way to this kind of partiality; for, after all, how imperfect the best of us are, and how frail are all our virtues, unless they are derived from the only source of true strength, a principle of religion in the conscience. I have no faith in any virtue which arises merely from natural impulse, because, though frequently amiable

and excellent in appearance, we are sure to find that it partakes of the variability
of our present weak and corrupt nature, and on this account can never stand
the test of trials, as that virtue will which has its basis in Christian faith. Now
I have sometimes thought, from thy natural impulses being remarkably good,
there is some danger of thy depending too much on thyself, and not sufficiently
seeking for assistance and direction in thy conduct from that Source of light
and strength which alone can ensure thy continuance and progress in the best
things. I know Hannah's happiness is completely dependent on thee. I
know, too, how deeply and increasingly she feels the importance of religious
principle; therefore, for her sake as well as thy own, I am most anxious that
thy mind should be equally impressed by the importance and the necessity
of seeking to possess it, as the foundation of all your future comforts. I am
quite sure that Hannah, with her feelings on the subject, never would be
completely happy unless it were the constantly regulating principle of action
in thy mind, in preference to any particular affection.

"Don't suppose, dear Fowell, I mean to lecture thee. I only mean to advise
thee not to depend too much on the gifts of nature, but to look to the Power
from whom these gifts are derived, and by so doing learn the true means of
turning both the one and the other to thy own and dear Hannah's ultimate
advantage.

"Our dear friend and favourite, Mr. Wordsworth, has been paying us a
visit of two days; we have enjoyed his company exceedingly. How beautifully
the influence of religious principle, united with deep learning, appears in his
character. Such examples ought to be encouraging, and stimulate us to act
according to the talents bestowed on us.

"This morning we had some delightful hours, sitting with him altogether
in the dressing-room, talking on different subjects, and then he read to us
in Taylor's *Life of Christ*. What wilt thee say to this long letter? Thee
must excuse it, and believe me, dearest Fowell, thy truly affectionate

"Catherine Gurney."

In the summer of 1806 several members of the Earlham family set out on
an extended tour of Scotland. The girls, Hannah and Louisa, were accompanied
by their intended husbands, Fowell Buxton and Sam Hoare, and their brother
John, who was in a despondent state caused by the refusal of his advances
to Miss Susan Hamond, daughter of the squire of Westacre, near Swaffham,
in Norfolk. The reason may seem curious to those who only know the
subsequent history of the Gurneys. It throws floods of light on the social
background of the year of Trafalgar. It was the Hamond family who refused
the match, the select land-owning circle did not consider this son of the wool-
stapling and banking city family a proper person for an alliance with their
daughter. He was not rich enough.

Can it have been a coincidence that his sisters invited their cousin Elizabeth
Gurney to be one of the party? We have a description of her from a friend
of the family, Pitchford:

"Elizabeth of Keswick is a most sweet girl. Her manners are uncommonly
elegant; her beautiful hair between flaxen and auburn; her lovely blue eyes
beaming with intelligence and full of unexpressible sweetness; her complexion
exquisitely fair and her whole countenance full of the glow of youth."

Again, Daniel Gurney's reminiscences tell us:

"She was striking and very handsome—a profusion of rich auburn hair, a regular and intelligent countenance, and beautiful and simple manners."

This then was the atmosphere in which young Fowell spent his vacation! Nor must we be misled by the constant recurrence of biblical phraseology, and preoccupation with evangelical ideas. They had their fun. Stopping for some days at Ambleside, Fowell and young Samuel Gurney dressed up as widows, and called on the Miss Gurneys to beg assistance for themselves and their offspring. Nor were they discovered until they revealed themselves.

And was that how young people went off together, in those strict days, it may be asked? Not a bit. They had a chaperon, none other than their semi-illiterate old drawing master, John Crome, founder of the Norwich school of painting, who brought them all back safe and sound. We know how they travelled by the following letter:

(Hannah Gurney to Elizabeth Fry.)

"Cambridge, 16th July, 1806—Surrounded by almost our whole party, I sit down to write to thee. We have had a most comfortable and pleasant day's journey, and we have all much enjoyed ourselves, none more, I think, than my father, who was quite delighted with the remarkably sweet party which I must say we are. We set off in three chariots, with Sam and Louisa in a whisky behind us; and most completely equipped for travelling we looked in every respect. Elizabeth Gurney enjoys our cheerful party. We arrived here to dinner about six, where we met John, who appears determined to be as agreeable an addition to our party as he can. We are sorry to part from Sam to-night, and wish he was to be our companion all the way; his visit has been most satisfactory and highly interesting; to have him and Fowell with us together has been more so to me than I can well say. . . . Fowell and I had a most comfortable ride in our chariot the first stage, and I have much enjoyed the quietness of travelling with him to-day. We are all very well and comfortable, and if our good minds do but last, we shall have a very uncommon journey; but in travelling with so numerous a party, there is much to try the patience, and great forbearance is necessary. To-morrow we see Burleigh House and sleep at Grantham."

Fowell told his mother that he meant to visit Weymouth before returning to Dublin, but, possibly because of the length of the tour, he was obliged to go straight from Scotland. His Hannah must have been a girl of almost prophetic foresight, for as a result of a discussion about alternative routes, she made him promise not to cross by the "Parkgate vessels." He reached Chester, all hot to get back to his preparations for his approaching exam. The captain of the Parkgate boat went so far as to assure him, when they met at Chester, that the sailing would take place in a few hours, with a fair wind, and that he hoped to make Dublin the following morning, while the Holyhead line was uncertain and involved a journey across North Wales. Fowell, however, stuck to his promise, and watched the Parkgate passengers go off to embark with bitter impatience. The result was reported in his next letter to the Gurneys:

"Have you heard of the dreadful accident which happened to the Parkgate packet? You will see by the newspaper the particulars. I have been talking to-day with the only passenger who was saved; he says there were 119 in the vessel, and mentioned many most melancholy circumstances. Had I gone by Parkgate, which I probably might have done, as we were detained some time at Chester, and expected to be detained longer, I should have been in the vessel, but I declared positively that I would not go. Can you guess my reason for being so obstinate ?"

The fair "reason," by sheer intuition, saved him for a further forty years of public work. Her satisfaction seems to have agreed with her, for we find that Fowell received a letter from his sister-in-law to be, Louisa :

"Little Parlour, October, 1806—I have been wavering for some time between spending the evening with Hudson and the family in the Great Parlour, or retiring here to enjoy your company. . . . I cannot make out why I do not find it easier than I do to converse with you in a letter, when it would be so great a pleasure to be placed by your side over some snug fire, with time to talk over all that has happened since you left us. I believe, however, the cause is that I feel as if Hannah told you everything, so that I am only treading in a dull, beaten track, but this is better than having no communication with you. I imagine you now poring over your books in your comfortable room. I long to take a peep at you. As the examinations approach, our interest will be doubly excited in all the accounts we have of your proceedings. I do not at all like to be so much separated from you as I have been for the last month, as naughty Hannah has only favoured us poor sisters with two sentences out of the last, I think, of these letters, and been very silent as to their contents, except in expressing her own enjoyment of them. I think her journeys to Dublin are more frequent than ever, and often, when we are both gravely seated at our History, with every appearance of the profoundest attention, I am obliged to rouse her, at certain intervals, by asking who she is thinking of, and where she has wandered to. . . ."

"The Hoares were all struck with Hannah's improvement—the agreeable confidence she has acquired, and which they had the strange idea of attributing to you. I did not, however, much differ from them. I liked them the better for being so warm about you, and so pleased with the connection."

Hannah seems to have been able to keep up her spirits during his absence, for we find Rachel Gurney writing from Earlham to him, at College :

"Earlham, 9th December, 1806—We have had a very pleasant little dance, contrived chiefly for the purpose of bringing Mr. Pitchford here. Dr. Southey came with him, quite a new personage on our stage, full of life and spirits, and remarkably handsome. Pris, our little rosy Pris, has quite enjoyed a little flirtation with this fascinating youth. Happily he leaves Norwich in a few weeks, or I fear Cupid would again be making inroads amongst us. George Kett was in a very agreeable mind, flirted—who do you think with ?—thy Hannah! They were quite merry together. I do love to see her with other young men in your absence; she has all the ease that arises from having the heart wholly secured. How I longed for you, and how you would have added to the enjoyment of the evening! I hope it is not wrong to be a little proud of you. Mr. Pitchford was most agreeable, so truly kind and sympathising about Louisa, and so affectionate to us, yet so inflexibly steady in the forbearance and self-denial that he has prescribed to himself. I earnestly hope he may find his reward in that which can never fail, and I hope that we all (I include my brothers) shall be real friends to him through everything. . . . I doubt not Hannah has told you how valuable our mornings have been lately to us. We have spent the greater part of them together (we six girls) in the dressing-room, and have enjoyed each other's company. It is wonderful to think how nearly the separation approaches. We greatly rejoice in having spent so many quiet and happy years together as have fallen to our lot since Betsy's marriage. It has so cemented that union which exists amongst us, and has given so much time for our minds and sentiments to grow together, which could not have been the case had we sooner dispersed. If I had married when I wished to do so, I should hardly have known the girls in their present state. Thus there is generally a mixture of good and evil in all things. Louisa's heart is very full, and she is at times oppressed by the near approach of so great a change, and she has often lately been drowned in tears.

"To-morrow Hannah and I go to Northrepps for a few days, to see our new sister-elect. John's last visit to her seems to have been a very happy one, and our uncle a little more favourable to him towards the close of it. Elizabeth writes as if she became more and more dependent on him."

In fact, the Hoare marriage came off about Christmas of 1806, in the plain little meeting house, at Tasburgh, some eight miles south of Norwich, still to be seen by motorists who cross the small Tas stream, on the main Ipswich Road, a little east of the bridge. Rachel Gurney described the ceremony to him:

"Earlham. 31st December, 1806—Louisa and Sam returned yesterday from Cromer, where they have been spending nearly a week in retirement, so that they have now the effect of married people who have begun their career together. Louisa looks sweetly and Sam truly happy. I never saw a greater mixture of dignity and sweetness than in our bride. How we did long for thee, dear Fowell, to be with us. The love that prevailed amongst all deeply concerned was delightful, and the uncommon solemnity and yet sweetness of the Meeting seemed to sanctify their union in a manner never to be forgotten. It was a most pleasant sight to have so long a train of brothers and sisters in wedding garments. The whole day was without a cloud—so seriously and quietly conducted, and yet so truly cheerful. The troops of young people were very enlivening, and the old most kind and sympathising. Our greatest regret was not having our dearest Fowell with us."

The marriage did nothing to disturb the warm family feeling that existed between the girls, and into which they seem to have drawn their young mates. By this time Fowell was regarded more as a brother than a prospective brother-in-law, and elder sister Rachel had to tell him all about the homecoming of the happy pair, after a honeymoon visit to relatives of both bride and bridegroom on the Norfolk coast. She was writing from "Betsy" Fry's:

"St Mildred's Court, 14th January, 1807—Hannah will have told thee all about Louisa's visit to Earlham after her return from Cromer, and of her finally leaving home, and how much she felt it, which is not to be wondered at, considering what a happy home she leaves, though her prospects are bright. She had in Sam almost all that she can wish, yet the pain of entering a new circle and leaving all those she is so very closely united to, must be expected to take at least from her present enjoyment. I have no doubt she will become happier and happier in proportion as she is familiarised to the change. Thee must be prepared for a few tears when thee runs off with Hannah, though I do not think that she or any of us will feel it so much as Louisa's marriage. Thee has been too completely one of the family, and for my part, I look forward to thy wedding with pleasure, as uniting us to thee more nearly."

Then the married sister took the, as yet, unmarried one into her confidence, and it is touching to see so recent a bride able to immerse herself in another's affairs, and feel so warmly about a sister's love-making:

(Louisa Hoare to Hannah Gurney.)

"25th January, 1807—I have a great deal to say, but do not know whether to begin with myself or thee. . . . I am at last beginning to feel the pleasure of our quiet establishment and the happiness of a union with my dearest Sam. In that and in all other things there are feelings of flatness which you will not misunderstand, for you know how happy I feel in him, and how affectionately and dearly I love him. Housekeeping and servants are still a weight, but I have advanced gradually, and am much encouraged by what I now imagine my own cleverness. With experience, however, I may prove the fallacy of this imagination. I have much wished, dearest Hannah, that thee would have persevered in thy housekeeping and cutting-out plans in spite of all discouragement, for I should have been far more painfully at a loss had I not attended the little I did, and it is no small relief to be pretty free from these cares just after marrying, when the mind is ever occupied; indeed, I strongly feel what an inestimable advantage it is for everyone to be well prepared in things both great and small before marrying. Seeing how much the little I have is now called into use, and how much what I want is seen and missed, makes me feel the importance of perseverance and vigilance, even when I do not perceive the immediate good effects from them. It also makes me more earnestly wish that thee may not give way to discouragement in anything till thee marries; but pursue with spirit all thy good and useful plans, even if thee seems to thyself going on but poorly in them. I have at times felt more, I think, than any one of us imagined I should, entering a new family, and having to act as Sam's wife before them all. How I wish I may endeavour to obtain a right independence of them, together with a sincere wish to consult their real happiness and wishes, as far as I reasonably can.

"We dined at the Heath on Wednesday, and though I was much depressed in the morning after a fatiguing expedition to London, the day was the easiest I have yet spent, and I felt cheerful and comfortable amongst them all. Engaged as we now are, few days indeed fall to our share to be spent quite alone, but I hope this now will subside. At times, however, I am a little discouraged by the multiplicity of the new calls upon us, as if we should have so very little time quite to ourselves; and I do not think this reasonable. Yesterday was my first full company-day at home, and it was highly interesting to me, and many parts truly pleasant; but being so unused to it, I was a little confused by the number of interesting persons and having to entertain them all. It was Sam's day out, so I determined to enjoy dear Betsy and all her darling and noisy flock. They arrived in a hack, about one, with dear Chenda, and before dinner we four rode up to see our house, which I liked better than before, and with which they were all much pleased. Fowell walked in with Dan at his side, a little before three, and soon after that we dined, the children in the drawing-room and we in the dining-room; I quite 'mistress,' anxious about my dinner and the nice entertainment of all my dear guests. It was so very strange to me to find myself in this capacity with all of them. We chatted pleasantly in the afternoon, and, after an early tea, Betsy, Catherine and brats left us three to a truly snug and happy evening. But I must first tell you how very sweet the darling children were, and what a treat it was to me to have them routing about the house. They all seemed thoroughly to enjoy the novelty, and were quite happy with their exalted ideas of 'Aunt Hoare' and her house, which little Rachel said was almost as fine as the King's house. But now for our evening. Imagine dear Fowell stretched on the sofa, which was wheeled close to a cheerful bright fire, and Chenda and me sitting by him. After a little very pleasant and interesting conversation, I read thy letter to Betsy to him, and determined to talk as well as I could on the subject, feeling so earnestly desirous that it may not be put off, but effectually thought of and acted upon. He seems, certainly, very desirous of being a member of the Society from approving their doctrine in great measure, but still more, I think, from admiring and valuing the effects of it upon their conduct. His sentiments on some of the chief points seemed, however, unfixed. We advised him not to perplex himself so much to settle them, but seriously to weigh what he thought best, considering the present state of his mind; to exert himself about it, and to remember the most important consequences of his being in the Society, and how far he would like to submit to them, even if there were temptations to the contrary—as to oaths, arms, etc.

"About eight dear Sam came in, looking most sweet and cheerful, rejoicing to be at home and delighted to see Fowell. I think I never saw them on more happy or brotherly terms. We all sat round the fire, talking, laughing, and easy and happy, Fowell looking truly one of us again. I told him a good deal about our wedding, and pictured him through the different scenes of the same transaction. We longed for thee, dearest Hannah, to share the pleasure, and felt it was almost unfair that we should have it first. After a snug supper, and a little more comfortable sitting over the fire, we went to bed. This morning we met again at breakfast, and then Chenda and I walked with Fowell and Sam part of the way towards London.

"We rather hope we may see Fowell on Monday to breakfast, but this is uncertain. I think I never saw him look more sweet and innocent in manners than he does now; indeed, I do think thee has got a delightful husband. I did think what two prizes they were when I saw him and Sam walk off arm in arm this morning, both looking so very agreeable, handsome, and delightful.

"One more hint about marrying. I trust thee will not have thy wedding clothes begun without telling me, as from experience, I think I could give thee some useful hints. I rather long for the complete regulation of thy mind, which I could now do to a nicety! . . . I walk out constantly, sometimes round and round the gardens, sometimes part of the way to London with Sam. I enjoy Chenda's company, and Catherine's company too is increasingly valuable to me. I am fully convinced that her coming was the wisest plan: it is so great a help to me. When we are quite undisturbed, we generally get up about seven, and read very comfortably till breakfast, after which Sam goes off to London. Then I go into the kitchen, order dinner, and devote myself for a time to thinking of household concerns; an hour or two of quiet reading and thinking follows this, after which I walk, and often read a little later—for the good of my mind— till dressing-time. I am almost always ready to receive my dearest Sam on his return, and to attend on him while he is in his little dressing-room. Catherine— except at dinner and tea—often leaves us most of the afternoon and evening, which are more than filled up in talking, enjoying the rest of being together, and reading lighter books, such as *Walton's Lives*.

"I do hope you are careful about mad dogs (for the number of people bitten is shocking), and that you will make Joseph go out in boots, for they generally bite men's legs."

"The Heath" at which they dined was the Hoare parents' mansion.

"I do think thee has got a delightful husband." Did ever married sister show more generosity to an unmarried one?

"One more hint about marrying" is more in the conventional style. Yet even at this moment of concentration, the wise Louisa did not forget the danger to young Joseph's legs from the mad dogs, apparently then a public danger, as we shall see later.

If anything were needed to emphasize the atmosphere of marrying and giving in marriage with which Fowell was thus surrounded, it may be found in the fact that his first Earlham intimate, John Gurney, was married to his cousin Elizabeth, not without considerable expostulation from her father, Richard of Keswick, who held to his strict Quaker tenets against first cousins marrying. He and his son-in-law, Sampson Hanbury, "ostentatiously" walked away from the bridal party at Northrepps, so as not to witness the ceremony they would have liked to forbid.

Fowell now came to the most momentous decision of his life, on which all his future career was based. There was no longer any point in his preparing himself to be an Irish landlord. We may wonder what effect he might have had on the chequered history of the next hundred years had he devoted his budding vitality, vision and resources to healing the perennial wounds of that tragic land. As it was, he turned away, refusing a request to stand for Parliament for Dublin University, set aside the encouragement of his friend North, and on 7th May, 1807 was married to Hannah Gurney at Tasburgh Meeting.

Here is the account in Rachel's diary:

"Earlham. 7th May, 1807—We all rose in good time, the weather mild and summer-like; our bride composed and cheerful. Many collected to read as usual before breakfast, and after it we dispersed till it was time to equip ourselves in bridal array. The house was overrun with bridesmaids in muslin cloaks and chip hats. We led our sweet bride to the stairs, where our men joined us, and we had all a pleasant drive to Tasborough. To me the Meeting was solemn in its beginning, and striking from such a circle of brothers and sisters so united in affection; it might well recall a verse in the Psalms, 'Behold how good and pleasant it is for brethren to dwell together in unity.' Our dear couple spoke with much feeling, and Fowell with his usual dignity. Preparing for dinner took up the rest of the morning, and nothing could be prettier than the train of bridesmaids dressed alike in white, with small nosegays, except the bride, who looked lovely, who was still more white, and was distinguished by one beautiful rose. At dinner were my father's fifteen children, and four grand-children. Afterwards the whole party dispersed in different parts of the house. Hannah sat with Elizabeth in her room. At tea all reassembled. Our dearest Fowell was most affectionate and sweet to us all; I think there was scarcely ever such a brother admitted to a family."

"19th May, 1807—I accompanied my father to Northrepps to visit our three dear pairs. The sight of them all so happily married—John and Elizabeth, Sam and Louisa, Fowell and Hannah—was delightful, particularly to see the sweet and happy looks of my dearest Fowell and Hannah."

While this happy and comfortable domestic settlement was taking place, a converted dandy called William Wilberforce and an unconverted rake called Charles James Fox were pressing through the unreformed parliament whose chief preoccupation was fighting, almost unaided, a Hitler-Mussolini called Napoleon, a bill to stop the crimping of negroes in West Africa, by British ships from Liverpool and Bristol. There is no evidence that at this time, Fowell knew much about the subject, or guessed what part it was to play in his life.

CHAPTER II

The Prospect Before Him.   1807—1823

WE NOW SEE FOWELL, AS HIS FAMILY, AND ESPECIALLY HIS WIFE'S FAMILY, ALWAYS called him, entering manhood, married life, and a business career all at once, in 1807.   He was twenty-one years of age, a magnificent figure, four inches over six feet in height, broad-chested and powerfully built, as yet an outdoor sportsman, only just beginning to discard his hunting and shooting in favour of wide reading, deep thought, and the strain of evangelical emotion.   We have no portrait of him at this moment, and must beware of those of some years later, which show only too plainly what physical sacrifice he dedicated to the causes he espoused, so that we find him bespectacled and stooping, while the *Memoirs* speak constantly of his illnesses, his weakness, and exhaustion, though characteristically, the nature of his ailments is not specified, and perhaps the medical science of his day did not know.

In 1807 he must have been a very striking young bridegroom and one who took his responsibilities seriously.   His immediate financial position was most discouraging, and again we must rid our minds of the conception true in later life of the successful brewer and large landowner with a pocket so well furnished that there was no apparent limit to his benefactions.   Very different was the outlook when he sought an establishment for himself and his young wife. We know vaguely that his mother's expectations of an estate in Ireland had proved groundless.   She seems to have been unwise in her choice of investments of the family funds.   Finally she married again, this time an Essex neighbour of the name of Henning and went to live at Weymouth, where for a few months Fowell and Hannah set up housekeeping in a small cottage.   He gave up all hopes of being called to the Bar, and is quoted as saying: "I longed for any employment that would produce me £100 a year if I had to work twelve hours a day for it."

Nothing came immediately to hand, and his Hannah seems to have felt her separation from the Earlham circle, and Catherine Gurney, the "little mother" of them all wrote to him in these terms:

"1807—Your going has been deeply felt, dearest Fowell, and nothing can make up fully for the loss of our dearest Hannah but believing she is happier with thee than she could have been with all of us.   We therefore depend upon thee for making her so, and knowing thy love for her and for us, as well as thy principle, we have the firmest reliance upon thee.   This is by far the greatest earthly consolation in the pain of separation, and I have every hope that your mutual happiness will more and more reconcile us to it.   Yet I wish you to know, my dearest brother, how much we feel we give up for thy sake.   Do feel for dear Hannah in the sacrifice she makes of such a happy home as hers has been, and the trial of entering amongst new scenes and people; all these things affect a woman's feelings more than men are always aware of; so do be very watchful over her, and never let her be long without thy company and soothing, supporting influence, for who can do her half as much good as thee can ?   Not one of us can have the same power to cheer and comfort her.   I hope thee will not dislike my writing a little to thee now and then in my letters to her; I feel you both so very near my heart."

And again a little later to Hannah Buxton:

. "Earlham, 1807—I have just seated myself in my own room immediately after breakfast, whilst the others are taking their turn round the garden this beautiful morning. Nothing can look more bright and cheerful than the place, and everybody seems in a happy mind.

". . . I am far from thinking that the pleasure of being together again will be in any degree lessened by our separation. It seems to me as if nothing could lessen it, but, on the contrary, as if the variety of circumstances in which we shall each have been placed would make it more delightful. I am almost surprised at myself for being now satisfied in leaving thee at Weymouth, and so little impatient to have thee within reach. Thy being treated with so much respect and kindness in thy husband's family is a blessed proof of thy own prudence and principle, and in this light particularly valuable to me. Thy being enabled also to be so contented and usefully employed in thy solitary house, is another source of real satisfaction to me, and the capability of happiness between you and dear Fowell when you are undisturbed is more than either of these perhaps. . . .

"My father always enjoys hearing parts of thy letters which we read to him, and I like that his interest about thee should be kept alive constantly. If it is only on this account, I hope that thee will always write and inform him of thy plans."

Later, Priscilla, her younger sister, stayed with her, and in spite of the sedulous privacy and circumlocution then in fashion regarding intimate matters, we soon become aware of the real cause of Hannah's lonesomeness. She and Fowell were founding a family, and although she was two and a half years his senior, she was very young in many ways. Her father was quite perturbed by the situation in which she found herself after "quitting this sheltered home," and mutual reassurances went backward and forward, the Earlham servants joining in.

"Thee hath the satisfaction, dear Hannah, of knowing that the love of the whole household attends thee. Judd (the housekeeper) was quite enthusiastic in her lamentations, saying 'thee wert a lady she could live and die with'."

Fortunately, all went well. On 25th February, 1808, the eldest child of the marriage, baptised "Priscilla" after her dearly loved aunt, was born "in Mrs. Catherine's chamber" at Earlham.

Soon after this, Fowell visited Brick Lane brewery. "My uncles Sampson and Osgood Hanbury were there, and revived my old feelings of good nephew-ship, they treated me so kindly. This morning I met Mr. Randall and your father," he told Hannah, "I think that I shall became a Blackwell factor."

The Hanburys, however, knew better. They offered him a year's probation in their brewery.

In July he wrote to his Mother, "I was up this morning at four, and do not expect to finish my day's work before twelve to-night—my excuse for silence."

Thus strenuously did the young brewer found the firm we know to-day as the successors of Truman Hanbury and Buxton.

In 1811 he was made a partner, and his seniors delegated to him the task of remodelling the whole administration of the firm. Little did they anticipate the use he made of this. He soon began to track down discrepancies in the books, old and outworn methods among the staff. One employee who withstood this "new broom," was bidden to meet his young master at six o'clock in the morning and after an interview which may well have been long and difficult, was induced to mend his ways. The long-term result was that the growing business ran without so much direct supervision, and that is how Fowell had for most of his life an assured income, and could devote himself to national and international affairs. These had already begun to attract his attention in the earliest period of his married life. From somewhat wide and discursive reading, *Tristram Shandy* and *A Patriot King*, Machiavel and Fenelon, he began to concentrate on such matters as . . . "the general propriety of introducing Christianity into India . . . but is this the proper season?—— The result which I have come to is that it would be highly expedient, and perhaps the only measure which could reinstate our declining power in the East."

Further, we find:

"The Poor Laws are the next question I shall consider." These points he put to his Mother. But he had also formed a friendship with William Allen, Quaker, philosopher and philanthropist, which led him to join "a small society for the purpose of calling the attention of the public mind to the bad effects and inefficiency of capital punishment." In this at least we can see the influence of his sister-in-law, Elizabeth Fry, and the circle in which she moved. He also enumerates "the Bible Society and the deep sufferings of the weavers," the latter being the descendants of Huguenot refugees who had settled in Spitalfields. We shall hear of them again. We are now surveying the germs, but by no means the substance of his lifework, and it must never be forgotten that he did not approach these matters from the economic or political point of view, but from that dictated by his burning evangelical christianity. This leaning of his character is the most difficult for us to understand to-day.

Yet in the case of the powerful group of wealthy, well-educated and influential people with whom he now became more and more closely associated, this, to us, remote creed, produced the very opposite result to that which might be expected. "The Clapham Sect," as the brilliant circle over which Wilberforce presided had become known, and the immediate friends and relatives of Elizabeth Fry knew, somehow, the means to turn all this morbid introspective soul-searching outwards, so that it embraced with the warmest humanity the East End poor, the victims of the unspeakable prison system of that day, the building of a boys' school, and so perhaps, through the cursory interest in the natives of India, a line not destined to be followed, to the dark-skinned underworld of the West Indian islands, and other dependencies of the Crown.

Two perceptible points can be discerned in this progress—his first public appearance on any English platform, as distinct from those at Dublin University, and a peculiar series of personal misfortunes which, unthinkable nowadays, had then a most pregnant influence on his private character. Of the personal misfortunes which, if they happened to a member of the best provided and cared-for class of that day, must have been infinitely more devastating to the general average of the population, and account for the urgent and plaintive belief in an incalculable Providence, rather than in collective effort, the earliest was the death of his brother Edward Buxton.

This brother had been sent to sea in one of the East India Company's ships, under the command of a relative. The boy seems to have run away and joined the army. For five years nothing was heard of him, then Fowell received a letter from a shipmate of Edward's to say that the latter had arrived at Gosport, dying of dysentery. There followed all those harrowing death-bed scenes, familiar to us in the pages of Dickens, the total incompetence of the medical aid of that day, the regrets for wasted life, the readings from the Bible, the prayers for forgiveness of the relatives whose love and good counsel he had

EARLHAM HALL, PRESENT DAY.

HANNAH, LADY BUXTON.

From a portrait by G. Richmond.

neglected, the last words—"he hoped God would soon be so very kind as to take him!" The words are still affecting. Small wonder that they caused Fowell to feel the "increasing power of religious principle." This seems to have been accentuated by attendance at "Wheeler St. Chapel," in the small thorough-fare that runs parallel with Norton Folgate, where the Rev. Josiah Pratt was carrying on his earnest evangel. It must have been reinforced by a severe illness, the nature of which is not stated, and perhaps was not known, which led him, within twelve months, to the brink of the grave into which he had seen his brother sink. The medical gentleman who attended him observed that he must be in low spirits. "Very far from it. . . . I feel a joyfulness at heart which would enable me to go through any pain . . . from faith in Christ." He even went to the length of greeting his brother-in-law with the words: "Sam, I only wish you were as ill as I am!"

However, he took the sensible precaution of removing his young family, increased, by the date of Waterloo, to four, to a house at North End, Hampstead. He himself was obliged to be at Spitalfields, where a great explosion of gun-powder, in a house adjoining the brewery, cost eighty lives and caused great damage, endangering the premises by the fire that resulted. Meanwhile his house was robbed; then, on going to Weymouth, about the affairs of a friend who had fallen into a desperate situation in business: "I can suffer my own misfortunes with comparative indifference," he declared, "but cannot sit so easily under the misfortunes of those near to me, but in this I hope to improve, to be able to look upon trials, in whatever form they appear, as visitations from the merciful hand of God."

He needed all his fortitude. Happening to survey some repairs in progress at the brewery, "we were standing upon a plank, with only room for two, face to face—as soon as we changed places, several bricks fell upon the roof, and one struck (Mr. Back's) head . . . he never recovered from the injury, but died shortly afterwards." Nor was it only the fabric of the brewery which was unsafe—"I went into town this morning some thousands of pounds richer in my own estimation than I returned at night!"

Such were the vicissitudes of the early years of his management of the brewery and founding of a young family. Small wonder that he felt the need of that direct appeal to supernatural power in a world which threatened the human life, even of so fortunate and physically imposing a person as he was. It is difficult to estimate how far the history of these years, in his private life, or in that of the nation to which he belonged, with its sombre background of the Peninsular and Waterloo campaigns, influenced the whole course of his future career. Or how far it was inevitable that anyone of his lively intelligence and masterful character should be swept along upon the crest of what was, at that moment, the newest and most powerful current of thought and feeling?

For what we are really witnessing in the person of Fowell Buxton, is the setting of character in nineteenth century scene. It is always dangerous to date a century of human progress by the calendar. The eighteenth century, for instance, was coloured by the dynastic problem created by Stuart autocracy, at least until 1714, and had not got rid of it until 1745, if then. Our own twentieth century began abruptly with the change from Victoria and the Imperialism of the South African war in 1901, to the surge of social legislation and political ferment which filled all the years from 1905 to 1914.

The transition in which Fowell Buxton found himself enveloped was a longer and even more drastic process. The nineteenth century was already

C

visible to him in the years that culminated in 1815 in the very clothes he wore, the trousers and top hat, which had already supplanted the kneebreeches and three-cornered hat that his father wore, in the umbrella which had replaced the sword. But the confirmation of the new time did not come until the very end of his life, in the railways and financial legislation of the forties, and indeed only attained its marked characterisation in the Crystal Palace, after his death.

It is no matter for surprise, therefore, that he did not know, in his twenties, what it was that would place his name on his nation's roll of honour, or cause his memorial to stand in Westminster Abbey. He must have heard of the putting down of the Slave Trade, by the Ministry of All the Talents, who inherited a promise Pitt had made to Wilberforce, and were in a position to override the opposition of Liverpool shipowners. It would have seemed strange to him, the young country gentleman who had given up his shooting to devote himself to business and to social welfare in a Parliament mainly recruited among his sort of person, to know that Parliament would, in a few years, be composed from Prime Minister, down to the benches, of people who were coming upwards, socially, through ship-owning, and brewing and manufacturing, to be the landed and titled gentry of the latter end of his century. He seems to have come to public life, all unconscious of what was its nature and possibilities in this unlikely manner. Indeed his first public appearance in the county which was to be his home, was made, at the instance of his brother-in-law, Joseph John Gurney, at a meeting of the Norfolk and Norwich Bible Society in September, 1812. He had to be induced to leave his sporting engagements to make a speech "distinguished for its acuteness and good sense." But the result seems to have been to make him the defender of the new society from the attacks made upon it by Dr. Marsh, later Bishop of Peterborough. At the moment, however excellent may have been the matter with which he dealt, the impression he made was rather due to his imposing physical presence. "Elephant Buxton," he was called, on account of his great height and the breadth of his shoulders. In any case, this somewhat obscure effort in the provinces either gave him a confidence and direction he had previously lacked, or the report of it filtered through Quaker evangelical circles. Anyhow he found his place amid the acute industrial depression that succeeded the Waterloo peace. It was at this period that the East End as we have known it, became almost a separate country, the extent of its poverty and overcrowding gradually impressing itself on the slow-moving imagination of the public, and superseding the older "Alsatia" and "Bankside" slums, generally relics of unpoliced clerical or monastic property, along the river from the Fleet to the Temple, and opposite on the southern shore. Anyone who cannot imagine what Spitalfields and Bethnal Green, Whitechapel and Wapping became in a few years, as industries that had been characteristic for centuries declined, and the middle class population, of which Samuel Pepys had been the type, moved out, can read it all in the passionate indignation in which Fowell Buxton described it, in letters reprinted in the *Memoirs*. It culminated in a meeting at the Mansion House at which, after he had spoken, over £40,000 was raised on the spot. Fowell Buxton's speech attracted so much attention that the Prince Regent sent £5,000.

This, however, was not the most important result of the new and unlooked for publicity in which he quite suddenly and without premeditation found himself singled out. Wilberforce wrote from Kensington Gore on 28th November, 1816—"I must in three words express the real pleasure with which I both read and heard of your successful effort on Tuesday last on behalf of the hungry and naked.   It is partly a selfish feeling, for I anticipate the success of the efforts which I trust you will one day make in other instances, in an assembly in which I trust we shall be fellow-labourers, both in the motives by which we are actuated, and in the exertions which will be directed."

Such were the words in which the benevolent philosopher of the eighteenth century joined hands with the new social evangelist of the nineteenth.   Yet it is clear that neither man realised the true nature of the train of events they were setting on foot by this salute.   So little indeed, that for a further two years Fowell Buxton remained apparently quite unconscious of the particular target which the older reformer had in mind.   On the contrary.   We find him with his brother Charles, his brother-in-law, Sam Hoare, and his sister-in-law Fry, deeply struck by the awfulness of the Newgate prison of those days.   The impulse appears to have been sudden and common to all the group.   As we search the voluminous letters, the constant prayers and efforts at self-dedication, there seems to be no clear reason why this particular philanthropy, irrelevant to his subsequent actions, should have taken so strong a hold on him just then.   The *Memoirs* gives it the air of fortuitous occurrence.   "One day while walking past Newgate with Mr. Samuel Hoare, their conversation turned upon the exertions of Mrs. Fry and her companions, for the improvement of the prisoners within its walls."

But how was it that the handsome and vigorous Norwich banker's daughter herself was already so deeply immersed in the life work by which she was to be so well-known?   If we follow this clue, a possible explanation suggests itself.   Elizabeth Gurney might have remained a beauty and a distinguished member of Goat Lane Meeting, with no doubt considerable philanthropies in her own district, and a brilliant place in county society.   But marriage had pitchforked her into the narrow streets, the new over-crowding and industrial problems of the post-Waterloo East End.   It is not credible that anyone of her abounding vitality, and with her memories of the perfect English home at Earlham, could fail to notice the dismal contrast between her new surroundings in St. Mildred's Court, and the pleasant and peaceful view of Colney church tower across the valley of the Yare.   It was easy enough to see God amid the chestnut groves and wide vistas of her childhood, but how dreadfully was He obscured in the terrible miseries left by the Napoleonic War in a London which still contained nearly all the squalor Hogarth depicted, and was hardly touched by the nascent humanitarian sentiment that informed her and all her circle?

Very similar influences would seem to have been in operation in Fowell Buxton's case.   The sport-loving, country-bred boy found himself tied for most of his days to the drab surroundings of Brick Lane.   Small wonder that he is reported to have said:

"I want to be living in a higher key, to do some good before I die."   The opportunity lay ready to his hand.

But we must allow ample scope for the other side of him, which might possibly have acted in any case as a tremendous stimulant to any form of "good works." The evangelistic impulse which had taken so strong a hold on him and all his relations and associates saw all human life as a critical preparation for another life to come.   It was redeemed from morbidity by its passionate urge to throw the gates of Heaven wide, not for the individual or the few, but for all mankind. That is why we find Buxton and his set not specially interested in education or hygiene, as any of us may be nowadays, but impelled towards them from sheer horror at the idea that thousands of their fellow-creatures were unable to read the gospels, possess the clothes and habits that were the outward example of the pure and cleanly life, or were unable to earn the income on which alone honesty and leisure for prayer and reflection were possible.

There may also have been a kind of symbolic relationship between the literally-rendered Gospel phrases about prisoners, the bond and the free, and the wretched half-clad and debased creatures thrust pellmell into Newgate and the numerous mid-London prisons by the repressive political and police measures of the time.

However it may have been, a few weeks after his Mansion House speech had made him "news" as we should say now, he and his brother Charles and the reformer Peter Bedford visited Newgate.

"I saw four poor creatures who are to be executed on Tuesday next. Poor things! God have mercy on them! The sight of them is sufficient for the day," he wrote to his wife. . . . "It made me long that my life may not pass quite uselessly . . . if I were now to begin to serve Him . . . might be the means of some good to my fellow creatures. . . . My mission is evidently now abroad. . . . We would sow the spirit, and we would sow to the flesh; we desire Heaven and we are chained."

Such were the quite mistaken feelings engendered by seeing the condemned cells, or rather ward, in which, on Sundays, those destined for the scaffold were marched to service, and seated opposite a black coffin instead of an altar.

As to the actual venue of all this enthusiasm, it turned out that Wilberforce was right. The wholesomely nurtured Fowell, who felt no doubt a physical nausea, which he instinctively translated into a spiritual aspiration, at the sights and smells of Newgate, soon became aware that to be a minor disciple meant, in the second decade of the nineteenth century, being a Member of Parliament. We are not told what exactly caused this revelation. He doubtless put it down to prayer and meditation. We may think that the practical instincts of the son of the squire turned brewer were aroused. Surely the latter do him almost as much credit as the former. Anyhow his thoughts turned, perhaps naturally, to his mother's influential position at Weymouth. No later than February, 1817 he went down at the invitation of Mr. Williams, presumably the local banker of that name. He seems to have expected to stand as an "Independent" candidate and found that "the word Independent has been the obstacle on this occasion." He did not despair of maintaining his independence. Indeed, like his cousin R. H. Gurney, and his brother-in-law J. J. Gurney, and most of the partners in the Norwich Bank, he was really detached from party politics, and held the electioneering methods of the day in abhorrence. How fluid the situation was can be seen from two unconnected facts. One was noted by Trevelyan, who describes the Liverpool Ministry of that day as "Tory, becoming Liberal after 1822," and the other was the impending struggle for electoral reform, which struck at the privileges of the real eighteenth century Whig grandee as much as at those of his Tory counterpart. Although Fowell Buxton hardly mentions such matters, the burning question of the day lay between those who believed in repressing the sometimes fatuous and sometimes dangerous subversive elements which had lingered ever since the French Revolution, and those who believed in ventilating the many crying and obvious social grievances. Fowell Buxton and most of his near relatives and friends were concerned with something which lay far ahead, and is to-day called social welfare. He seems to have presented himself, in the spring of 1818, as candidate for Weymouth, and certainly wore the blue ribbons of the Tory party. So little was he concerned with mere electioneering, that he said: "It appears to me to be the sphere in which I can do most for my Master's service." How far that is from Walpole and Pitt, Burke and Fox ! He was soon made to realise what was involved. In June he wrote:

"I think we shall have a contest, and a sharp one, and the result is doubtful. . . .

"I am very sick of the bustle, and my expectations of success are considerably diminished. . . . I am exceedingly popular with my party. . . . We have made some most bitter attacks upon Sir (name left blank); I expressed in my speech the disdain I felt at promoting my cause by slander. . . . The violence of my party could hardly bear this . . . and gave some indications of disapprobation. I told them plainly that I would do what I considered an act of public justice, though it offended every friend I had in the town."

Evidently he was no party man.

And yet, in spite of the gutter methods, the majority of illiteracy, the tiny and biased electorate, there was, even then, some undefined commonsense moving in England. In the face of every disadvantage and improbability he was elected, and it is safe to say that a very small minority, if any, of those who cast their votes for him had the faintest inkling of the use to which he would put political power.

"The election is over, I am now going to the Hall to return thanks to my constituents," he wrote to his wife on 29th June. "And so I am a Member of Parliament. . . . I only wish you were here to see me chaired. . . . (This was the process by which the victor in an election was placed in a specially adapted chair, on a small platform provided with handles. A number of stalwart supporters carried him in this, round the marketplace, and at intervals, on a given signal, jerked him aloft, and caught him again more or less) . . . The town is in an uproar. The bugle-horn is at this moment playing, and hundreds of persons are collected on the Esplanade. Everybody has blue ribbons."

It does not seem to have occurred to him to ask how many of that noisy, tipsy crowd knew or cared about the battle for electoral reform, in which they were shortly to be engaged, that for Prison reform, then nearest their new member's heart—or the remote and unmentioned matter of Slavery in the colonies, to which he was to devote most of his parliamentary time and energy, during the next twenty years.

He seems to have established himself in the attention of the House at an early date. The matter of the intolerable conditions in convict transport ships occasioned some two or three debates in which he took part. This seems to have given place to a motion by Lord Castlereagh for a committee to inquire into the state of Prison Discipline, which was succeeded by one by Sir James Mackintosh for a similar inquiry into Criminal Laws. Fowell Buxton rose to second this. He told Joseph John Gurney:

"I spoke for nearly an hour. I was low and dispirited, and much tired (bodily) when I rose. I cannot say I pleased myself. . . . I rose with the cheers of the House and contrived to give much of what was on my mind. Everybody seems to have taken a more favourable opinion of the speech than I did. . . ."

This shows how modest he was. Little as we can now recall the urgency of his case, the accents in which he spoke, we cannot but be impressed by the fact that all sorts of members came up to him and introduced themselves.

Not merely his brother-in-law, Sam Hoare, his cousin R. H. Gurney, and his associate William Smith (the two latter the members for Norwich), but all sorts and conditions of men.

"The House is prepared to receive him with respect and kindness," Smith wrote to J. J. Gurney. ". . . . I recollect very few who have made their début with so much real advantage, and seem likely to maintain the station thus early assumed."

It is the more surprising when we remind ourselves that this was the old unreformed House. Only a dozen years before, Fox was still to be seen there, while that eighteenth century scene, the trial of Queen Caroline, was yet to be enacted nearby before the eyes of many of its members. In an incredibly short time, its figures were to change from a general flavour of port wine and gambling debts, the House of Fox and Pitt, to one of prayerful earnestness, and commercially successful rectitude, the House of Gladstone and Bright and Lord Russell. Fowell Buxton still found it necessary to warn his college friend, North, who was contemplating entering parliamentary life:

". . . . the House loves good sense and joking and nothing else, and the object of its utter aversion is that species of eloquence which may be called Philippian. There are not three men from whom a fine simile or sentiment would be tolerated; all attempts of the kind are punished with general laughter. An easy flow of sterling, forcible plain sense is indispensable; and this, combined with great powers of sarcasm, gives Brougham his station . . . Canning . . . his reasoning is seldom above mediocrity . . . but . . . language so wonderfully happy . . . manner so elegant . . . wit so clear . . . Wilberforce has more native eloquence than any of them, but he takes no pains and allows himself to wander from his subject; he holds a very high rank in the estimation of the House."

There we have the initial judgments of the new member for Weymouth. He must have concealed these somewhat critical opinions very well from the more eminent and powerful of his fellow members, those of whom he spoke with such detachment, but with whom lay all the initiative in getting things done. For, as the result of the two motions of the 1st and 3rd of March, 1819, he found himself nominated to a place on the two Select Committees on capital punishment which resulted. He found, as he told a correspondent:

". . . no man goes so far as I go—namely, to the abolition of the punishment of death, except for murder, but all go a very great way, and if we merely make forgery, sheep-stealing and horse-stealing not capital, it is an annual saving of thirty lives, which is something, and satisfies me in devoting my time to the subject. I am confident that our opinions will ultimately prevail; in short, I am in high spirits on the whole matter."

There we see two things. One is the condition of public opinion amid which he made his parliamentary reputation. To make the matter more vivid, let us remember had he chanced to visit Norwich at that time, he might have seen, at the foot of the bridge over the ditch of the moat of Norwich castle, half a dozen pitiful creatures, some dumb with panic, some with a brute stoicism, strung up in a line, one a girl who had stolen ribbons, others, men who had stolen sheep or horses. Nor was this in any way exceptional. He might have seen a similar sight in any county town, after the assizes. He did not need to see such sights. His humane imagination was sufficiently strong. The other thing is, that while so many of his thoughts and words were concerned (as were those of his sister-in-law, Elizabeth Fry) with Eternal Salvation, in practice, it was the sparing of human life that he was in fact so anxious to achieve. It was no sentimental or visionary other-worldliness that drove him on.

The second Committee could not proceed so swiftly. This Committee did not publish its first report until 1820, when the government brought in a bill for amending the prison laws. After reference to a further Committee, on which he sat, a bill was prepared which became law and marked one of the numerous milestones in the long road to prison reform.

His work received a violent interruption later in the year. On 16th August occurred that charge of the yeomanry against the peaceful meeting of both sexes in St. Peter's Fields, Manchester, remembered as the massacre of Peterloo. It resulted in a full dress debate, which Fowell Buxton reported to J. J. Gurney:

"We have had a wonderful debate; really it has raised my idea of the capacity and ingenuity of the human mind. All the leaders spoke . . . but Burdett stands first . . . the finest . . . clearest . . . fairest display of masterly understanding. . . . Canning was second . . . exquisite, eloquent and kept the tide of reason and argument, irony, joke, invective and declamation flowing without abatement for nearly three hours. Plunkett was third . . . clear and bold. . . . Next came Brougham—and what do you think of a debate in which the fourth man could keep alive the attention of the House from three to five in the morning, after a twelve hours' debate ? Now, what was the impression made on my mind ? . . . First, I voted with the Ministers, because I cannot bring myself to subject the Manchester magistrates to a parliamentary inquiry; but nothing has shaken my convictions that the magistrates, Ministers and all have done exceedingly wrong. I am clear I voted right . . . the bias being on the other side." "P.S. Bootle Wilbraham (who is a Lancaster magistrate) was defending his brethren in the debate, but did it in so low a tone of voice that nobody could hear him; somebody whispered about that he was reading the Riot Act."

This gives us some insight into his attitude towards his parliamentary duties, a very English attitude of using the machinery for what it might be worth, even of taking pleasure in its working, without allowing himself to be rushed to extreme views by the sinister condition of repression then in vogue and which threatened the very means he was beginning to use, for influencing public opinion, namely public meeting and discussion.

In this he may have been in advance of his time. And what a time! A little earlier than the events related above, on going to his brewhouse, to look into the matter of Sunday shifts kept by his work-people, he discovered, apparently by accident, that a vat containing 170 tons of beer had become insecure. He noted the need for repairs and passed on to religious exercises at Wheeler St. Chapel. The effect of prayer, curiously enough, was to increase his uneasiness, and he went back to the brewery. This time there was no mistake. The iron pillars supporting the immense weight were bending. He sent for the surveyor, who confirmed his worst fears. He had just ordered the emptying of the vat and seems to have avoided a very serious accident by about five minutes. But now the ominous faculty of chance struck nearer home. In the early days of 1820 he was considering the question of further representation of Weymouth. The matter was brought home to him by the death of old George III which caused a dissolution of Parliament. He decided to stand and was re-elected. Then his thoughts were suddenly switched away. His doubts about his devoting his time to Parliament were at least in part occasioned by the fact that he was now the father of eight children. Hardly had he made his decision than his eldest son was sent home unwell from school, and died from some unspecified disorder. The younger children, after a bout of whooping cough, developed measles. In a few weeks three infant daughters were dead.

"Thy will be done!" was his broken-hearted exclamation. "Cannot He who rules the universe decide what is best for the children he has lent me ?"

Such was the helplessness of the more fortunate classes on the accession of George IV. We may well wonder how far these constant reminders of the extreme precariousness of life, as then lived, affected his determination to improve it.

He took "the fragments of the family," as he mournfully described the survivors, to Tunbridge Wells, and it seems that for some weeks he was so affected that his reforming zeal found no concrete outlet. Any Parliamentary project he may have nursed was in any case interrupted by the sordid story of the relations of George IV and his Queen. It was the accidental cause of his second intimate meeting with Wilberforce. Foreseeing the disgusting nature of the disclosures that the inquiry into the "disgraceful scenes in the Royal family on both sides" must produce, he called his senior out of the House, and persuaded him to move an adjournment, which he himself seconded. The sense of the House was with him and the Ministers were obliged to give way. Even the tough Brougham said: "You may live fifty years, and do good every day, but you will never do as much as you have done this night!"

About this time, and we may think, partly on account of his meticulous and devoted management, the actual work of the brewery was delegated to others, he gave up residence, and also relinquished the house he had taken as a country residence at Hampstead, and moved to the old hall at Cromer, on the Norfolk coast. This house, long the seat of the Windhams, has now disappeared, but the move was a decisive one and linked him permanently with the district from which his wife had come. To emphasize this, shortly after he had installed his sadly depleted family, he received his sister-in-law, Priscilla Gurney, who had become a hardly less assiduous "Friend" than Elizabeth Fry. Again we are met by the, to us, insoluble problem: How was it that the country-bred girl, with all the best advantages that the age could provide, fell a victim to tuberculosis ? Was it some inherited weakness from far back, or can it have been an over-straining of the spirit ? She seems often to have led the Meeting. However, as things then were, all that a tender-hearted brother-in-law could say was: "As for dear Priscilla, I feel her given to the Lord." Yet the remembrance of her single-hearted piety was with him for the rest of his life, transmuted in the energy with which he waged his many humanitarian campaigns.

He must have torn himself from her bedside. "A flood of business has overtaken me," he wrote to his wife, and a fortnight later, "I have had my hands brimful of business last week, but it has not fatigued me as parliamentary business does; there is no stress on my mind."

The business seems to have been a dinner at the Duke of Gloucester's, and a morning with Wilberforce, who was beginning "to share the seat in my mind which Joseph has so long occupied." This must have been an allusion to his constant correspondence and community of views with Joseph John Gurney. But he found time to tell one of his boys:

"I have had a fine gallop this morning on your capital horse Radical. I ride him with Abraham (Plastow ?) every day, and always as fast as they can go because I have so much to do that I cannot behave like little Lord Linger. . . ."

The rest of the letter was concerned with an account of the poverty, ignorance and helplessness of the poor among whom he was working. But it ends again on the note which must have made him a delightful companion to his growing sons:

"I don't much like to bring you a horn, because I am sure you will disturb the hen-pheasants, and so we shall have no young ones." Thus amid the continual references to the Bible, and adjurations to charity and well-doing, comes a whiff of keen Norfolk air from the bare February copses on the low hills behind Cromer.

Fortunately we can form some idea of the sort of establishment which the young pair set up at Truman's brewery in Brick Lane, Spitalfields. Much of the house has survived, although altered. The sometime entry has disappeared under the necessity for increased office accommodation, but the old staircase still mounts to the spacious corridor on the first floor, where some half dozen rooms still contain the fine Adams style overmantels, and many of the cornices and mouldings. The original mansion must have been built in the middle of the eighteenth century, a typical three-light window, arcaded in the centre, marks the first floor front. The stairhead is lighted by an oval skylight, while at the northern end, the present board-room with its highly ornate ceiling, window-seats in recesses, and magnificent fireplace, gives us a very good idea of the elegance amid which the young family began to grow up. Many portraits of the founders of the business, in oils, or engraved reproduction, are here preserved. There is also a bust of Buxton, in later years, now occupying an appropriate niche on the stairs. Most of the surrounding district has been rebuilt since his death, and it is no longer possible to trace what garden space then surrounded the house, or to picture, without effort, how it must then have dominated the neighbouring dwellings and business premises. But it was an English home, clear, in the best tradition, if smaller and less happily situated than Earlham.

On 30th January, 1821, he had been back at his native Coggeshall for the last of the shooting, but just after this we find the first mention of the African Institution, the new kind of outside-parliament propagandist body, which Wilberforce had been among the first to use, and which apparently, had languished ever since the initial victory of 1807, when the active trade in negroes destined for slavery had been outlawed.

If it did not then find as large a place in his activities as it did subsequently, the reason is not far to seek. Here is a specimen week's programme he reported to his wife:

"Thursday, the Brewery; Friday, Cape of Good Hope Slave Trade; Saturday, Lord Lansdowne's; Monday, Prison Bill; Tuesday, Brougham's Bill on Education; Wednesday, I make a speech to the children of Spitalfields; Thursday, Brewery and Mail coach; Friday, home!'

Truly, there were giants in those days. Later, he was "working very, very hard." Prison Discipline, Criminal Law, again a mention of Slave Trade. But amid so much, he took up the report of a Baptist Missionary, the Revd. Mr. Peggs, just returned from India, on the subject of Suttee. Apparently only in British Madras was this custom allowed to persist unchecked, but in spite of his attempts, the government side-tracked the matter, as being within the province of the East India Company. He seems, meanwhile, to have spoken strongly about the African Institution, and to have drawn a step nearer

Wilberforce, whom he found "warm to excess; he thanked me for the boldness of my remarks." They had dined together during the month of March, and in reply to a question as to who was the greatest man he had ever known, Wilberforce, who was "quite delightful" told him, "Out of all comparison, Pitt; I never think of his superiority without reflecting that he who is least in the Kingdom of God, is greater than he!"

So the evening must have passed, and it would be temptingly picturesque to say that , in the growing intimacy of the two reformers, the eighteenth century handed on its torch to the nineteenth. However, it is not quite so simple as that. Wilberforce did not live to see the accession of Victoria, but he was a long way removed from the period of Hogarth and Walpole, and even Smollett, more nearly his contemporary. Yet he does typify something of an earlier age, which was about to disappear, its last traces lingering in Palmerston for a further twenty years, the world whose politics, expressing its social progress, were entirely in the hands of the titled, the landed and the wealthy. The elegant little man had won himself a hearing by his sweet temper and bewitching voice in an assembly in which such qualities were still appreciated. Fowell Buxton would have made two of him physically and had no need to disguise himself in the arts of persuasion. He was one of the then relatively small number of what we should call to-day, city men, a practical brewer, who, though he might sit for Weymouth, knew Spitalfields street by street, its poverty and its problems. It was his speech on the Bill for the Abrogation of the Death Penalty which seems to have finally decided Wilberforce, after reference to his friend, Stephen, to request Fowell Buxton to press the campaign which had originally aimed at the prohibition of a trade, largely carried on by British personnel, and which the new consciousness of the time would no longer tolerate, to the logical conclusion of the Abolition of Slave-owning.

So perhaps there was a continuity of interest that connected the otherwise unlikely-looking partners. Fowell Buxton had been told by his mother of the iniquities of slave-owning. His sister had refused to eat slave-grown sugar. He had been struck by many things, as we have seen, in the conditions of the coloured populations of those lands, far overseas, in which British adventure and commerce had laid up so heavy a British responsibility. No young Member of Parliament could fail to be impressed by Wilberforce, the associate of so many great figures of the political scene then closing. It was with such preparation that the critical letter passed from the elder by thirty years, to the younger, in these terms:

"London, 24th May, 1821.

My dear Buxton,

It is now more than thirty-three years since, after having given notice in the House of Commons, that I should bring forward, for the first time, the question concerning the Slave Trade, it pleased God to visit me with a severe indisposition by which indeed I was so exhausted that the ablest physician in London of that day declared that I had not stamina to last above a very few weeks. On this I went to Mr. Pitt and begged of him a promise which he kindly and readily gave me, to take upon himself the conduct of that great cause.

"I thank God I am now free from any indisposition; but from my time of life, and much more from the state of my constitution, and my inability to bear inclemencies of weather and irregularities, which close attendance at the House of Commons often requires, I am reminded, but too intelligibly, of my being in such a state that I ought not to look confidently to my being able to carry through any business of importance in the House of Commons.

"Now for many, many years I have been longing to bring forward that great subject, the condition of negro slaves in our trans-Atlantic colonies, and the best means of providing for their moral and social improvement, and ultimately for their advancement to the rank of a free peasantry; a cause this, recommended to me, or rather enforced on me, by every consideration of religion, justice and humanity.

"Under this impression I have been waiting with no little solicitude for a proper time and suitable circumstances of the country, for introduction of this great business; and latterly for some Member of Parliament, who, if I were to retire, or be laid by, would be an eligible leader in this holy enterprise.

"I have for some time been viewing you in this connection, and after what passed last night, I can no longer forbear resorting to you, as I formerly did to Pitt, and earnestly conjuring you to take most seriously into consideration the expediency of your devoting to this *blessed service*, so far as will be consistent with the due discharge of the obligations you have already contracted, and in part so admirably fulfilled, to war against the abuses of our criminal law, both in its structure and its administration. Let me than entreat you to form an alliance with me, that may truly be termed holy, and if I should be unable to commence the war (certainly not to be declared this session) and still more, if when commenced, I should (as certainly would, I fear, be the case) be unable to finish it, do I entreat that you would continue to prosecute it. Your assurance to this effect would give me the greatest pleasure; pleasure is a bad term—let me rather say, peace and consolation; for, alas, my friend, I feel but too deeply how little I have been duly assiduous and faithful in employing the talents committed to my stewardship; and in forming a *partnership* of this sort with you I cannot doubt that I should be doing an act highly pleasing to God, and beneficial to my fellow creatures. Both my head and heart are quite full to overflowing, but I must conclude. My dear friend, may it please God to bless you both in your public and private course. If it be His will, may He render you an instrument of extensive usefulness; but above all, may He give you the disposition to say at all times 'Lord, what wouldest Thou have me to do or to suffer?' Looking to Him, through Christ, for wisdom, and strength. And, while active in business and fervent in spirit upon earth, may you have your conversation in Heaven and your affections set on things above. There may we at last meet, together with all those we love, and spend an eternity of holiness and happiness complete and unassailable.

Ever affectionately yours,

"W. Wilberforce."

It may seem astonishing that anyone who had spent his parliamentary career in an atmosphere of Burke, Sheridan and Fox, should walk so closely hand in hand with God. On the other hand, there is the authentic prolixity, the feeling that anything worth saying, was worth saying well, characteristic of one who, however mercantile his origin, had long been an English gentleman, addressing an exclusive assembly of English gentlemen. A modern Englishman would find such an appeal insufferably longwinded, and probably suspect in its evangelical urgency that any legislative act could possibly be so closely scrutinised in realms above. A modern Frenchman, on the other hand, while agreeing with the latter suspicion, and prone to rate the verbiage as an example

of English perfidy, would, one feels, nevertheless, listen with some attention
to periods so well turned, and delivered with a certain stateliness.   This appeal,
then, seems to lay bare, better than any comparable document, the change that
had come over the world, of which the typical figure had until lately been,
let us say, Horace Walpole, and was turning it into the world of which Spurgeon
and Theodore Parker were to be some of the best known public figures. Doubt
less many unrelated but confluent sources lay at the back of such a change.
Wesley comes to one's mind, and if we admit Wesley, we may be reminded of
many another humbler gospeller, stretching back through Bunyan, possibly as
far as Wycliffe.   For the select company that filled the House of Commons,
the county administration, and the Court of the Georges, was only part of
England, if the more visible, can we say superficial part!

Had he needed any further urging, Fowell Buxton might have found it in the
last words of his dearly loved sister-in-law, Priscilla Gurney.   In spite of the
convulsive coughing characteristic of her dread disease, she was able to pronounce
the words: "The poor, dear Slaves!"   Such was the dying legacy of one of the
seven pretty daughters of Earlham, who in their scarlet cloaks and purple boots,
had been wont to join hands across the road to prevent the Norwich coach from
passing.   We have seen how important a place family life had always had in
Fowell Buxton's feelings.   It is difficult to apportion the weight which this
dying injunction may have had with him, and that which belonged to
Wilberforce's exhortation.   But from this point matters came to a head.
Zachary Macaulay (who had been asking the Friends' advice as to the training
of his son in oratory) Dr. Lushington, the veteran of the earlier Slave Trade
campaign, and Lord Suffield, head of the Harbord family, the North Norfolk
Whig grandee, met at Cromer Hall.   The plan of action seems to have been
decided then, about 1st October, 1822.   Wilberforce (most of whose letters
to Fowell Buxton have perished) wrote enthusiastically about the lines then
laid down, and shortly after proposed a further meeting at Marden Park, his
new country house.   "Long and deep," we are told by Wilberforce's
biographer, "were their deliberations how best to shape those measures which
were to change the structure of society throughout the Western World."

We cannot keep this note too continually in mind in studying the motives
that led Fowell Buxton on his way.   At the very time of this meeting, both he
and Wilberforce were bitterly reproaching themselves with prayers and
repentance for not having been more active in the matter.   Fowell particularly
seems to have been driven on by an almost morbid feeling of the worthlessness
of so much of human life, that is hard to comprehend in a man so otherwise
sane and normal, who could at the same time write to his eldest surviving son:
"How are the pheasants, and the baby, and the rats, and the ponies, and all the
other animals ?   Love to you all!"

Yet the moment he turned his thoughts to the Slavery question we find him
crying out to God, "for guidance that, renouncing sin, I may walk worthy of
my high vocation, in and through Jesus Christ my Lord."

Such was his impetus, and he does not even seem to have glanced at the fact
that one at least of the major considerations governing the whole status of
negro servitude was the prosaic one of the taxation tariff on East Indian grown
sugar, about to be repealed, and leading on to the larger issue of Free Trade.
But no! He saw the whole matter from a visionary standpoint.   He never set
eyes upon the black thousands for whom he laboured, never visited either
the country of their origin or that of their bondage.   He seems to have looked

on them in the light of human souls in danger of damnation rather than as human bodies in need of civil rights, congenial conditions and a more easy-going occupation. Nor had he the least first hand knowledge of the victims of Suttee. "The Slave Trade, Slavery, Indian Widows, Criminal Law, Prisons, Police!" he assured his Maker should have his earnest and unremitting attention. He would renounce the world for their sake. Thus did the prosperous young brewer and country gentleman dedicate himself.

The first steps were Wilberforce's "Appeal on behalf of the Slaves," and the foundation of the Anti-Slavery Society for the purpose of collecting evidence and spreading information, of which Fowell Buxton became Vice-President. He was even conscious of this break or duplication in his mind. About this time he told his wife:

"I am very earnest about Slavery; it seems to me that this is to be the main business of my life—this and Hindoo widows: I am well contented and want no other business. How odd are the transitions of the human mind! How occupied mine was with pheasants and partridges till I left Norfolk!" He made this naïve confession after an interview with the Under-Secretary of State, who made an appointment for him with Lord Bathurst "relative to my Slave Bill."

The current business of the Society was to arrange the signature of petitions, and in this the Friends lent them aid. It was their appeal, urged by Wilberforce himself, that was to form the opening of the action.

The scene on that March day of 1823 can be imagined. The old House, ripe for Reform, but still dominated by the historic class that had wielded power since the English Revolution and even earlier, were there in strength. The House in which the debate opened must have been stuffy in any case, and few of us who prefer modern ideas of ventilation, can regret on these grounds, the fire of 1848 which destroyed it. Most pictures we have of it show three windows behind the Speaker's chair, and show them always hermetically closed. They may well have been, for it was about this time that the Thames, just outside, was losing its historic character as a waterway, and acquiring that of a vast open sewer, while its tributaries, the Fleet ditch, and the stream we know as the Serpentine, discharged an ever-increasing load of "sludge" into it, until its stench was unbearable and sometimes fatal.

In the stuffy air of the House, too, lingered the passions of the debates of the period. How far material surroundings and habits of debate, even traditional appearance and methods of men, have created a special atmosphere, it is difficult to say. Many of the members who listened to Wilberforce that day had grown up in the presence of a continual battle between a sovereign who would have liked to be an autocrat, and an executive determined to govern in their name. Across this lay an entirely different influence, the urgency forced upon such an assembly by thirty years of standing with few or dubious friends against a continental military tyranny quite as ominous to them as anything we have known in the Twentieth Century. This may account for the fact that, when we search the intimate records of the time, the many lives and memoirs of George Canning, Secretary for Foreign affairs, and leader of the House, we find little or no trace of Wilberforce's speech. Canning was concerned with what were, to him, far graver matters, the critical "Post War" settlement of those days, the ambitions of France in the Peninsula, the attitude of the Czar towards Turkey. When Wilberforce introduced the petition by reminding the House that it was nearly thirty years since he had presented the first of its kind, against the "kindred iniquity of the Slave Trade," and followed this up by affirming it to be "the first stone of an edifice which would stand at some future period, an ornament to the land," Canning asked if it was the intention to found a motion upon it. He may well have been nervous of the effect upon the delicate situation in the Spanish and French overseas possessions, then in a state of turmoil. Wilberforce replied:

"It is not, but such is the intention of a friend of mine." Fowell Buxton then gave notice that on the 22nd April, (he actually said 22nd April, but apparently the date was altered), he would submit a motion, that the House take into consideration the state of Slavery in the British Colonies. He seems to have prefaced his motion by a letter written to Wilmot Horton, Secretary to Earl Bathurst, the member of the Cabinet charged with the conduct of the Colonial office. This contains the main lines of Abolitionist policy as then foreseen. They are:

(1) The making of the slaves into nationals of the islands in which they were at the time living, and even giving them some interest in its soil.
(2) That they cease to be chattels in the eyes of the law.
(3) That they be considered credible witnesses in a court of Law.
(4) That owners must be prepared to prove their title to any slave they claimed.
(5) That manumission be permitted.
(6) That the Spanish practice of fixing the value of the slave by competent authority be followed.
(7) That no governor, judge, or attorney-general should be a slave-owner.
(8) That provision be made for the religious instruction of slaves.
(9) That marriage be sanctioned and enforced.
(10) That the slave's Sunday be free for rest or religious instruction, and that time be allowed him for cultivation of his own ground for food-stuffs.
(11) That the authority of the master to fix punishment be regulated, and a substitute found for the driving system.
    There was also included a plea for determining a date, after which children born in slavery should be considered free and have provision for their education.

The reply from Wilmot Horton was a proposal for delay, which Fowell Buxton, with studious politeness, rejected. He told his Norfolk neighbour, Mrs. Upcher, of the confidence with which he set out for the House. His opening speech seems to have been timed for 5 o'clock on 15th May. Before he spoke several petitions, and one counter-petition, were read. The formal resolution he moved was: "That the state of slavery is repugnant to the principles of the British Constitution and of the Christian Religion; and that it ought to be gradually abolished throughout the British Colonies with as much expedition as may be found consistent with due regard to the well-being of all concerned."

He seems to have asserted that the intention of the body of opinion for which he spoke was Abolition, but by slow degrees which "shall partly conduct us to the annihilation of slavery."

He began by explaining that he stood in the place of Wilberforce at the latter's invitation. He glanced at the difficulties of West Indian members and their fear of possible agitation among the slaves. He went on to give details of some revolting floggings. He then declared that the aim of Abolitionists was nothing less than total emancipation beginning with those now children. He quoted the examples of this practice in some of the New England states and that of the islands of Ceylon, Bencoolen (the district subsequently ceded to the Dutch) and St. Helena and Colombia, South America.

"Now, Sir," he pleaded, "let the House observe the moderation with which we proceed. We say 'make no more slaves—desist from that iniquity—stop—abstain from an act, in itself full of guilt, entailing in its consequences as much of misery as any felony you can mention'."

Having established this point, of the freeborn status of negro children, he went on to deal with the adult slaves, admitting that many slaves were hardly fit for emancipation, for which he blamed the system. From this he went on to demolish the claim of the owner, declaring it to be similar to that of the receiver of stolen goods, because it originated in theft and kidnapping. He deduced from this that the negro slave's child was even less attachable as the property of the master. His peroration ran: "We do not say 'Retrace your steps,' but 'Stop.' We do not say 'Make reparation for the wrong you have done' but 'Do no more wrong, go no further; complete what you have commenced; screw from your slave all that his bones and muscles will yield you—only stop there': And when every slave now living shall have found repose in the grave, then let it be said that the country is satiated with slavery, and has done with it for ever."

Thus was the matter placed before the House, and caused, we are told, a long and lively debate. Mathieson, one of the most penetrating historians of the movement (see *British Slavery and its Abolition*) is critical of the way in which Buxton framed his case and considers it made slavery more iniquitous than the Trade, and was the least persuasive way of inducing West Indian plantation interests, who had, he says, a representation of over fifty members in the House, to accept any alteration in the status of their human property.

The person who had to deal with the matter was, however, Canning, leader of the House and Foreign Secretary in the government of Lord Liverpool. It does not take much imagination to see why he was not really very deeply impressed by Buxton's speech. He had spent his whole adult life in the House, at one of the most strenuous periods of its existence. He may have been a humane man, but he had as much time and energy to spare for the wrongs and disabilities of coloured people he had never seen and any change in whose condition might turn fifty votes against the government, as any other Cabinet Minister in a similar predicament. West Indian interests were already alarmed at Fiscal motions tending to destroy their monopoly of the sugar trade. The shadow of the Repeal of the Corn Laws, twenty years away, was already cast over the right little, tight little island which had challenged the whole military world by very nearly starving its own labouring classes. Canning may have felt that Slavery was a bad thing. He had the upper-class eighteenth century upbringing which made it easy for him to speak in terms of classical disapproval of bondage. He and his sort of person had just been aiding the Greeks to regain some degree of national independence, and had also, at the instance of the very people who were backing Buxton's motion, been engaged in altering the criminal law and the conditions of penal servitude at home. He could hardly, even had he been inclined to do so, have come out frankly as a supporter of slavery, bluntly so-called. But we may well feel that he must have been obsessed, like any other political leader, with the smallness of current majorities, unlike the massive disparities of our day, and with the disquieting stirring of political alignment into new phases, Whigs and Tories beginning to think of, if not call, themselves

"Liberals" and "Conservatives." We can perhaps enter into his mind as he listened to Buxton, thinking, "This is a private member's motion. If I give it government support, I lose at least fifty votes, of the West Indian interest and its associates. On the other hand, if I withstand it I shall have against me this new vociferous body, in and out of the House, mainly dissenters and evangelicals, which has such formidable means of moving public opinion, and will enlist all the East Indian interest, plus the people who think that the labouring classes should have cheap sugar."

He took what any parliamentarian will consider the natural course. He proposed an amendment which led on to the resolutions, which were carried:—

"(1) that it is expedient to adopt effectual and decisive measures for ameliorating the condition of the slave population in His Majesty's colonies.

(2) that, through a determined and persevering, but at the same time judicious and temperate enforcement of such measures, this House looks forward to a progressive improvement in the character of the slave population, such as may prepare them for a participation in those civil rights and privileges which are enjoyed by other classes of His Majesty's subjects.

(3) that this House is anxious for the accomplishment of this purpose at the earliest period that shall be compatible with the well-being of the slaves themselves, with the safety of the colonies, and with a fair and equitable consideration of the interests of private property."

Anyone who has had anything to do with the support of the great progressive movements of the nineteenth century will recognise the tone, familiar to the debates on Home Rule or Women's Suffrage, the inevitable but desperate antagonism between the shifts of the parliamentary strategist, and the emotion, thrilling but slightly vague, of the full-blooded reformer. He assented to Buxton's statement that Slavery was repugnant to the Principles of the British Constitution and the Christian religion, but pointed out that both had tolerated it for centuries. Canning's sentiments were unexceptionable. The three clauses might be paraphrased—"Amelioration of the negro's condition as soon as he is fit for it, without upsetting the value of the owner's property."

Of the clauses which Buxton and Wilberforce were said to have derived from the proposals of Dundas, and which were set out in the memorandum to Wilmot Horton, and of which the final one, the immediate emancipation of children born in slavery, had actually been proposed in 1807 by Earl Percy, not one was fully implemented, unless the general conciliatory tone may be taken to mean that Nos. 8 to 10, favouring religious instruction, sanctioned and enforced marriage and free Sundays, were to be proceeded with at once.

Abolitionists at least were under no doubt as to the direction in which Canning's resolution was tending. This policy was dubbed "amelioration" —a title which indicates the stately pace, as of a cosmic process, at which it was hoped the negro might emancipate himself. Like all such pronouncements it made all too obvious the fact that most negroes then alive would emancipate themselves by the normal course of death, without finding their earthly conditions sensibly modified.

The debate was continued by Ellis who had the difficult task of representing the West Indian opinion in the House. He was, however, accustomed to the task, for as long ago as 1797 he had been the mover of a motion reproaching

"THE SLAVE MARKET."

From a picture in the possession of the Anti-Slavery Society.

NORTHREPPS HALL, GARDEN FRONT.

From a pencil sketch by Priscilla Johnston.

the assemblies in the West Indian islands with having failed to implement the measures of amelioration then enacted. He referred to this, and to several other acts, chiefly concerned with granting religious instruction to slaves. He was able to make play with the appointment of curates and coroners' courts. He stated, on his personal authority, that the whip was carried as a badge of authority. He was able to assent to the proposal for the free Sunday, but told the House, and it must have been his strongest point, that members must expect modifications of detail in any enactment, or to put it more plainly, that they were legislating for unknown conditions thousands of miles away.

This brought up William Smith of Norwich, who complained that the returns that might have justified Ellis's assertions were uncompleted and even more disappointing, and brought the debate back to the vital point of the fact of ownership of man by man. Sir George Rose, another West Indian, gave details of the progress of religious instruction, in the estate he had inherited. The parochial clergy were "too highly educated for the missionary task among human beings so utterly ignorant and narrow-minded." He had found the Moravians and Wesleyans far more effective, presumably because they were less highly educated.

But his speech, quaintly as it may read to-day, brings up the very quality of the debate most difficult for us to seize. Sir George, a practical planter, talked about the negroes in terms of souls to be saved, just as much as Fowell Buxton. He gives us some vivid, if unintentional, side-lights.

Next came Mr. Bright to justify the planters against the unmerited obloquy to which they had been subjected. The attack he described with such candour was apparently the Revd. William Cooper's *Negro Slavery*, and he endeavoured to controvert the statements made therein from the official returns on the table.

Then Mr. Sykes brought the discussion back to the main question of emancipation, supporting the view advanced in *Negro Slavery*, and throwing doubt on the willingness of the Colonial legislature to implement the resolutions. Against this, Mr. Marryat read the House long extracts from the reports of these legislatures, asserting the happy results of the cessation of the Slave Trade.

This aroused Brougham, and with him we pass into a different atmosphere. Border by birth, he was partly Scottish by parentage and wholly by education. He was one of the earlier examples of the new Scotland. There is nothing in him of the picturesque if outmoded Jacobite of two generations earlier. Brougham made his way, forerunner of the new invasion of England, not by Divine right and the claymore, but by superior education and ferocious logic. He had established himself as a person to be listened to, by the bold but dangerous course he had taken at the "trial," as it is always called, of Queen Caroline, actually the debate on the Bill of Pains and Penalties brought in to the House of Lords against her. It is a marked coincidence that his associates in that famous episode, Wilberforce, Lushington, Denman, were all among the Abolitionists. Brougham dealt with the Ameliorationists with the savage satire of which he was master. He took one by one, the favourable reports that had been quoted, the fears that had been expressed, and turned them upside down, or showed them to be groundless, He even ran to earth one hopeful statement as to the number of negroes baptised by a hard-working curate, and which spoke in terms of thousands, and suggested that this remarkable result had been brought about by a fee of a dollar a head baptised. He was followed by Bernal and Baring, both pleading conciliation, which was their name for Amelioration, and Buxton replied with some heat pointing out that nothing in the resolutions relieved the slave from his chattel condition, or his child, or protected him from the lash.   These are his words:

"What then! does the slave require any hint from us that he is a slave, and that slavery is of all conditions the most miserable ?   Why, Sir, he hears this, he sees it, he feels it, too, in all around him.   He sees his harsh uncompensated labour, he hears the crack of the whip; he feels—he writhes under the lash. Does not this betray the secret ?   He sees the mother of his children stripped naked before the gang of male negroes and flogged unmercifully; he sees his children sent to market, to be sold at the best price they will fetch; he sees in himself, not a man, but a thing—by West Indian law a chattel, an implement of husbandry, a machine to produce sugar, a beast of burden!   And will any man tell me that the negro, with all this staring him in the face, flashing in his eyes, when he rises in the morning and when he goes to bed at night—never dreams that there is injustice in such treatment till he sits himself down to the perusal of an English newspaper, and then, to his astonishment, discovers that there are enthusiasts in England who from the bottom of their hearts deplore and abhor all negro slavery ?   There are such enthusiasts; I am one of them; and while we breathe we will never abandon the cause, till that thing—that chattel—is reinstated in all the privileges of man!"

There can be no mistaking the authentic note of evangelical vision in such words, and oddly they must have rung under that roof that had contained so much sophistry and sturdy courage, on the ears of men who, only a decade earlier, had been listening to the meagre and painfully growing confidence that Britain might remain unconquered and perhaps uninvaded.

Abolitionists felt so dubious of the government's intentions, that Buxton, Wilberforce, and William Smith had an interview with Canning, of which a detailed account was drawn up, submitted to Canning, and returned with his comments.

Either as a result of being so closely catechised, or from motives of expediency connected with the general political outlook, the Colonial office of those days showed a surprising agility.   By the end of the month a circular had been addressed to the governors of the West India islands, which dealt with the points of Buxton's original programme, apparently as implemented by the resolutions of the House, though in a rather different order, which may throw some light on what was thought advisable to suggest to officials and administrators on the spot, so many thousand miles away, which British Legislators were dealing with:

(1)   Religious instruction was put first,"Christian education."
(2)   To make this possible Sunday markets and Sunday labour were to stop.   This meant that where subsistence was not provided by the master, time had to be allotted during the week for the slave to cultivate his plot.
(3)   Acquisition, possession and disposal of property.
(4)   Marriage to be legalised and protected.
(5)   Separation of families by sale or otherwise to be prevented.
(6)   Power of owner to punish to be regulated.
(7)   "To abolish the degrading punishment of females."
(8)   Testimony of slaves to be admitted in court.
(9)   Slaves not to be detached from the plantation to which they belong.

(10) Manumission at a fair price.

(11) The use of the whip to be abolished, either as an emblem of authority or a stimulus to labour.

(12) To establish Savings Banks for the use of slaves.

A comparison of this effective outcome of the first full-dress debate, shows us what modification the politicians in power had imposed on the demands of those whom Buxton had rightly described as "enthusiasts." The first demand that slaves should be attached to the island, presumably that in which they were living at the time of the passing of the resolutions, was allowed, but the next, that they should cease to be chattels before the law, was only indirectly met. The third concerned the value of their testimony and was conceded, but the fourth again, which really was the basis of ownership, was denied. The fifth, for manumission, and the sixth, basing it on the Spanish system, were practically granted. The seventh, aimed at slave-owning officials, was ignored, which was perhaps inevitable, for Mathieson states that the Governor of Demerara, General Murray, was one of these. The eighth, ninth and tenth dealt with religious instruction, marriage and the free Sunday and were all granted, they were, in fact, placed first. The eleventh, that sought to limit, but very vaguely, the power of the owner to punish, was not only granted, but the "degrading" punishment of females was prohibited, and most remarkable of all, the use of the whip was to be abandoned. This last alarmed so old a campaigner as Wilberforce, who knew by experience how grave a break with tradition was involved.

The memorandum was in fact, if not in intention, a most astute political manœuvre, for while it did not give way on the crucial point to all slave-owners —their property in the negro—it did attack all the lesser incidents of slave-owning that could no longer be defended in the new humanitarian nineteenth-century England. Who was going to rise in Parliament to support the flogging of stripped women, the break-up of families? Who was going to attack, in that atmosphere, the organisation of religious instruction, thrift and ownership of a home and plot of land? The West Indian party was deprived of all its best debating points. The Abolitionists had all their most spectacular demands granted, except one—and that was one which brought into question the depriva-tion of the individual of his private property, duly bought and paid for—a proposition not within the compass of the imagination of the members in 1823.

Alas, that anything so shrewdly planned and plausibly phrased should run up against the living flesh and nerves of human nature! Wilberforce knew with prophetic insight that what looked so moderate and timely had in fact made inevitable a fierce conflict. And at the meetings of Abolitionists at his house Macaulay echoed his fears. For while Buxton and those behind him felt that they had been cheated of the substance by a grant of the shadow, the actual Slave-owner, when he learned what was proposed, went in fear of his life. We must try next to see what so devastating a theory as Abolition meant on the spot in which it was to work.

CHAPTER III

THE DARK BACKGROUND. 1823—41

IF WE REALLY WANT TO SEE WHAT IT WAS WITH WHICH BUXTON WAS DEALING in the main effort of his best years, we must now summarise what were the conditions of Slave-owning that he attacked. This is rendered obligatory by what most modern minds find most extraordinary in his attitude. For half his life, practically all his parliamentary career, the fate of the African negro slave was always in his thoughts, nearly always on his lips, or the subject of his writing. Yet he never saw a plantation, or a negro slave at work. In the weeks of suspense which followed the sending out of the House of Commons resolutions with Earl Bathurst's explanatory memorandum, he seems to have considered "an invitation from Lord Huntingdon to visit the West Indies in person; but when this plan was referred to Mr. Wilberforce, he gave a most decided opinion against it."

So says the original edition of the *Memoirs*. A note adds:

"Mr. Buxton could not, as yet, have been aware of the reception which his proposed reforms would meet with in the West Indies, and the deadly hostility with which their author would be regarded, or he would not have entertained for an instant the idea of this visit. Captain Studholme Hodgson of the 19th Foot, in his work called, *Truths from the West Indies*, after mentioning "the volumes of abuse lavished upon Sharpe, Wilberforce, Lushington, Stephen, Buxton and Admiral Fleming" continues: "This enmity seems to be more deadly towards the two latter, than even that entertained for the others; and I will undertake to say that were these two gentlemen to arrive in any island in the West Indies, and venture to move out unsurrounded by a guard of those grateful beings, who night and day implore blessings upon them, they would inevitably be torn to pieces by the Europeans who would all vie as to who could most mangle their bodies."

However exaggerated this may have been, Buxton did not go, and it is hard to believe that his visit would have made much difference to his convictions. Certainly threats and abuse would not have disturbed him, for we have seen that he had more than the average share of physical courage. Further than that, it does not seem that any actual contact with plantation negroes would have altered his views or modified his strong emotions. He did not look at the problem as a modern reformer would, in terms of political equity and welfare. His actions sprang from his strong reaction to the wave of Evangelical Christianity just then sweeping the country and involving him, parallel but distinct from the great resurgence of Quaker thought and feeling that involved so many of his relations. Quaker and Evangelical alike, as we survey their actions and peruse their writings, strike us as beginning by regarding prisoners in British gaols or negroes in British plantations, more as eternal souls to be saved, than as creatures of legislation and administration. From that attitude there is a most sudden leap to the most practical acts of material charity. For instance, Elizabeth Fry had hardly ceased reading Holy Writ to the irreclaimables of Newgate and The Fleet, before she was helping them to decent clothes as any good housewife and mother of a young family well might. In the same way, Buxton could declaim against the slave's loss of his personal rights over his body, as if he were speaking of a lost soul, and the moment he stooped to frame his proposals, these were concerned with where and how the negro was to live, how many pounds, shillings and pence he was to pay for his redemption, and how often he was to be whipped. Nor is it very wonderful when we consider how often in the gospel narrative, which was seldom long absent from his lips, the loftiest spiritual exhortation we know stands in the next sentence to some act of practical charity, whatever we may think to-day of its sometimes alleged miraculous character, some matter of feeding the hungry and curing the sick. It may well be that the work of Buxton, and that of his relative Elizabeth Fry, and of the Americans who, a generation later, were to achieve their own Abolitionist victory, springs ultimately from the unique dissemination of the English Bible. But there may be contributory causes. No logical-minded Frenchman, or well-administered German will ever understand something that is earlier than even our biblical habit, the English ability to say one thing and do another, which has earned us so much incomprehension and abuse, and still makes us *Perfide Albion* in so many foreign eyes.

Now of whom and of what was Buxton thinking and speaking? Partly of the confused condition of subject races in the great vague territory now roughly included in the Union of South Africa, and the island of Mauritius, in both of which Great Britain was becoming by various fortuitous circumstances the dominant power, and remains as it were, relatively a newcomer to-day.

But principally he was concerned with the West Indies, in some of which we had been the first European settlers, and to which we, or in certain cases our forerunners, had carried bodily, under conditions from which the twentieth century mind shrinks, hundreds of thousands of very primitive dark-skinned natives of tropical Africa.

To survey this territory to-day, and its main outlines are unchanged since Buxton avoided it, we should probably embark by passenger plane at George-town, Demerara, or British Guiana as it has come to be called. This settlement of Dutch origin had been ceded to us in 1815 and was administered as a Crown colony, its adjacent part of Berbice being incorporated with it. Flying almost due north about a hundred miles from the western extremity of Guiana we should see below us the largish island of Trinidad, roughly fifty miles by fifty, also a Crown colony, of Spanish origin, but ours since 1802.

From this point northward for over 600 miles stretch the Lesser Antilles, a chain of islands which mark off the Caribbean Sea from the Atlantic, in a series of very varied size and history. None approach the size of Trinidad, and two of them, to this day, Guadeloupe and Martinique, remain French. The others, in order as we fly north, are Tobago, which we took from the French in 1815, Grenada, French until 1763, St. Vincent, also acquired at that date, and a little east of it Barbadoes, the oldest of all our possessions in the region, held since 1625. Next comes St. Lucia, taken from the French in 1815, and a Crown colony, in distinction to the rest of the islands which from Tobago onwards all have their own two chamber government, Council and Assembly under a Governor.

Between the two French islands lies Dominica, French until 1763. North of Guadaloupe is Antigua, settled in 1632, with tiny Nevis and Montserrat of the same date, while the slightly larger St. Christopher or Kitts came from the French in 1712. The chain ends in the seldom heard of Auguilla, Barbuda, and Tortola or Virgin isles, with several small islands under French, Dutch, Spanish, and Danish regime. Yet another six to seven hundred miles north-west lie the Bahamas, British since 1670, and nearly a thousand north of these, the isolated Bermudas, British from 1609.

But by far the most important, is Jamaica, ours since 1655, quite detached, south of Cuba, and incorporating, in Buxton's day, the territory of British Honduras on the mainland.

Thus, the subject of the Abolitionist campaign was the condition of a negro population, variously computed, but considered by Buxton to amount to some three-quarters of a million, nearly half of them in Jamaica, and one-tenth in Guiana, the remainder dispersed over the archipelago. In any case it outnumbered the insignificant white-skinned population, consisting of a few clergy and officials, some resident planters and slave-owners, the managers or overseers of non-resident ones, and a floating scum of "poor whites" of dubious origin and debased character. The negroes themselves had not become sufficiently mixed by irregular unions with the whites to lose their distinctive character, but spread over this territory of thousands of miles, with the most various history and traditions, they had little cohesion beyond their instinctive feelings and common servitude. Yet partly owing to the widely differing past of the separate territories, and partly to idiosyncrasy of individual owners, there were great discrepancies in their actual state. Buxton could give chapter and verse for the nauseating atrocity stories he quoted, mainly outrageous, vicious, and we should think sadistic use of the lash (but were they any worse than contemporary naval and military punishments ?). Certain well-meaning owners could, no doubt, show that they treated their slaves as well as many an English landed proprietor treated the labourers on his estate, except for the basic fact of purchase and sale of their bodies. In fact, one of the pleas of the West Indian party in Parliament was for a gradual solution of the state of bondage as villeinage had been solved away in England in Plantagenet days, but even the unreformed House of 1823 found this process somewhat outmoded.

Ruling over, administering, or owning this displaced African element, were white men, mainly British, if shading off into what were vaguely called mulattoes, or "people of colour" or "brown," in the less considered posts and social circles. This equally alien population was just as various in its aspirations and outlook. The higher officials had to keep pace with the movement of opinion in the home Parliament, which had been moving, unequally if steadily, towards emancipation for nearly half a century and might always endanger their places, to put the matter in the most cynical light. The larger planters had the sentiments natural to any set of landed proprietors, coupled with an apprehension common to racial minorities, though the negroes were so far from being organised, much less armed, that it is hard to believe that white lives were in danger. Still, we know what white opinion still is, in the Southern United States. The managers, overseers, store-keepers, many of them with different degrees of colour, are described by Mathieson, as "Despising the blacks and cringing to the whites."

One thing was plain, and so basic that it went further than Christian principles or broad humanity. The negro, considered as a labour force, was continually decreasing. After the main source of recruitment by the "legitimate Slave Trade," was stopped in 1807, the plantations had to rely on slave smuggling, which at certain times and places assumed large dimensions. This stern fact accounts for the insistence by the Abolitionists on standard marriage and domestic conditions. The slaves lived under most diverse regimes. After the original discovery of the West Indian territories by Spanish pioneers, some had passed into Dutch or French hands before becoming British, with the exception of Barbadoes.   There were, then, not only the individual characters and methods of the planter owners, but various inherited systems to be taken into account. Oddly enough, the writers most critical of slave-owning, seem to agree that the Spanish system had been the most liberal, at least in the matter of freedom by manumission, and this is confirmed by the fact that Dundas, who had been the first British statesman of prominence to contemplate Emancipation, far back in the eighteenth century before the Slave Trade had been extinguished, was really only the mouthpiece of Burke, who at the very birth of the movement seems to have been impressed by the merits of the Spanish system.   In other territories British administration had inherited the Dutch view of slave labour, which has often been spoken of, both in Guiana and what is now South Africa, as being harsh.   This may sound unlikely, in face of the excellent reputation which the Dutch East Indian administration has earned for itself in our later day.   It is, however, sufficient for our purpose that, in dealing with the matter in hand, Buxton was faced with a variation of tradition in method which may be broadly called the Dutch system.

Further, there were territories in which the French had been in power for periods of varying length.   There is no need to emphasize the eternal difference between British and Gallic points of view in almost every department of life. We have to allow for the fact that in some of the plantation islands with which Buxton was concerned, the existing outlook was not the characteristic British amateurishness, under which the planter, even if resident, and to a certain extent his subordinates and representatives, white or dusky, thought of themselves as gentlemen first and planters incidentally.   Not so, we may be sure in any island of French development.   Under rigid logic and a cast-iron administration, a slave had been a slave, a planter a tradesman, an official an official, a priest nothing like a lay preacher.   The French influence, for what it was worth, was further complicated by the fact of the French Revolution, which had begun by disturbing the whites, and finished by completely upsetting the slaves of the neighbouring large and sometime prosperous island of San Domingo, where to-day we see, as a long distance result, the republic of Hayti.   We have to allow for the fact that behind the absurd-sounding talk of slave risings and massacre of the whites, with which Buxton was faced, was the present and terrifying example of the French terror and the bloodshed and destruction in one of the larger units of the West Indian group, all of which had happened in the lifetime of most of the Members of the House of Commons that debated slave-owning, or tried to set in motion the altered administration resulting from the lofty sentiments of Abolitionism.

On the top of this heterogeneous mixture of racial instinct and differing systems, had been clamped down, under stress of the Napoleonic Wars, a British administration of the partially democratic character so familiar to us. Guiana, Trinidad and St. Lucia were amenable to the "democratic" House of Commons of that date, which could call a Minister to account for what happened under his direct jurisdiction in a Crown Colony.   But otherwise there were a dozen island "Assemblies," miniature parliaments, in which, naturally, the narrower local opinion was not only strong, but practically unopposed.

Such were the "West Indies" to which Earl Bathurst, as Colonial Secretary, forwarded an account of the Resolutions passed by the House of Commons, and a report of Canning's speech.   But he wrote a special letter to the recently appointed Governor of "Demerara," as Guiana was then called, and Mathieson surmises that slavery conditions may have been worse than the average in that ex-Dutch colony. The recipient was Sir George Murray, a slave-owner, though it is said that he was personally liked by his slaves in contrast to his "manager" who was not, and this may have been true in other cases. When he found himself enjoined to prohibit the flogging of females, and his "Court of Policy" was expected to abolish the use of the whip, he may well have been surprised; if he was not, far away in London, Wilberforce and the older Macaulay, we are told in the Life of the former, certainly were, and called such a hastening of a reform so revolutionary, "positive madness." Their forebodings were soon justified. Although Governor Murray did his best to keep secret the communications he had received from Bathurst, the news leaked out in a distorted form. It is not hard to imagine what fantastic ideas the average negro of that date formed in his head of the far-off King of England, whom they dimly knew as the authority set above their masters, even above the island assemblies or the Governor of such a Crown Colony as Guiana. The longer Sir George Murray hesitated the worse the rumours became. Many factors contributed to a result that Abolitionists in England could not have foreseen. Some planters deprived their "drivers" of their whips, others defied the suggestion. Meanwhile sailors from ships lately arrived from the home country gave their own, probably not too concise, account of the debate in Parliament. The negroes seem at length to have made up their minds that the "King of England had set them free," and that their masters, or the colonial officials, were withholding the promised boon. It meant only one thing to them, and that was, that they were no longer obliged to work. Up to then, no one had been sufficiently advanced to give them any interest in their labour, and it may be that racial instinct disinclined them to do more than was necessary for mere subsistence, at any time. But coincidence happened to make the moment unusually inauspicious. While the clergy officially allotted to the new colony do not appear to have concerned themselves deeply with negro welfare (after all, the settlement only became British in 1814), there were, however, a number of humble "missions" supported by the already large variety of Dissenting bodies in this and other countries. The character of these "chapels" or "bethels" had indirectly a considerable, if remote, effect on the Abolition campaign. We know well enough to-day, if the men of 1823 did not, the capacity of the transplanted African native for certain types of religious emotion and its expression, highly biblical and finding vent in singing and preaching rather than in the sonorous periods of the Anglican Prayer Book. Added to this was the fact that, as in the home country, these "meeting-houses" were identified with progressive or democratic political ideas. Long before the news of the Emancipation debate reached them, the negroes of Guiana had come to regard their "chapel" as a place not only for worship but one at which their disabilities and grievances would be heard and understood. This was so well known that the officials and owners in most of the islands and settlements almost automatically came to look upon "chapel" as a place in which some sort of primitive sedition was being preached quite as much as some deleterious religious doctrine. Mathieson quotes instances in which they had punished negroes, if not very drastically, for attending chapel, had deprived them of their hymn books, and made them observe a system of passes which permitted attendance only when an overseer was present, so that he was to be seen riding to service with a crowd of enthusiastic black licensed worshippers trotting beside, or hanging on to his mount. These missionary centres are described, some as being supported by Wesleyans, some

by Moravian brethren, some by "Independents" whom we should pro
"Congregationalists" to-day. Cobbett, in his well-known manner,
the whole missionary effort as "Methodism," one of the deepes
reproach in his blustering vocabulary, and the London Missionary Society
had perhaps a general, if not always an immediate, influence over them all.
In any case it was at, or around, a chapel maintained by this body that the
trouble which was to have such far-off repercussions originated. It was situated
in the Berbice district of Guiana, at a place called in some records, *Le Resouvenir*,
and described in others as "belonging to a Mr. Post." Some slaves
were to be sold here, and this was one of their most clear-cut grievances,
since it involved breaking up such family or friendly ties as they had, and
the dislocation of what, in happier circumstances, might have made a very
different picture of slave-owning, the direct personal interest of the master
in his serfs. It is said that sermons preached here caused the negroes to
congregate and procure arms of some description. When General Murray
came out hastily from Georgetown, he seems to have acted with courage and
discretion, but matters had gone beyond the point of verbal appeasement.
The negroes demanded "Emancipation" on the spot, and after some argument,
he felt obliged to return to Georgetown and place the district under martial
law. This meant calling out the Militia, consisting of the white inhabitants,
and the summoning of the regular troops available. Though the negroes,
who left their work during the following days, were met, it is stated, with attempts
at parley, they were now beyond control to the number of 13,000. They ill-
treated some white persons, killed two overseers who resisted them, but in the
main they were, by this time, chiefly concerned to obtain arms. In this they
failed, except for a few muskets and pistols, and the troops had no difficulty
in dispersing them. A hundred were killed. Martial law, however, was
maintained for five months and savage floggings were inflicted. But as we
know so well, it required some one personal incident to seize the low average
intelligence of the public, and give the incident what many in the home country,
just as the aggrieved white class in the colony, looked for, a scapegoat.

Both of these very human demands were satisfied in the person of Smith,
an "Independent" missionary serving the Bethel Chapel at which it was stated
the rising had been plotted. He seems to have been a good pastor of his
kind, helpful in epidemics and a real minister to the negroes. He was reported
as speaking in biblically critical terms of the official and owner class in the colony
and it may be that he was more forceful than tactful. But he completed the
requirements that all such phases of human history make upon some unlucky,
if afterwards canonised, individual. His health was poor, the climate deadly
to such a one. When arrested he made a spirited defence before the Court
Martial that tried him, and which may, as the Governor, Murray, subsequently
said, have been more impartial than a jury of white slave-owners. We can
readily imagine the atmosphere of such a court, in such a climate, against its
social background which had been threatened by violent, if ineffective, revolt.
The proceedings of justice, when called for, are said to have been tampered with,
and it would seem probable that his real crime in the eyes, not only of his accusers
and judges, but of a whole section of the population, was not what he had done,
but what he was. He put the finishing touch to the climax he provided in his
person, by dying in his unhealthy tropical prison, after being sentenced to death,
but before the recommendation to mercy, which the Court forwarded to the
home country, could receive assent.

The authorities seem to have been apprehensive that he might become more dangerous dead than alive, and tried to prevent the funeral, or the grave in which he was buried, from becoming the focus of further demonstrations. For that was what we know to-day by hundreds of parallel instances. At a moment of heated passions, leading to bloodshed, he, a slightly abnormal specimen of his type and nation, had died as the result of legal proceedings. In many countries it would have been enough to cause a revolution.

This was the story which could no more be kept from the public at home, than the emancipation debate of the month of May could be from the negroes. It became a rallying point for the Abolitionists, and by the spring of 1824, they were reinforced by a wave of petitions and popular demonstrations they badly needed, for members of the cabinet were deeply alarmed by the strong resentment the pledge they had given, and the resolutions they had passed, had created among the owners in the West Indies. The Smith case, as it came to be known, and the rising in Guiana of which it was the climax, were not isolated expressions of the sharp conflict the proposals for emancipation had produced. The big island of Jamaica, with its large proportion of the total African negro population, could not be ordered to implement the resolutions of Parliament, as a Crown Colony could. It could only be recommended to consider them, and its Assembly had no doubt about its opinion. A "plot" was discovered, which, although testified by the most dubious types of witness, was sufficient to cause the hanging of eight negro suspects in one parish and three in another. In Dominica a meeting of whites promulgated a desire for separation from the Home country (and there were men alive who remembered the United States holding similar language). In Barbadoes a riotous crowd pulled down a Methodist Chapel. However factious such demonstrations may seem, they were sufficient to intimidate Ministers. This was shown by the fact that, when Parliament met on 3rd February, 1824, there was nothing in the King's speech to mark any progress in making the resolutions effective, unless talk about religious instruction being extended could be so interpreted.

A week later Fowell Buxton wrote to his wife with the particulars of the disturbances in Guiana, and Smith's case, and saying he meant to "go to war" with Canning over them. He had never forgiven the astute parliamentarian for having suggested that the Colonial Assemblies, if they made difficulties about putting into practice the resolutions of 1823, should be brought to reason by authority. Two days later he was complaining of over-thought and over-work, a most enlightening confession from a powerfully built and open-air man. He next had to report that "the Government means to forfeit their pledge." At that point he had a second interview with Canning, and extracted a promise that no declaration of policy should be made until his plan had been scanned. He brushed aside kindly advice to avoid the violent abuse with which he was assailed.

"You folk think too much of your good name. Do right and right will be done you," he retorted.

Yet another two or three days elapsed, and at a further meeting he found Canning "had determined to yield to West Indian clamour and do nothing, except in Trinidad where there is no Colonial Assembly." This was the important point which Brougham was later to use with such effect. It appealed to a mind no less prone to all the arts of forensic strategy, and no less engrossed in the excitement of debate, than Canning's. If it had been possible to manœuvre the West Indies Assemblies into the position of defying the King's Government and talking separation from the Mother country, as some Assemblies had already talked of censure on the King's Ministers, then the dignity and authority of the House would have been brought into question. But that the Cabinet was resolved to avoid. In vain Buxton quoted Canning's own words, "if the Colonial legislatures would not consent to these ameliorations—if any resistance should be manifested to the expressed and declared wish of Parliament, any resistance which should partake, not of reason, but of contumacy—it would create a case upon which His Majesty's Government would not hesitate to come down to Parliament for counsel." And now the Cabinet withheld its hand. Buxton drew a picture of amelioration so gradual that it might take "ten centuries before the negroes were freed." Against this, he set a long and apparently authentic story of atrocious ill-treatment, physical brutality and moral contempt. He was, of course, employing the strongest satire of which he was capable. It was to be but ten years before at least a reasonable semblance of Emancipation was granted.

He was backed up by what Wilberforce called the "small but sturdy band of Abolitionists." The "Saints" were mobilised under Wilberforce, Dr. Lushington, Brougham and Denman, the lawyers, William Smith and Sam Hoare, Evans and the rest. But as so often happens, however worthy a project, however stimulating the rhetoric, the House was moved by the stern necessity of keeping the government in power lest worse befall.

Meanwhile the new technique of exerting pressure from without was growing, as we have seen, by question and petition. Sir James Macintosh brought one of the latter from the London Missionary Society on the subject of the unfortunate Smith. Buxton was justified in calling it "a good case," for it gave scope to the pugnacity of Brougham, who made the penetrating point that Smith and his kind had been teaching the negro the very kind of merciful and restrained conduct which had spared the West Indies the horrors of a full dress negro rebellion, and was able to rely for his testimony on the word of a clergyman of the established church. Once again Lushington spoke, this time supported by the rising figure of Denman, his colleague in the Queen's business, Wilberforce, of course, Williams, and the bearer of the petition. The struggle in Parliament was prolonged, but the new, restive public, which was to make its weight felt behind the Reform agitation of which the first tremors were already perceptible, was now awakening. The Abolitionists, in this matter, scored a tangible, if limited, success, for the Order in Council, forcing on certain of the reforms, which Buxton lamented was only intended to apply to the island of Trinidad, was extended to St. Lucia as well as Guiana.

It was a step, though a small one. But it was also noteworthy as being the last Parliamentary debate in which Wilberforce took part. Its general effect was to make sure that a bill on Ameliorationist, or gradual Emancipation, lines would be brought in, to replace the downright Abolitionist case for which Buxton was pleading.

A sidelight is thrown on the economic aspects of the subject by Whitmore's further attempt to alter the sugar bounties, from which the House nervously drew back. The matter was getting out of control of the ordinary channels of parliamentary business. Petitions came pouring in. Reverberations of the Jamaica and Guiana disturbances of the preceding year were felt. Buxton's colleague, Dr. Lushington, had no difficulty in showing that two coloured men of a certain position, since they were both sergeants in the Jamaica Militia, and had businesses of their own, had been deported under conditions that offended every axiom of British justice, on what was little more than suspicion, and interested suspicion, of having assisted, or meant to assist a "rising "of slaves that had never come off.

Then in June, Sir James Macintosh brought up the "case" of Missionary Smith. This was "ordered to lie upon the table," but a fortnight later, Grenfell, the member for Falmouth, returned to the charge with a petition from his constituency. This was a famous "case," for Brougham and Lushington had no difficulty in pulling the evidence to pieces and discrediting the methods both of trial and imprisonment in the West Indies. Great eloquence rang for hours on the heated air of the House. One debate was adjourned by acclamation in the early hours of the morning, but, on its resumption, although the Government was still able to command a majority, and prevent a formal petition to the King resulting, it was clear that a new crystallisation of popular opinion was taking place, and that petitions from the constituencies of sitting members were less important than those from larger amorphous bodies such as the London Missionary Society and the Society of Friends.

A further element of evidence came in with a Customs question regarding the island of Mauritius. It was shown, in the spring of 1825, that this island was being used as a kind of smuggling depot for evasion of the prohibition that had been placed on the Slave Trade. After this, Buxton stepped aside from his main purpose, to support Hume on a petition regarding the practice of Suttee in India. He returned to the West India question, however, in the matter of the Missionary Shrewsbury of Barbadoes. The facts on which the case rested were already nearly two years old, and formed a third after-result of the forwarding of the House's resolution by Bathurst to the Colonial Assemblies. Shrewsbury was not only a Missionary of devotion and exemplary character, but had begun by earning the respect of local authorities in the smaller of the Leeward Islands. There may be several elements peculiar to their several characteristics to account for the fact that these, St. Vincent, Grenada, St. Kitts, seem to have had a more seemly and enlightened public opinion among their white "master" populations. It is difficult to know how far this depended on local conditions, and social custom, how far on mere size, for in a small community it is often possible to preserve a more interdependent family feeling than in larger and more mixed populations. Moreover, the worst results of economic distress, which was a latent but powerful factor behind the owners' attitude, may have affected small self-sufficient communities less.

Buxton did not let himself be impeded by any such considerations. He attacked from his habitual lofty standpoint of abstract justice. Here was an English Methodist pastor, who had been first established in tiny Tortola, and had apparently gone on to the rather larger Grenada, earning golden opinions from "Colonels" and "Respectable merchants" in those places by his work in rendering the negro more sober, honest, and intelligent, as by-products of this evangelistic zeal. In 1820 he moved on to Barbadoes, much larger, possibly more traditionally British, and set in the mould which original seventeenth century colonisation had lent it. But Shrewsbury, who had married into a West Indian planter family, was, even so, the best man for the place. He seems to have won the respect of the clergy and of many owners, while a rowdier section of the white population had treated him with horse-play, interrupting the services he conducted with a growing congregation of black and mulatto children. But in October, 1823, that is, after an interval for the news of the first Emancipation Debate and the forwarding of the resolutions to have become common knowledge, he was the object of a series of attacks in local newspapers, and finally an organised assault was made upon his chapel, with chemicals and ordure, and fireworks, if no firearms were discharged, though it may have been with the intention of frightening rather than of wounding the members of the congregation, mainly of women and children.

The rowdy section, possibly because after some days no effort was made to punish or prevent this persecution, then became completely out of hand. Some of the local magistrates and tradesmen joined them, and when Shrewsbury appealed to the Governor for protection of his services he was advised to apply to the Magistrates, which was doubtless the correct course, if futile in the state of island opinion. On the other hand, visiting officers are reported as siding with Shrewsbury, and at least one Anglican clergyman gave him support and excellent advice—to apply to the Council of the island for redress.

Here the worst element in the planter circles put itself completely in the wrong, by forming a secret committee with the object of an organised attack on the chapel and manse. And when these were demolished, amid scenes of formidable violence, they issued a mock "Proclamation" in which they affirmed the intention of "putting an end" to Methodism, and invited inhabitants of the neighbouring islands to concur and complete this design. The Governor issued an appeal for detection of the rioters and pointed out how dangerous a precedent was being set, and what might be its effect on the minds of the negro population. As in the Smith case, the worst part of the mob attitude was that its members plainly opposed the education and improvement in status of the negro, and tried to bolster up the ancient ignorant and semi-bestial servitude inherited from the very beginnings of the existence of the Colony.

Although the facts were two years old, Buxton was able to make a weighty case. He was able to show that Missionary Smith of Demerara had died in gaol because, unsuccessfully, he had tried to prevent negroes rioting, and that it would be only just that those who had been unsuccessful in preventing whites rioting in Barbadoes should equally be punished, and no one can envy the unfortunate under-secretary, Wilmot Horton, who had the task of replying. He could not controvert the facts, for the anti-Abolitionist section of the island population had made no secret of their intentions, and the England of 1825 knew well enough what an anti-dissenter riot was like. Nor could any member of the House, listening to the laboured and half-hearted explanation of the Government's inaction, be in any doubt of the atmosphere in which the events that were so undeniable had taken place.

Within a year of this debate the same House had passed legislation against bull- and bear-baiting, but it was not so easy to frame an enactment against-Missionary-baiting. The embarrassed Secretary tried to throw some of the state of feeling in Barbadoes on to the Wesleyan Missionary connection, which had, not unnaturally, been active in defence of their agent. This only made matters worse, for it brought to their feet Smith and Butterworth, both dissenters, and both early representatives of the new movement of public opinion which was shortly to remove the ties and civil disabilities from Unitarians and Wesleyans alike. They were on their own ground, and made mincemeat of Horton's unlucky tactics. Canning was obliged to intervene and we see at once the consummate skill with which he conducted off the current of anti-government feeling, by speaking in the severest terms of this "unjustifiable, indefensible—violation of law and justice—a defiance of legal authority—a flying in the face of Parliament and the country."

Having thus got the House on his side, as the champion of its injured dignity, he proceeded to distinguish between "unknown persons in Barbadoes who had personally committed the outrage," secondly "the insular magistracy who it was impossible to say had done their duty," thirdly "the Governor of the Colony;" lastly "the government at home." The last was, of course, the count upon which he was really in earnest, and he plausibly argued that the reason Bathurst had not demanded the dismissal of the magistrates involved in the riot was because there might be no one to replace them. He absolved the governor and spoke of the mere mass of the rioters in no qualified terms. But eventually it came out that he was moving an amendment. This avoided the awkward question of spending government money in rebuilding a Methodist Chapel, and rallied the members to the unexceptionable principle of religious toleration. It was cleverly done, but it gave Brougham an opportunity to castigate the newly appointed Bishop of Jamaica who had hardly forwarded that principle by showing gross sectarian feeling in his reports on the religious situation in the islands, and by appointing a notorious character, Bridges, apparently in Holy Orders, but of no very holy order of character, to be his Chaplain. After making great play with the unlucky Bishop's report, he threatened that if the West Indian islands did not show a change of mood, he would bring in a bill regulating flogging, negro evidence and attachment to the plantation in the next session. He was followed by two of the West Indian section who did their best to show that all Barbadians must not be tarred with the same brush and that some missionary institutions had received considerable support in the islands, points much too fine to affect the course of the debate.

Buxton showed a combination of generosity and parliamentary wisdom in withdrawing his original motion. After all, he had drawn from the government spokesmen admissions that would have the strongest effect on public opinion in the country and without. He had enabled Brougham to give notice of a possible fresh instalment of his own Emancipation plan for the next session, and all he had to relinquish was the rebuilding of the chapel and the word "astonishment" for which Canning substituted "indignation." Thus, although the debate placed no specific legislative act on the statute book, it furthered considerably the real movement by the conviction of the essential rightness of his theory, which may be broadly summarised at this point as that of levelling-up Colonial civilisation, instead of levelling it down. This, more than matters of detail, marked the difference between amelioration, which left the slave rather better off in his original station, and moving him up to this category of a more responsible human being.

It was now two years since the first Emancipation debate had resulted in Canning's ineffective resolutions and, aided by the marked advance in public opinion, Abolitionists now prepared to force the pace, and oblige the government to redeem, however tardily and partially, the undertakings which had induced them to relax their early intentions.

What the actual legal position then was can be seen by the following advertisements.

Public Advertiser of Jamaica, 14*th October,* 1826

SIXTY DOLLARS REWARD

Absconded from the subscriber on the 11th inst. a brown man named Sam. He is about 5 ft. 7 or 8 in. high, 26 years of age, stout made, full face, with sulky countenance. Had on, when he went away, a new blue round jacket, brown drill trousers and a straw hat, is well known about Spanish town and Kingston, being barkeeper at the Ferry Inn for some time.

It is supposed he is gone to Trelawny as his family was sold some years ago to Robt. H. Scott, Esq. for Kinloss Estate. One pistole will be paid for lodging him in any work-house and the above sum on proving to conviction by whom harboured. Having been off the island for some-time years, he may attempt to pass himself as new. Masters of vessels are cautioned against taking him off the island.   John Macdorman.

6*th October,* 1826

Runaway from the subscriber, a sambo woman named Ann, who has been about with her child (about twelve months old) about two weeks. She is about 5 ft. 4 in. in height, stout made and slovenly in appearance. It is strongly suspected the above mentioned woman is harboured by her husband a sambo man living in Golden Street and employed by Mr. Naar, Tobacconist. Any person giving information of the said runaway, or proving to conviction by whom she is harboured will be suitably rewarded.   Jos: Maparbe.

The autumn of 1825 was spent in conferences and plans. Macaulay, Lushington, Brougham and Macintosh were in communication with Buxton, and it was determined to take an opportunity, early in the new year, to press the government to broaden and enforce the resolutions, and if possible to pass some portion of the twelve Emancipation items, although Macintosh thought that the whole programme was too much for one session. Buxton, however, was full of fight. He intended "to bring forward one or two enormities" and these were not far to seek, for however slowly or unevenly justice might move, in British Colonies it did move. Not, we may think, through any inherent respect for its principles and certainly not from any love of logic, but from a mixture of that sporting temper always agog to see if the "other side," in whatever might be the contest, could put up an adequate appearance, with a certain devotion of local officials to their jobs, which remains the wonder of the world. Thus, the Fiscal of Guiana had been receiving the complaints of the negroes of their ill-treatment and had made his summary of them, revealing many cases of inhuman cruelty. Moreover, the detailed account of the "plots" discovered in Jamaica, which had resulted in eight executions and some expulsions from the island, offered a field for stringent criticism.

These matters, reprinted at length in the *Anti-Slavery Reporter,* had now become common knowledge and Buxton marshalled his attack by a preliminary preparation through petition. This mode of keeping Parliament in touch with public opinion had itself been the object of controversy on the floor of the House, and was destined, within a few years, to fall into some degree of contempt, when the petitions of the Chartists were shown to be signed with false or duplicate names. The original of the Emancipation petitions may have been better guaranteed by the Quaker and Evangelical sections by which they were fostered. Not that such people were liked, but they had the characteristic of sterling honesty, more remarkable then than it would be to-day. Thus among many others we find, on the 28th February, 1826, Lord Palmerston presenting one from the University of Cambridge. He spoke on it, asserting slavery to be opposed to the principles of the British Constitution. He told the House, in his well-known manner, that "having abolished the traffic in slaves, they were not to rest there . . . he would state to the colonists that there appeared in this country a strong feeling to deal tenderly with their interests, and that they ought to take advantage of that feeling while it lasted. . . . It was vain for them to think that they might retard, they could ultimately defeat, a measure supported by the concerted sentiments of Great Britain."

No one need suppose that Palmerston felt very deeply touched by the sufferings of distant coloured people. But he had that shrewd horse-couping common-sense with a touch of a gamble in it, which made him put his money on Abolition and give a second place to Amelioration. It is illuminating, also, to note that he spoke of the University for which he was acting as the school "of those who were to be the future legislators of Great Britain."

Yet more petitions had been presented on the next day, when Fowell Buxton rose to present that which came from the inhabitants of London, and was said to bear 72,000 signatures, which he stated to be the largest number any such document had ever borne. He laid hold of this point first, and made it the fulcrum for his demand to know what the goverment intended to do about the pledge they had given, nearly three years previously, when they had induced him, and those whom he represented, to confide the matter to them. He insisted that Canning's resolutions had meant nothing less than the raising of the negro to the status of a British subject. He taunted the leader of the House with having foreseen that the several Assemblies of the West Indian islands would never implement such proposals. He summarised the somewhat piecemeal advances which had been made by these bodies, for instance, in Tobago, the admission of negro evidence by the Courts in some cases, the regulation of Sunday markets, protection of negro property and against the indiscriminate use of the lash; in the Bahamas the legalisation of marriage and prevention of dismemberment of families by sale; in Barbadoes, negro evidence had been partially admitted. He was confining himself to the self-governing islands in which Jamaica and Barbadoes were, out of all proportion, the most im-portant instances.

He drew from this the conclusion that the House must either renounce its pledge to the public on behalf of the negro, or take the matter into its own hands. He concluded by quoting Canning's own words, "Trust not the masters of slaves in what concerns legislation for slavery. However specious their laws may appear, depend upon it, they must be ineffectual in their application. It is in the nature of things that they should be so. Let them, the British House of Commons, do their part themselves. Let them not delegate the trust of doing it to those who cannot execute the trust fairly. Let the evil be remedied by an assembly of freemen, by the government of a free people, and not by the masters of slaves."

This clearly demanded a reply from Canning himself, for none saw better than he, that, behind the charming compliment which Buxton paid him on his eloquence, still more by quoting it, lay the threat to raise the country against the Cabinet. At the rate and size in which public petitions were arriving there was substance in the threat. That was why Canning employed what would be called to-day "elastic defence." As the clerk of the House proceeded to read the petition in an abbreviated form, or "short," Buxton requested that it be read at full length, and when Members raised cries of "short," Canning himself intervened to have the "wishes of the petitioners complied with." This enabled him "to concur with the sentiments contained in it, and he must admit that it appeared to him to be most unexceptionable, and to be stated with great propriety and moderation."

This was polite, for the petition stated in unqualified terms that "the Colonial legislatures have either treated the recorded wishes of Parliament, and the recommendations and remonstrances of His Majesty's Government with neglect, or met them with the most determined opposition." It characterised the ameliorations that had been effected as "in their practical operation . . . an instrument of grievous injustice, cruelty and oppression." The "general treatment" of the slaves was "harsh and disgusting." But it did not rely on humanitarian sentiment alone. It attacked this "unjust and immoral system" which "derives great support from those commercial regulations which, by means of bounties and protecting duties in favour of the produce of slave labour, not only materially enhance its price to the British consumer, but augment the miseries of the slaves, and render their liberation more difficult."

The petitioners pledged themselves to pay an amount equal to the loss of property, presumably by taxation, for the extinguishing of the system.

Thus did the forward-reaching shadow of Free Trade project across the debate.

Canning began by calling for the resolutions of the House of 1823. It was soon clear why he did so. If the conditions of slavery really were contrary to the British Constitution and the Christian Religion, they ought not to exist another minute. He was not prepared to interfere until the Assemblies had had another chance, and felt three sessions not too much to give them.

Any of us who are in the habit of trying to follow the processes by which aspirations towards human betterment become political issues, from political issues, party questions, from party questions to items in a programme, and from thence subjects of debate, on a time table, and so legislative enactments or lost causes, can see why Canning took this line. From a lofty aspiration of Buxton's to raise up the oppressed to the stature of a British citizen, the question had inevitably followed the channels that eventually made it an attack upon the government. There is no need to doubt that Canning was a humane man and as sensitive as anyone can be who has spent his life in what is aptly called the political arena, swayed by the excitement of crowds, the keen competitive stimulus of divisions, the disillusionments that accompany the unmasking of human emotions. But at all costs he must not allow a division which might mean a government defeat, or worse, a government victory leading to a contest with the island Assemblies, to make them do what they were disinclined to do, except in their own spacious time. He had to show that the human tragedy resulting from their dilatory or obstructionist course, was not very tragic. After tracing the actual handling of the instruction that conveyed the Order in Council to the Assemblies, he recorded that the religious instruction clause had been adopted, by eight out of twelve, that regarding negro evidence in the Courts, by seven, marriage, five, security of property, eight, manumission he found had already been conceded by most before they received Bathurst's communication. The clause concerning the dismemberment of families by sale, had been implemented by only four; it was, of course, the matter which, most, directly arose from the chattel status of the negro, but he stated that the difficulties in the way were "rather of a legal than of a moral nature," while non-separation of females from their children had been adopted by eight. With regard to the clause abolishing the corporal punishment of females, "he was sorry to say that but five had acceded to it." He knew well enough that this was the point which would raise most feeling. He made a graceful gesture of almost preferring Buxton's motion on this point, allowing no moral advantage

E

to those whom he had to placate. Finally, Saving Banks did not seem to have
been founded by any colony.

He passed on to a yet more difficult question, the trials of slaves as a result
of the alleged "plots" in Jamaica, in which unsworn evidence of blacks had
been sufficient to support death sentences. He had, however, private information that the Jamaican Assembly was now likely to pass more equitable
legislation on this point. He, therefore, proposed to submit a bill which would
offer the framework of an act to the Colonial Assemblies, which they could
adopt, reject, or modify. He justified himself for the quotations from his own
speeches of thirty years before on the Slave Trade, with which Buxton had
confronted him, and invited the House to give the Assemblies their chance to
do what was expected of them without being forced. Incidentally, he included
in his list of settlements the island of Mauritius with its French traditions.

Brougham then rose to push his long nose through this able parliamentary
screen. He wanted a plain answer, yes, or no, about manumission, slave
evidence, and the whip, and the dismemberment of families. Canning gave
him the facts as shortly as possible. Buxton came next, to know about securing
bequests to negroes in Jamaica, and got an even shorter answer.

It was then the turn of William Smith of Norwich. He was able to quote
the Duke of Manchester who, it appeared, had told the Assembly of Jamaica
bluntly, "Another year has been allowed to pass away without your having
taken one effectual measure for the improvement of the negroes. It does not
become me to anticipate the results of the disappointment of the British
Government when it learns that reiterated representations which it has made
to you to do that which your own interests require, no less than the comforts
of those who depend on you, have totally failed. In obeying the instructions
which I have received from His Majesty's Ministers I earnestly press upon you
the necessity of doing something, if not to disarm your enemies, at least to
satisfy your friends."

So apt was the quotation that Mr. Secretary Peel had to intervene, and those
who listened to him can have had little idea that he would give his name to the
Police Force or the silver coin worth twelve pence.

Peel's pleading was for moderation in language and he was successful in
shortening the debate. It must have been clear that the government, while
it was moving, was going at a pace which the Emancipationists would find
it hard to adopt.

The strong emotions of Buxton, the destruction of the legal and logical
side of amelioration, particularly as it had been practised in Jamaica, by
Brougham and Denman were irresistible and had, of course, a considerable
long range effect on public opinion, but, taking the shorter view, the House did
not see its way to passing legislation so drastic as to overrule the government.
So the general intention of giving the Assemblies at least a year to implement
what was clearly now the unmovable will of the House, went up to the Lords where
Earl Bathurst had no difficulty in getting it endorsed. Although Emancipation
had many friends in the upper House, from the Duke of Gloucester, descending
among famous names such as Lansdowne, its members were necessarily more
remote from vivid appreciation of the actual conditions of the case, which made
so strong an appeal to the Commons. Lords were inclined, even more than
Commoners, to think in terms of landed estates, and Bishops in terms of religious
conformity rather than of personal liberty. But if the debate at this level
provided no very novel instance, on one side of the question dearest to Buxton's

heart, it revealed that the inhabitants of Barbadoes had been visited by second thoughts on the subject of Mr. Shrewsbury's meeting house. Evidently they, or perhaps the soberer part of them, regretted the excesses in which certain of their number had disgraced the good name of the island. It may sound, at this distance, a very small matter, and only indirectly connected with Buxton's deep convictions and lifetime's devotion. But it helps us to understand the contradictory and uncertain currents amid which he worked. It also is a testimony to the progress the cause was making. Nor was it the only one. On 14th April a petition was received voicing the views of the Council and House of Assembly of the island of Antigua. This was one of the smaller of the islands, and had, on the whole, a fairly good name for the treatment of its negro population, which may possibly result from the circumstances of its area, leading to a more personal relationship between owner and slave. Such at least was the feeling of the islanders, who threw back upon the merchants of the home country the responsibility for the slave trade, which, so they alleged, obliged them to receive their coloured population, in spite of protest. They quoted chapter and verse and date of the endeavours they had made to be rid of the traffic, and asserted that they had done well by their dependent classes. But the real object, little stressed but uncompromising, was the demand for compensation.

The same memorial reached the Lords, where it suffered an odd and irrelevant fate. For while the facts may have been just as true, the atmosphere in which they were to be debated was one in which the members were far more particular about their privileges. The thing which struck the noble lords was that the memorial was signed only by the Speaker of the Antiguan Assembly and this caused a great exhibition of learned eloquence, Scottish Lords at least being inclined to regard it as a personal missive from the Speaker only. They were brought to a closer view of the matter in hand by Lord Calthorpe, who was at pains to reject certain strong expressions aimed at the Abolitionists and apparently at Stephen, Wilberforce's associate, whose pamphlet had been so widely read and discussed. Lord Liverpool, however, pointed out that, if the home parliament was to retain its power to legislate for the Colonies, they must be accorded the right of petition on usual lines. This intervention enabled Lord Dudley and Ward to put the important point, "where slavery ended, compensation began." "The West Indian proprietors had claims to indemnification which stood upon far better grounds, as to right and justice, than any which those gentlemen who trafficked in political influence could set up." He seems to have been an advocate of the gradual introduction of free labour. Apparently Lord Calthorpe had expressed a desire that Emancipation should be granted during the life of Wilberforce. This, in view of that veteran's age, had precipitated the anxiety of the petitioners, for it looked like an attempt to promote legislation within a year or so at most. But such is the nature of second chambers that the debate petered out with a question of privilege, and the petition was referred to a committee to be discussed from that point of view.

Yet more evidence of the degree of success which was progressively attending Buxton's efforts can be seen in a petition which Baring presented to the House on 20th April. It came, not from the islands of the Caribbean, but from "the Merchants of London trading to the West Indies, Mortgagees and others having claims on West Indian Estates." It prayed "the interference of the House to give them some further protection for their property or else compensation." This phraseology has at least the merit of frankness, and it shows us three things about the problem with which Buxton, from his lofty standpoint, was dealing on such apparently simple lines. The first is the precarious nature of the West Indian Trade. Begun in a romantic blaze of glory, when tough Elizabethan filibusters talked as though they were going to discover some Aladdin's cave of jewels and precious metals, and actually brought back sugar and tobacco, coffee and rum, it had long passed on to be a very profitable business for the few lucky or astute or unscrupulous. Nor was enough known about economics and their application to industry for any wide and settled view to be adopted. The infant commerce of the eighteenth century had grown up under what is generally called "Mercantilism," and is, in fact, a system of controls, tariffs, bounties, navigation acts, whatever they may be, not dissimilar to those into which we ourselves have been reluctantly forced in the years between the wars, and which may, for all we still know, be the natural symptoms of a disturbed time. For many years before the Emancipation campaign, many plantations had been in difficulties. This is the meaning of the term "mortagees" in the petition. They had been forced to rely on artificial financial support and "protective" legislation. This led on directly to a second condition. Plantations in the condition above described were not the family homes of their financial backers in London. The latter had no personal stake in some far-off sugar-producing estate. They had lent money on it, in the faith that it would be "liquid," saleable, the pledge on it redeemable. But would it retain that quality if, instead of a chattel labour force established on it, there was nothing to depend on except a scarcely tried "free labour"?

The third element is revealed in the verbal framing of the petition, and is a compliment to Buxton and his party. The mention of compensation shows that London creditors of West Indian estates thought that total and imminent emancipation might well become law, and were in haste to secure the solvency of the security on which they relied.

Baring's introduction underlines all this. There were only a few sentences in justification of the case of the London Merchants. Most of his speech was taken up by an attack on the Emancipationists, of whom he must have considered Buxton the leader.

This line of argument, or lack of it, brought William Smith to his feet. He made no bones about his part in the debate. A strong henchman of Buxton, "he rose merely to repel the insinuations of the hon. member against the Abolitionists, and to deny every word and every assertion to their prejudice uttered by the hon. gentleman, or contained in the petition on the table."

He took the House through the strongly worded Antiguan petition of the week before, and showed that the rather better condition of the dark population in the island had been the work, not of the owners, but of the Moravian missionaries.

He was followed by Warre, who gave away the real cause of the heated language that was being used. James Stephen, forbear of Leslie Stephen, an old associate of Wilberforce, was, perhaps, a stronger advocate for emancipation than even Brougham. For he had gone straight to the new rising British public with its reformist aspirations and sporting temper, in a pamphlet entitled, *England enslaved by her own Slave Colonies*. The second edition had been just printed and it requires an effort now to draw from its yellowing print the emotions of a time when the French Revolution, and the Cause of Independence in the states of North America were still living issues, and memories of eye-witnesses, and when many members of the public to whom

Stephen and his colleagues appealed were suffering still at that date from disabilities resulting from their religious and political opinions.

Mixed in, therefore, with the strong humanitarian sentiment, which makes all the difference between the world of Smollett and the world of Dickens, was a more personal feeling. Many readers of the pamphlet, unlike Buxton himself, felt for the negro under the lash, because they, or their associates, had been charged by yeomanry or spied on by "informers," a type of public scourge whose presence, however illusory, was the cause of the violence done to Mr. Pickwick in the early stages of his career.

"The constitutional and effectual path is plain," Stephen had told the restless and largely voteless public of the day. "You are soon to be solicited for your votes by those who wish to be your representatives in the House of Commons. Let your first question to every candidate be: 'Are you a proprietor of slaves, or a West Indian Merchant?' If the answer is in the affirmative, I would recommend to you a positive refusal."

Probably some of the members who took part in the debate had had such interviews with their putative constituents. Small wonder that the pamphlet, rather than specific enactments on the Emancipation question, formed the chief subject of the debate. And on nearly every one of its pages the pamphlet cites Buxton or his speech of May, 1823, and the attendant consequences. But mixed up with that were, what are to us, dead issues, the double revolution in Hayti, our relations with the French, the incursion of rum on the English brewing trade, the losses in men and ships in maintaining the West Indian possessions. The Spanish Inquisition was then a bogey to frighten the simple, though we may find it difficult to recognise its counterpart in the London Merchants or West Indian Planters.

Thus Bernal, member for Rochester, was entirely concerned, not with the case of the London Merchants, but with specific statements made in Stephen's pamphlet, particularly the charge of the branding of the ordinary negro worker as distinct from the class charged with misdemeanour, and of not giving facilities for the free Sunday.

In reply to this, Sykes brought out a copy of the *Jamaica Gazette* in which negroes were advertised by the brandings they bore. William Smith followed with other instances. Finally, after a battle over the accuracy of the details of the pamphlet by Stephen, Wilson brought the debate back to the point of protective duties on slave-grown sugar, which was, after all, very much the matter of the original complaint. So the London Merchants had their petition printed along with the others.

William Smith was up again on the same day with his petition regarding the Slaves of Guiana. He showed the complications arising from the recent Dutch ownership and the principal case he cited was against a Dutch manager. He had no difficulty in showing that the Protestant Missionary was attacked (as in the case of the unfortunate Smith) for doing what the Roman Catholic was enjoined to do. This unlikely looking plea, was, at that date, of great importance in an anti-Catholic House of Commons. Smith, being a Unitarian, sharing the disabilities of the Catholics of the day, naturally seized the argument. His main weight, however, was thrown upon the most searching argument that Buxton had employed, namely, that the overdriving of slaves to produce such a quantity of sugar per head that was only saleable by virtue of a protective duty, was wasteful to the point of actually decreasing the black population.

Wilmot Horton, the under-secretary, was obliged to reply, lest the closing words of the petition should bring about a decision the government would find embarrassing in the extreme. The words were:

"This House is led to conclude that no legal enactments (this referred to the various measures and offices promoted for the protection of the negro) can prove sufficient for such effectual safeguard of the slave, unless the officers . . . shall be appointed and supported by the government at home, and absolutely prohibited from possessing or employing slaves in any capacity. . . ."

Horton made a detailed defence of government policy, instancing what had been done in Trinidad, and which had apparently been extended to the Demerara district of Guiana, but not that of Berbice. In fact, he did his best, and gained a measure of support from Ellis, who may be taken as the home country apologist for the slave-owning interest.

Denman had no difficulty in applying destructive criticism with all his armoury of legal tactics. He taunted the government with having, "struck out of the grammar of the planters the future tense. Every abuse was now said to have happened formerly, to belong to time gone by." He made a counter attack to the allegations against Stephen's pamphlet and kindred anti-slavery publications by appealing to the evidence of West Indian papers, that slaves were still being used as materials for distraint upon debtor owners. He supported the main tenor of the resolution against ownership by officials. Baring then intervened to try to slow down the persuasive weight of Denman's argument. This in turn brought up Brougham, and once more the subject became submerged in questions of tactics, of the fairness of anti-slavery propaganda, and his own actions in giving notice of a motion. Canning, as usual, was the only government spokesman who could follow Brougham, and he was at his most conciliatory, admitting most of the instances of cruelty and injustice complained of, but maintaining the government's good intentions. He persuaded the House to drop the motion. His efforts at conciliation, or rather at maintaining the government, could not obviate the fact that the hunt was up. Only five days later, the House found itself faced with a petition, submitted by Joseph Hume, on behalf of one, Augustus Hardin Beaumont, a planter and slave-owner of Jamaica, now resident in London, praying that no measures he passed respecting the West Indian Colonies, by which the property of planters and slave-owners might be injured.

Hume presumably believed in him and the case which he made out was not similar to that to which the House had already listened.

Beaumont, so Hume said, had repeatedly signed petitions to the legislature of Jamaica for the bettering of the condition of the slaves, and even of granting emancipation, provided the owners' property was protected against injury. Hume felt that such proprietors were entitled to such a guarantee, basing their claim on the fact that early attempts at Abolition of the Slave Trade in the Colonies had been resisted by Parliament. He dared Canning to put forward an act for the coercion of the island Assemblies without, at the same time, guaranteeing the losses. . . . ". . . the abolition of slavery" he said, "would remove what was now a stain on our nation," and he quoted from the petition, "that, as the black man was by nature entitled to the mercy of the legislature, so was the white man entitled to its justice."

This brings vividly before us the stage which Buxton's campaign had reached. The petitioner actually inherited his West Indian property by some roundabout channel, was no longer resident, and seems to have been anxious to divest himself of it, and was apprehensive that he would find himself faced with emancipation without compensation. Canning put him off on the plea of Brougham's pending motion on the subject.

Before Brougham's motion came on, Buxton himself took the floor to move upon another flank of what he had styled the battlefield. His motion related to the island of Mauritius, where, he stated, the slave trade was being continued in violation of the Acts of 1807, which had abolished it, of 1811, which had made it a felony, and 1824, which made it a piracy.

The island was only recently a British possession. Its main historical interest had been as the base from which France supported her long contest with the United Kingdom, over the domination of India. It became finally British after 1815, and Buxton's earlier items of evidence concerned the military and naval occupation of pre-Waterloo days. He quoted various authorities who gave various figures of the traffic, he passed on to quote the three recent British governors of the island, and the point of his attack, on which he was sharply interrupted by the Chancellor of the Exchequer, was that the authorities in the island favoured or failed to prevent it.

One of these, Sir Robert Farquhar, was present in the House.

He went on to show that forty vessels were employed, and that they used the neighbouring island of Bourbon as a rendezvous. He produced depositions of a corporal in the 82nd regiment which gives even to-day a vivid picture of a French schooner, largely manned by Madagascans, landing boatloads of naked blacks in the jungly coast creeks, and defying authority, with the sure knowledge that local magistrates would connive. But he did not leave the matter at these individual depositions. He produced figures to show the huge preponderance of males in the island population, a well-known sign of importation. There was also the large disproportion between "foreign," that is, not island born blacks, and creoles or native people of colour. There was, further, an increase in the export of sugar, a commodity which could not be increased without fresh supplies of black labour. He passed on to the Seychelles, the islands lying nearest, though not very near by European standards. Here the official returns showed a sharp increase in the negro, that is, non-native, population, and he had figures, though not such exact ones, of exportation, and made out a very strong case, on this basis alone, for a regular, if illicit trade in human beings. Added to this was the difficult question of bounties paid on slaves illicitly imported. He was able to show how a high figure, relative to that obtaining in the West Indies, argued a very large illicit trade.

He then recapitulated the horrors of the actual voyage, with which some of his hearers, at least, had been nauseated nearly twenty years before, when the Trade itself had been made illegal, and indeed subject to the severest penalties. Even to-day most of us are familiar with the harrowing tales of primitive blacks, torn from their villages by Arab and other bands, packed as we should hardly pack merchandise to-day, starved and kept waterless, and thrown to the sharks, if it became apparent that their terrible condition rendered them unmarketable.

At the root of it all lay the main fact, which to Buxton overrode all considerations of detail, expediency, even political sagacity. It was the treatment of a living human being as a chattel. The measure of world disturbance in the nineteen-forties can be gauged by the fact that there have been symptoms of this attitude towards human creatures in Europe itself. It requires no great effort of the imagination on the part of those who have had to deal with modern, relatively humane prison and internment camp conditions, to realise what the voyage of the slaver can have been like a hundred years ago.

Having recited the facts Buxton tabled his motion, that a Select Committee be appointed to inquire whether the Slave Trade has prevailed at the Mauritius, and to what extent, and the causes thereof, and to report thereon to the House.

Sir Robert Farquhar rose at once, and took the speech as an attack upon himself. As we read his speech to-day, we feel that he protested too much. If there had been nothing in the complaint, why not let the Select Committee proceed to vindicate him ? He spoke at length, but the House must have had an uneasy feeling that if he cleared himself, he did not dispose of the matter. For Wilmot Horton followed, and engaged in what amounted to a heated argument as to some of the relevant facts and dates, and it required the suavity of Canning to wind up the debate. "Viewing the motion in the light of a public question, and not as an individual charge, he was not disposed to offer any obstruction to it."

In the light of this indication of government support, even Brougham had to acquiesce. The motion was carried, and the Committee appointed.

Brougham's own motion did not come on until mid-May. It was in effect an attempt to speed up the forcing upon the Colonial Assemblies of some action on the lines of the resolution of 1823. The words he put down are significant, both in showing what had been going on, and in throwing into relief his relation to Buxton: "That this House has observed with deep regret that nothing effectual has been done by the legislatures of His Majesty's Colonies in the West Indies in compliance with declared wishes of His Majesty's Government and the Resolutions of the House of 15th May, 1823, touching the condition of the slaves; and this House will, therefore, early in the next session of Parliament, take into their most serious consideration such measures as may appear to be necessary for giving effect to the said Resolutions."

He had no difficulty in making out his case. Indeed in many cases the less worthy colonists had made it out for him. He went over the colonies one by one, and over each head of "Amelioration" as Earl Bathurst had indicated them in his first despatch, already just three years old.

Wilmot Horton did his best, in reply, but he was no match for Brougham. Even had he been, the party of Emancipation could call upon the almost equal ability of Dr. Lushington, who was concerned to attribute deliberate obstructionism to members of the ministry. After him, Bernal and Ellis, both connected with the plantation interests, did their best to ensure gradualness. As we have seen, West Indian opinion varied a good deal, from those who felt sincerely that they were hardly used, to those who were chiefly alarmed about the amount and means of compensation. By the time Butterworth spoke on church establishment in the islands, and Denman had elaborated the argument for legal compulsion, there were cries of "question" and "divide." Canning, however, allowed him his full sweep, and then came in on the very lofty note of "the state of slavery is repugnant to the principles of the British Constitution and of the Christian religion." He had no hard task to show that all three institutions had coexisted for centuries. But if there had been any doubt as to the intentions of the government, it was dispelled by one of his concluding phrases:

"The great difference between the plans of His Majesty's Ministers and those of the hon. gentlemen (he was alluding specifically to Buxton) who are desirous of a more rapid progress is this, that those hon. gentlemen would risk great dangers, would risk even the frustration of their own object, for the hope of arriving at it immediately, whereas we would rather postpone a little the attainment of the object, in order that we may arrive at it with greater assurance of safety."

Brougham's motion was lost by an adverse majority of sixty-two, and the Emancipationists had to resign themselves to an interval of at least twelve months, during which the Colonial Assemblies would have an opportunity of reflecting on the wisdom of doing what was expected of them, before they were compelled.

So ended the first major battle for Emancipation.

"We will go to war with Canning," Buxton had declared, and the battle had raged across the floor of the House, the crowded benches, and on to the division lobby. It was more like a siege than a battle, and while the government emerged victors, in the sense that no division had been carried against them, there were ominous signs of the progress made by the attackers. The phrase which occasionally still slips from the lips of a Member of the House about "raising the country" had a real meaning in the Emancipation campaign. Something had happened to Britain, or more exactly, to the British, and Buxton was the expression of it. The condition of slavery, which, but a generation earlier, hardly caused comment, had become repugnant to the average citizen and voter-to-be. Dimly, he saw an abhorrent thing, and even more important for him a menace to himself, his liberty and his standard of life.

Mixed in with these opinions, was a strong personal urge towards reform in representation and in the fiscal system. Again and again we come upon the phrases, "trafficking in political influence," and "restraint upon trade." Cobbett might bluster, but his conception of a self-sufficing island, engaged in subsistence agriculture, was an outworn one. The people he despised, dissenters, visionaries, industrialists, reformers, were in the ascendant. In a few years, not only the slavery against which Buxton fought, but the very composition and appearance of the House in session was to change. We must now go back to the private life of this prime mover in the national story, seen against the dark background of the African negro populations for whom he worked.

CHAPTER IV

FROM FRUSTRATION TO REFORM. 1823—1832

WE MUST NOW REDRESS THE BALANCE, AND QUALIFY THE PICTURE OF BUXTON, dominating the House of Commons and endangering the plans of Ministers, and laying the foundation of a great popular reputation, which was destined to expand far beyond the limits of his native land. Behind this façade lay the private life of a deeply religious man, and the social life of the head of a family, a country gentleman, who, if he cared little for social occasions, in the ordinary sense of the word, was never happier than when, gun in hand, or mounted upon one of his favourite horses, he turned out into the fields of East Anglia. When he was able to be absent from London, where in 1825 he had taken a house in Devonshire Street, and seems also to have retained a room at the brewery, for we find letters dated from "Spitalfields," and the mention, "dressed at the brewery," he was often to be found at his brother-in-law, Samuel Gurney's house at Ham in Essex, or at his sister-in-law, Louisa Hoare's home at Hampstead. But he was devoted to the real country, out of reach of London, at Cromer Hall for preference, which he and his family shared with the Hoares.

It is related that the pheasants of the neighbouring coverts came right up to the drawing-room windows, over the lawn. Perhaps on account of his great size, we shall see that he had a special gun-stock built for him by the gunsmith at Holt, the neighbouring market town. As a rule, he suffered little from the average poacher; it may well be that he had so thoroughly identified himself with the life of the countryside that those who might have trespassed on his land, forbore to do so. On one occasion, at least, he was witness of a very different kind of depredation. A well-dressed young man entered one of his fields, before his very eyes, and shot a partridge. Buxton rode up to him, and demanded, first, his name and address, second his licence, and thirdly, his permit to shoot over that land.

The "poacher" politely gave the answer to the first question, but in response to the others, asked to be excused and made off. It says much for Buxton's sense of humour, amid the grim preoccupations of his public career, that he let him go with a laugh.

Another story told in the *Memoirs* concerns the figure of Thomas Coke, afterwards Earl of Leicester, the great agriculturist, one of the precursors of scientific farming, who had reclaimed so many thousand acres of hitherto barren land on the north coast of Norfolk. He also was a gigantic figure, as tall and broad as Buxton himself, and a great host to all and sundry, by no means only his own class of landed gentry and practised sportsmen. The anecdote of the sculptor Chantry's "brace of woodcock" will be remembered. Yet another instance of his wide hospitality related to a professor, who, unaccustomed to the use of firearms, was placed in a safe position and was heard to be firing continually. When the other members of the party drew near, to find out how he had enjoyed himself, it appeared that he had been shooting at an object he discerned moving in the undergrowth. It proved to be the gaitered legs of one of the beaters sent to head back stray birds. The Professor could not understand how any creature could withstand his fusillade. The beater, fortunately, was quite unaware that he had been a target.

This leads us on to Buxton's lifelong devotion to his dogs. One of the earliest anecdotes recalled by the *Memoirs* concerns his dog, Prince, and dates from his early days as a young brewer, living, with the Hoares, at Hampstead, while his wife and young family were in the country during the summer of 1816. He wrote to tell her the terrifying story: It was reported that Prince had turned very vicious, had been attacking the other domestic pets. He had the dog tied up and cared for, but on his return to Hampstead found it running wild, biting at every creature within reach, including two boys and a man. After some efforts had been made to corner and confine what was by that time recognised as a dangerous mad dog, it broke away and turned in the direction of London. Buxton rode after it, overtook, and kept close to it, dreading that it might enter the crowded streets of the then detached suburb of Camden Town. It turned into the gate of a house occupied by some people called Pryor, and Buxton flung himself from his horse upon the frantic animal, held it, changed hands so that he could force his gloves over his fingers, and finally managed to attract the attention of the gardener, who opened the gate with the query:

"What do you want?"

"I've brought you a mad dog!" was the answer.

Telling the man to fetch a stout chain, Buxton carried his capture into the yard.

"I was determined not to kill him, as I thought if he should prove not to be mad, it would be a great satisfaction to the three persons whom he had bitten."

This characteristic thought, at such a moment, throws floods of light on Buxton's character. He was so little overawed by the unnerving spectacle of a domestic pet in the last stages of dangerous derangement, that he had time to reflect on the possible after-thoughts of people entirely unrelated to himself. The gardener, on the contrary, "in a terrible fright" was bidden to fetch a collar and fasten it. There the wretched beast had to stay, with all the symptoms of hydrophobia. Buxton pinned him down between the prongs of a pitchfork to fasten a better chain to his collar, not a moment too soon, for at the next bound the old one broke. In two days the dog was dead.

"I shot all the dogs and drowned all the cats (i.e. those bitten by Prince). The man and boys who were bitten are doing pretty well; their wounds immediately attended to, cut and burnt out.

"Write me word whether Fowell (his son) has any wound on his fingers, and if he has one made by the dog, let it be cut out immediately; mind, these are my positive orders." Such were the vicissitudes of country house life, in the Waterloo era, and such the temper of the man who was to carry that same strong authority far beyond his social circles into the counsels of the nation.

Ten years later, amid the cares, disappointments, and occasional triumphs of the Emancipation campaign, he had retained his country-bred affection for animals. One day, standing in the entry of the old House of Commons, talking to his relative by marriage, Joseph Pease, the Darlington Quaker, a fine black and tan terrier rushed at his companion, barking furiously, and seems to have intruded upon the very floor of the chamber. The Members of that day, mainly dog-fanciers themselves, abandoned their parliamentary manners, and rose from their seats, "shouting and laughing, while the officers of the House chased the dog round and round."

In no other national assembly in the world could such a scene have taken place. The dog itself knew it, and sought sanctuary with Fowell Buxton, "who, as he could find no trace of the owner, took him home."

This unasked-for pet developed a marked character; we are told that it formed the habit of visiting the country houses of the Cromer neighbourhood. Buxton had christened him "Speaker," possibly in allusion to his demonstrated capacity to make the House rise. As if conscious of its dignity, it would never enter the kitchen, nor yet the cottages of the labourers. Such were the lighter moments of the Member of the unreformed House of those days. Its atmosphere has disappeared almost as completely as the building itself.

We read: "Once at rest in the retirement of Cromer Hall, Mr. Buxton began to lose the grave and careworn expression which usually marked his countenance while under the heavy pressure of business in town."

We may well believe it. From near the friendly coverts of Holkham there runs eastwards a low ridge of wooded hills that reach the shore at Sheringham and make a steep cliff above the beach as far as Mundesley. Almost in the centre lies Cromer itself, and just south-east the thickly planted woods of Northrepps, which was to be his eventual home. Anywhere over this wide stretch of undulating country, much of it covered with heather, being too light and stony for cultivation, much of it planted by Buxton and his relatives, with the plantations that make it the delight of the visitor to-day, there was abundant scope for engaging in all the field sports at which he was adept. Here were the fine view points to which the large joint family of Buxtons, Gurneys, Hoares and their widespread relatives, and those of parliamentary associates, could go to picnic, walk or ride. So numerous were the parties they made that at one time they produced a family newspaper. Other occasions indoors afforded the opportunity for reading and discussion of a variety of subjects ranging, from "Locke on the Human Understanding to William of Deloraine good at need" with, in the background, the serious moment of family prayers or the Sunday services, then so regularly attended.

A guest at Cromer Hall is quoted in the *Memoirs* :

"I wish I could describe the impression made upon me by the extraordinary power of interesting and stimulating others, which was possessed by (Sir) Fowell Buxton." On the serious side, it seems that he contemplated publishing a volume called *Maxims for the Young*, with a view to the education of his numerous children, nephews, nieces, friends and dependants. He gathered these aphorisms from Locke, Burke, Huskisson, Fox. But he added his own homely wisdom, the result of thoughtful daily experience.

"Vigour—energy—resolution—firmness of purpose—these carry the day," is perhaps characteristic. "Read *multum, non multa—homo unius libri*, the most important part of your education is that which you now give yourselves."

As the younger members of the joint families that stayed under his roof played on his lawn, shot and hunted over his land, grew up and moved out into the world, he sped them on their way with prayerful injunctions, quoting not merely the New Testament but the Old, as well:

"Deliver him, O Lord, from feeble and unstable purpose."

". . . . May he be able in after life to ascribe his success to the Lord, and to say with David, 'It is God that girdeth me with strength'."

Again "This mortification is a test to try your character . . . if Fortune will not give you her favours, tear them from her by force. . . . If you are sick at heart and can't sleep, and laugh and defy malicious fortune, then you may make a very decent banker, but there is an end of you. . . ."

Nor was such sage precept the mere gratuitous advice of one who has relinquished the conflict. He meant what he said and was a realist in action, if often something of an evangelical mystic in speech.

On 23rd October, 1823, just after the first Emancipation debates in the House of Commons, Buxton and Sam Hoare, who were regular members of the rescue parties that manned the life-saving apparatus in use on that dangerous coast, were warned that a collier, *The Duchess of Cumberland*, was ashore on what was described in the *Memoirs* as "the rocks off Cromer lighthouse." The fact is that these are beds of flint quite invisible at night, or in any but the lowest tides. The unfortunate vessel, in those days when there was no light on Happisburgh sands, had tried to pass, or been driven far too close in, and by the time the rescue parties arrived on the scene she was hard aground, close in shore. An attempt to launch the life-boat was a failure, the fishermen of that day, unlike the immortal Blogg of the twentieth century, would not man her. In vain did Buxton spring into the boat directly she floated, no one followed, and he was forced to abandon the attempt. The next expedient was "Captain Manby's gun," pictures of the operation of which can be seen in Norwich Castle Museum. The line attached to the rocket fell short, although the distance was so small that nine of the crew could be seen lashed to the rigging. At length she split open, her cargo "blackening the waters," we are told.

"Poor, dear hearts, they're all gone now," exclaimed an old fisherman. At that moment Buxton thought he saw a human form floating on a wave. "Without waiting for a rope, he at once dashed into the surf—caught the man—flung himself upon him and struggled against the strong drawback of the retiring billow, until others could reach him." In spite of his herculean strength, he was so exhausted that he had to be carried up the cliff.

Such was the man who conducted family prayers, compiled moral texts for the benefit of his young folk, shot and hunted with Lord Leicester, Lord Suffield and the rest of the county gentry, and held the noses of Ministers pitilessly over the unsavoury details of slave-smuggling and plantation conditions. He had a good deal to say that has a modern ring, about the reading of scripture; though he lived at too early a period to believe in anything less than the verbal inspiration of the Bible, we can trace already in his alert mind that very intensive scrutiny of Holy Writ that has led to our modern knowledge of it.

"An astronomer looks at the face of the heavens through a telescope and sees a harmony, an order, a profuse display of power and wisdom. An ordinary man surveys the same sky with the naked eye and observes nothing of all this. . . . And so it is with reading the Bible; if a man looks at it with naked, unassisted reason, he sees little and learns nothing: He wants the instrument, the Holy Spirit, to guide his inquiries, to enlighten his understanding."

The Prison Bill of 1822 did not fulfil all his hopes, but he was bidden to dinner with the Duke of Gloucester of those days, so often the patron of Emancipation activity.

All the time that Buxton's activities in Parliament can be traced in official records such as *Hansard*, there was another life of his running in a parallel stream. Its details are to be found in the older early editions of the *Memoirs*. First it is the Bible Society's meetings in Cromer, then it is the labourer and his pig, which he had to abandon if times were hard, and must often have asked the generous and well-known tenant of the Hall to help him out of his difficulties. "When they ask me to buy a bit, I buy two—one for myself, the other for them, they are so grateful and so pleased."

Again, as he stopped to speak to a friend who had been detained at the Court by business connected with the local bench, a crowd gathered round.

"I hope you will attend the meeting," someone called out.

"No, I do not understand Magistrates' business."

"Yes, Sir, you are the poor man's Magistrate!"

In other letters and anecdotes we find him full of concern for the fate of the wives of insane officers.

But after such remarks he would break off:

"John Ribbons is much to blame for not going to church, and must do it. He must not kill a rook on any consideration. I trust they will enjoy their matrimonial life; and I feel quite vexed at their being molested: in short, he must kill nothing but vermin."

There surely we have the authentic note of the real democrat of those days. He might be a land-owner and a wealthy brewer. He might be a Member of the unreformed Parliament. But he saw no difference between the Duke of Gloucester's dinner table and John Ribbon's attendance at morning service, and the matrimonial affairs of the rooks. He refused to go shooting with his old college friend, North, in Wales, although Wilberforce was there. We know that at the height of the Emancipation debates he had found time to applaud Martin's "Cruelty" bill that put an end to some of the more disgusting blood sports of the period. "All the dogs in England, and bears in Christendom, ought to howl us a congratulation," he said. And went on to write to a young clergyman about the principles that should guide him in planning the new house he was about to build.

Just before he undertook a special minor campaign that concerned the slave-smuggling at Mauritius, he had to stand for re-election at Weymouth. Personally popular, he took little part, and perhaps this was just as well for the scenes that took place were so violent that cavalry had to be called in, and were quite ineffectual in quelling the disturbance. One wonders if they were daunted by recollections of the blame thrown on the military at "Peterloo." In any case, the delay, expense and trouble to which he was put caused him to complain to Sam Hoare, "This is the sixth day of polling, and there is every probability of six days more. The election is carried on with the utmost violence, and at *monstrous* expense. It is said that ——— spends £1,500 a day; his party confesses to £1,000. He has nine public-houses open, where anybody, male or female, from town or country, is very welcome to eat and get drunk; and the truth is, the whole town is drunk. I send you a copy of a letter I wrote yesterday to the Chairman of our Committee, protesting against any such proceedings on our side.

"I will pay no part of the expense of opening houses. If any individual on his own responsibility does so, pray let him clearly understand that he will have hereafter no claim on me."

Such were the conditions under which a member of the unreformed House fought for Emancipation.

He was re-elected, the only Whig of the four Members who sat for Weymouth and Melcombe Regis, and it was as such that he embarked on what may be called the Mauritius campaign, to distinguish it from that more precisely concerned with the West Indies in the previous three years, the other subsidiary campaign, if we may so call it, that concerned slavery conditions in Africa, and which preceded the final and general assault on the whole surviving principle of slave-owning.

But here, in his life as in so many others, illness, pure coincidence, chance or Providence, stepped in, to play its part, call it what we will, at least it was an incalculable element. So far as logic takes us, this man of exceptional physique, and open-air training, with his home already fixed in one of the healthiest spots in these islands, if not in the world, should have been unusually capable of withstanding the fatigue of a parliamentary career. But such was not the case. By May, 1827, he was found to be "sinking under the weight of business, and the anxiety with which the whole case (of Mauritius) was fraught!"

What exactly was it, in this, as in the early instance of an "attack" and his subsequent all too early death, which laid low such a magnificent and fortunately situated specimen of manhood? We learn nothing from the *Memoirs*. No disorder is named, and again we may be forced to believe that the medical science of the day did not know. All we are told is from a letter from a friend: ". . . he was too ill to come downstairs, and Dr. Farre was sent for. . . . He appeared much oppressed with headache and very languid. . . . When Dr. Farre arrived he ordered leeches, quiet, and total abstinence from business. . . . At night he seemed very ill." He was moved from Devonshire Street to Ham House from which he wrote to Mrs. Upcher:

"I am far better, but rather feeble and incapable of exertion, and somewhat perplexed by the question—ought I to overwork myself or underwork my slave cause ? My judgment is for the second, but my inclination for the first, and the result will be that I shall do both. I am now going to take a ride."

Clearly, therefore, it was something which did not affect his limbs, and indeed all the meagre evidence the *Memoirs* afford seems to show that it was some form of nervous depression caused by the revolting details of slave-smuggling, which apparently bore down a constitution no muscular activity would other than have stimulated.

"I can't bear it, it's too bad!" he exclaimed, after reading some of the Mauritius evidence.

He resumed work under the threat of what the *Memoirs* called "alarming illness." "The frightful result which ensued," appears to have been that he removed to Upton in Essex, but was obliged to call in his physician who diagnosed his state by the words, "You are on fire, though you are not in a blaze!"

May we assume from this, that he suffered from high temperature ? Would a modern doctor have said: "Blood pressure and irregular pulse ?" We don't know. He goes on to tell us that on Saturday, 19th May, after going into a case of cruelty to negroes, he was so exhausted by excitement, that he had to cease this work. Next morning he was unwell. After some of the family had gone to Sunday morning service he ceased to have any clear memory of what happened, except that at noon he told his daughter who was looking after him to send for Dr. Farre. He then was seized with a fit of apoplexy and showed no signs of recovery until the following Wednesday. He then noticed the anguished faces of his family around his bed. He was able to give them some reassurance, but had none for himself when he discovered that the day for the Mauritius debate had come and gone while he was lying prostrate, apparently at death's door. He had not the comfort at that moment of any prophetic vision of how near to realisation were all his cherished hopes. For the time being at least the Mauritius case had to be abandoned.

That apparently is all that we shall know about this remarkable seizure, which then looked like having a far more disastrous effect on the cause he had so much at heart than was the case. Only those who have had medical training and experience can decide for themselves if it is possible that mere emotion, caused by reading what we should call "atrocity" narratives could, without other cause, induce what would be diagnosed as apoplexy nowadays. For the rest, this element in Buxton's life now supersedes the accounts of his physical presence and abounding vitality. He was forty-one, and the pictures we have of him in later middle age do not indicate his habitual fine stature and carriage. He is shown as a rather bent spectacled figure. The actual nature of the ailment remains a mystery enshrined in Dr. Farre's leeches and homely similes. The change which the illness produced was, perhaps, natural, although he seems entirely unconscious of it. On the one hand it increased the evangelical piety which had already coloured his thoughts so strongly. He spoke and wrote incessantly in biblical terms, and was abundantly articulate about the realisation of the thin veneer which the mortal scene interposes between us and the vast distances, silences, and mysteries of eternity. But on the other, as if by some divine compensation, he also developed more strongly than before what might have been thought an opposite and contradictory side—a rich delight in the half-wild life of the coverts of the North Norfolk coastal hillocks.

"The Lord is my defence, and my God is the rock of my refuge," he exclaimed at one moment. Almost immediately afterwards we find him saying that he chose the "divine silence," (his own words) of the woods. He even went further. He tried, how deliberately it is hard to guess, to reconcile the two tendencies. On one hand he told his children, and those of the related families who loved to join in his country excursions: "His (God's) hand is as manifest in the feathers of a butterfly's wing, in the eye of an insect, in the folding and packing of a blossom, in the curious aqueducts by which a leaf is nourished, as in the creation of a world, and in the laws by which the planets move."

How modern and how reasonable! But next door to it comes insistence on the routine of family prayers, and the extreme utility of the prayers of King David. One cannot but be intrigued by the speculation as to what he would have thought of that Syrian partisan, if he had ever met him, or what David's views on slavery might have been.

Once at least the growing duality of his nature, stimulated or not by the illness above described, brought him into a curious internal conflict. The great Mr. Simeon, one of the last of the high lights of Evangelicalism, then all powerful at King's College, Cambridge, and its neighbouring church, had been a great admirer of Rachel Gurney, "that dear departed saint," as he characterised her.

Now one of Mr. Simeon's vital concerns was with the Society for the Conversion of the Jews, and he expected Buxton to attend the powerful meeting organised in Norwich, to further this object, in October, 1827. But Fowell Buxton, mastered for the moment at least by the other side of his nature, persisted in going out shooting. Feeling perhaps that he owed his co-religionist some amends, he sent him a present of game resulting from his defection. This drew the following rejoinder from Mr. Simeon:

"My union with that whole family is near akin to the union of the saints in heaven, and my soul, in consequence of dear Rachel's experience being read to me, had been so in heaven, that I actually felt it a condescension to come down and dine with the party even though they had all been dukes and duchesses. . . .

"On these grounds, I thought that an act of condescension and self-denial on your part, if self denial it was, might not have been unseasonable. . . .

"Now, my dear friend, you see you have shot me flying, and penetrated my heart, and let out, not ill blood (there is none I assure you) but the stream of love, which was pent up there. . . ."

That was how friends sent and acknowledged a present of game in 1827.

With his main campaigns, that which concerned the West Indies, and that which concerned Mauritius, in abeyance, his health needing anxious care, Buxton still found time to approach the new Governor-General of India, Lord William Bentinck, with regard to another matter which was near to his heart. Years before he had been interested in trying to stop or abate the practice of Suttee, and one cannot withhold one's admiration from a conviction of mind which made him feel entitled to attack a religious practice of a people so many centuries older than his own.

The practice was abolished "at a single blow" by the new Governor-General.

There came in Buxton's life, at this point, one of those events we describe by the word chance, though many of us may find this an inadequate description. His landlord, Wyndham, wanted to rebuild Cromer Hall for his own

T. F. BUXTON WITH HIS FAMILY.

From a silhouette.

THE REFORMED HOUSE OF COMMONS, 5TH FEBRUARY, 1833.

From a picture by G. Hayter.

accommodation, and asked him to leave the house in which he had passed, as a tenant, eight eventful years. Where should he go ? Many members of his own, and of the larger inclusive family into which he had married, were settled in this neighbourhood, to which he had become deeply attached. A mile away, just south of the modern railway station, stood the rather smaller hall of the adjacent parish of Northrepps, owned by his cousin by marriage, R. H. Gurney of the "Grove" family. It was not only suitable in every way, but brought him into close touch with his sister, Sarah Maria Buxton, and his cousin, Anna Gurney of the Keswick branch. These two ladies had made their home in one of the most beautiful spots imaginable, Northrepps Cottage, a flint-walled dwelling, sunk deep amid the beeches and rhododendrons, about half a mile north of the hall, on the byroad that leads from the Norwich-Cromer turnpike, past the gate of Northrepps Hall, to the village church of the fishing hamlet of Overstrand. Not only were they the neighbours he would have chosen, and the situation as perfect as any in that beautiful stretch of country, but both his sister and cousin were almost as enthusiastic about his campaigns as he was himself.

It may seem obvious now that this was the place for him to choose, but there is no trace in any of his writings or speeches that he realised that it was at Northrepps that he would spend most of the remaining twenty years of his life, and that he would be buried in the little church of Overstrand (then largely a ruin, but since rebuilt) while his national memorial would be in Westminster Abbey.

It was, then, mere chance, so far as we can now tell, which led to his settlement here, not in the Essex in which he was born, or on the outskirts of the London in which lay his business training and his public career, nor down at Weymouth, where his family was established, and for which he sat as a member for so many years. His choice, so far as it can be called so, seems to have been guided by the congenial neighbourhood and congenial company which he must have felt he would find here. He rapidly became the patriarch, not only of his own family, but of the assembled Gurneys and Hoares, Quaker banking or brewing families, with a large acquaintance amid Evangelicals, Emancipationists and reformers. What the domestic atmosphere was can be judged by the two following rhymes, unsigned and undated, amid family papers :

(1)

A PORTRAIT: (*Anna Gurney*)

Possibly written by Charles, Buxton's younger son, and compiler of the *Memoirs*.

> A Lady I know, but I mention no name,
> For Ladies are apt both to blush and to blame,
> I will just try my hand her resemblance to catch
> And if I can hit it, I'll give you a sketch—
> She has (let me see, for I hate all romancing
> And my jade of a muse has no talent at prancing
> To mere matters of fact pertinaciously cleaves;
> To her betters, high fancies and fictions she leaves).
> Enough of your muse—pray proceed with your verse

F

And the charms and the whims of the Lady rehearse—
Of foibles and follies she had, I believe,
The portion assigned to each daughter of Eve—
When she's happy and matters go smooth to her mind
No creature's more pleasing, or playful or kind—
But a frown of impatience *will* darken her face
At the vulgar, the selfish, the cruel, the base.
Her character beams through her features, and hence
From her eye darts expression and feeling and sense;
And I tell you so great is her wit and her worth,
No better companion I'd wish for on earth.
No flatterer I—so I hint—if you're skilful,
You perhaps may discern just a touch of the wilful.
A keen critic may see from her gestures and tone
That our Lady so sweet, had a will of her own.
But come the just cause—arise the occasion
Which pity excites, or profound indignation.
Away go the terrors and tears of her sex,
No womanish weakness her efforts shall vex—
But sagacious in counsel—determined in deed
She has courage to dare, and persuasion to plead.
She has rescued the seaman,[1] the caffer,[2] the slave[3]
From the rapine of man, from the wrath of the wave.
Of her air, or her look, a just image you'll form
If you visit yon cliff in the rage of a storm—
Then a heroine she—with her eyes on that sail
While her hair wildly tossing out streams on the gale
Her forces assembled, her gun on the beach
If aid short of heaven those wretches can reach,
If they be not engulfed in the sea's heavy roll,
Their rescue will spring from her ardour of soul—
The truth I have told, but not half of what's true
Yet I must not, I dare not, the picture pursue—
My colours too coarse, and too harshly laid
May offend the nice feeling that covets the shade
Some who flee from no trial—from no sacrifice swerve
Yet shrink from the credit their actions deserve.
This only I add, may all who are here
Long rejoice in her wit, long regale on her cheer—
Catch her love of the right—her contempt of the vile,
At her whimsies indulge in a good natur'd smile
And with her for a guide, may each brace up his mind
And lay himself out for the good of mankind,
Let him study that art of all arts the most blest
Of befriending the weak, the forlorn, the distress'd.

*   *   *   *   *

---

[1] Haysboro' Lighthouse.   [2] Orders for the Restoration of the Adelaide Territory to Macomo and his People.   [3] Commercial Capabilities of Africa.

(2)

The second must be of later date, as it seems to refer to Buxton's baronetcy, 1840.

> A rumour hath spread both up and down
> The baronet had come to town.
> To stay awhile—not only he
> But[1] Chenda came and Lady B.
> No sooner come from far and near
> The family did all appear,
> Gurneys and Johnstons, Hoares and Frys
> With listening ears and wondering eyes
> For they had heard they came to town
> To pay their homage to the Crown.
>
> "Catherine dear,"[2] said Lady B.,
> "I want a little time with thee.
> Thee knows some clothes must now be bought
> In which I may appear at Court.
> My gown, my feathers and my train
> I wish to be both neat and plain.
> It would be a pity, dears, to spend
> Our money on a worthless end
> So all must help me and suggest
> What each would think to be the best."
>
> "I'll settle that," Aunt Catherine said,
> "Thy neat grey gown, and shawl of red
> And tidy cap upon thy head
> Will surely do, for who could bear
> To see smart feathers in thy hair ?
> I would not wear them, that I know
> For all the Queens that reign below,
> I only wonder what Hannah[3] can
> E'er have thought of such a plan!"
>
> "I quite approve, my sister dear,"
> Aunt Fry[4] rejoins, "thy coming here
> And shall be truly pleased to see
> Dear Fowell at the Court with thee,
> I to be sure when I did mean
> To go and see our dear young Queen
> Did only neaten up a little
> And wear my First Day gown and whittle,
> But yet I cannot quite repine
> With dearest sister Catherine,

---

[1] Richenda Gurney, Mrs. Cunningham.
[2] Catherine Gurney, the "Little Mother."
[3] Lady Buxton.   [4] Elizabeth Fry.

For I have always felt it due
To those who kindly favour you
To show respect e'en in your dress
And do the proper thing, not less;
My daughter Katherine, she would know
In what costume her Aunt should go."

To which her daughter quick replies,
"I really hope I can advise,
I'm often at St. James's Square,
And know *so* well what people wear,
And I confess, dear Aunt, I think
A Velvet Gown with train of pink
And ostrich feathers, I should say
Set in some brilliant head array
By some Artiste from France's shore
(By far the best is Isidore)
And Bessey hinted, though in vain
A Nigger boy should bear her train.
T'would show how Lady Buxton smiled
On poor afflicted Afric's child."

At last arrived the expected day
And all the Court in bright array
Assembled round the Throne, as gay
As singing birds in month of May.
At length arrived within the door
A pair, there never seen before.

"Pray who is that ?" 'twas whispered round,
"Full eight long feet above the ground
Of giant mould and bearing high
Stooping to greet the passers-by
And then that Lady, who is she ?
Such sweetness, it is rare to see
So mild, so gentle is her eye
And yet there's humour lurking by,
So truly Ladylike her mien
Though so unlike this giddy scene;
Her whole deportment of a kind
That clearly proves no common mind—
Who can they be ?   Sir Fowell he,
And that's his wife—My Lady B."

Evidently either this social environment, or the tonic air of Northrepps beechwoods and seaward cliffs, or the complete rest from parliamentary labours had their beneficial effect, and the "holiday" he enjoyed, from the early summer of 1827 until the spring of 1828, was another example of coincidence. For while both his West Indian and Mauritius campaigns were in temporary suspension, the former on account of the government's reluctance to bring forcible pressure to bear on the legislatures of the Colonies, the latter because of his inability to be present at the crucial debate, it so happened that Parliament itself was changing. Lord Liverpool gave up the premiership, but Canning, who naturally stepped into his place, was destined to live only a few months. What Abolitionists felt at this picture can be seen by a letter Wilberforce wrote to Lushington:

Highwood Hill, Middlesex,
23rd July, Wednesday, 1828.

My dear Dr. L.   You have manifested so warm and, I must add, considering your peculiar circumstances, so truly generous a zeal in the cause of the poor Negro slaves, that I cannot but take the liberty of applying to you and of imploring your exertions on their behalf, never, assuredly, were they more necessary.   The D. of Welln, declares indeed that he adopts as his own Mr. Canning's Resolutions; but then accompanies with the avowal that he looks to the Colonial legislation for carrying them into execution (telling these same Colonists that he is much pleased with what they have already done).   He even uses language which would almost convince anyone that he is not aware that we have the constitutional Right to pass Laws for the Colonies; nay, even to tax them under prescribed conditions.   In short, this looks as if we had all our work to begin again.   Do, my dear Sir, become again what I know you love to be, the advocate of distress and helplessness.   What a change has taken place since Dundas himself (afterwards Lord Melville) when the mouthpiece of the W. Indian Body proposd to the Hou: of Commons that about the 1st of Jany, 1800 Both Slave trade and giving birth to a slave should cease forever.   But you have no time to read or I eyes to write.   I therefore must lay down my pen begging my (read our Mrs. W. would require) to Mrs. Lushington and expecting and hoping that you will give us the pleasure of seeing you here for one day at least before you leave these parts for your Recess.   I hope Mrs. Lushn. will plead our cause.   The Excursion would do you good.   I remain ever

With cordial esteem and regard,
Yours very sincerely,
W. Wilberforce.

To an arena so changed in its dominating personalities Buxton returned in 1828.   Goderich's short-lived Ministry had replaced Bathurst, first by Huskisson, and finally by Sir George Murray, whose name we have already met with in West Indian affairs.   This Minister seems to have shown much more realism and decision in dealing with slavery matters than his predecessor, and had circulated what seems to have been regarded as an ultimatum to the island legislatures.   Wilmot Horton, freed from his under-secretarial responsibilities, moved to delay the Order in Council which had already been promulgated in the Crown Colonies of the mainland of Guiana to establish compulsory manumission.   The plantation owners thought they saw a threat to their available labour force.   This brought Buxton down to the House, feeling very queasy and unfit to undertake a full dress debate, even to master the mass of documents necessary to making an effective front against the delaying tactics which the plantation interests were employing.   To his consternation, when he arrived at the House, none of the major figures of the Emancipation body was visible save W. P. Smith of Norwich, a good, solid and honest man, but not of the calibre of Brougham and Lushington.   However, as the debate proceeded, the attacks delivered against the Emancipation party grew so violent, that he was roused to a pitch of alertness that made nothing of his enfeebled state. He chose for his main argument the well-worn, but unanswerable one, that, if the negroes were so happy as they were pictured, how was it that their numbers steadily decreased ?   He also made an avowal which was destined to be perpetuated in the final settlement of the question: "I am a friend to compensation . . . but on the widest scale."   He demanded, with unfaltering logic, that those who had borne the lash should be compensated as much as those who had wielded it.

He carried the House with him, and the Order was allowed to take its course. He was less fortunate, however, with Huskisson over the evidence in the case of Mauritius.   The Minister was convinced that the illicit trade had ceased and that the proper registration of negroes, which ought to have made it impossible, was being carried out.   Thus, until it was known what attitude the West Indian islands would take to Murray's reminders, both campaigns were once more in suspense.

Shortly after, as a result perhaps of this pause in his main activities, a new campaign was opened, this time in respect of the "Hottentots," as the original indigenous population of what is now Cape Province were called. Those who wish to have a full bird's-eye view of the whole question should refer to Macmillan's *Cape Colour Question.*   The facts with which Buxton was called upon to deal were a legacy from the history of white settlement in South Africa.   Dutch settlers had originally colonised the region in the middle of the seventeenth century, and there must be many memories in this country still of the degree of sympathy with which their history was viewed here and in Europe generally at the time of the South African War with which the twentieth century opened.   We know how strong is the Afrikander feeling at the present day.   It may at this distance of time be said without offence that the Dutch settlers who were to be the forefathers of the citizens of the Transvaal and Orange Free State were a sturdy type of colonist, who had crossed the sea rather than surrender their particular type of Protestant religion.   Soaked in the atmosphere of the Old Testament, foremost specimen of all that is frugal, practical and courageous in the national Netherland character, it is not hard to imagine their immediate conclusion from the discovery of a vast land of opportunity sparsely peopled by thriftless aboriginals.   They set about putting it in order by much the same means as Moses would no doubt have employed had he found himself their heaven-sent leader at the opposite end of Africa to that at which we read of him.   The danger of a Napoleonic occupation of this station on the route to India, as it was largely regarded a hundred and fifty years ago, led to the British seizure, and this brought in its train the visit of Dr. Philip as the agent of the London Missionary Society.

He found a state of life among the dark-skinned natives almost as bad, if widely differing in its circumstances, as that of their remote cousins who had been forcibly removed to the West Indies.   It must be remembered that the South African native was not technically a slave, though the patriarchal attitude of the early Dutch farmer may have given his fate an appearance not unlike that of the chattel negro on certain West Indian estates.   His status was nearer to that of the redskin in North America, while his numbers must have been greater. Buxton had had a glimpse of this problem some years before during one of Dr. Philip's visits to this country, and it seems that the enforced pause in his two main campaigns only now gave him the opportunity of mastering the detail, aided by the publication of Dr. Philip's *Researches in South Africa.* Buxton moved for an Order in Council setting down once and for all the status of the South African native. It is slightly misleading to see him quoted in the *Memoirs* as making "Emancipation" his aim, for the word bears a different meaning in relation to his other activities.

Possibly on account of the characteristic circumstances of European settlement in South Africa, possibly because he was fortunate in finding a farseeing and active Governor installed at the Cape, Buxton had a comparatively easy task before him. There was no solid body of South-African-owned seats in the House of Commons, no junior ministers who owned, or were related to the owners of, estates in South Africa; The Dutch, French or British colonist had no one to speak for him. Not that his case could have been made very convincing, since there was no question of the Mother country having deliberately put him in possession of the persons of the "Hottentot" natives, who had not been transferred to the Cape as a labour force, but were the historic population. In any case it is by no means certain that any effort they might have made to maintain a servile state beneath them would have resisted the strong action of Governor Bourke, who issued a ruling as to Hottentot status which Sir George Murray ratified by an Order in Council.

There is a certain pathos in Buxton's "jubilation" over this move. He evidently felt he had established the future of the native in what is now the Cape Province on a permanent basis. The references to this act are followed in the *Memoirs* by a description of the KAT RIVER settlement, at which the "Hottentots" were established as small farmers, "not surpassed by the peasantry of any country in Europe." They had dug 55 canals for irrigation, and were sober, industrious, and decent, a great contrast to his forthcoming experiment in West Africa.

Stockenstrom County perpetuates the name of the leader who first found the Hottentots on what was then the frontier of Cape Colony, wanting tools, education, and all the means to entering the world of Western civilisation. Buxton provided most of the funds, where, later, the Revd. James Read visited the village of "Buxton"; here Dr. Philip saw a native schoolmistress, mounted upon a stone block, tinkle a bell, and proceed to teach the fifty children who congregated, to spell from the separate leaves of a New Testament. A native convert, Stoffles, addressed a group of villagers comparing their fortunes to those of the Children of Israel, and the land they had taken from the Kaffirs as their Promised Land.

The political convulsions that marked the second quarter of the nineteenth century were now drawing nearer, and their importance to Buxton may well have appeared to centre upon the type of House of Commons before whom he, or one of the great lawyer orators, Brougham, Denman or Lushington, would end the long truce in the West Indian campaign, with an effort to insist on compulsion of such Colonial Assemblies as had failed to implement the resolutions of 1823 on some one or other of the eight main heads of Emancipation. He was confronted by a Duke of Wellington, who had made up his mind to another kind of Emancipation—that of Roman Catholics—from their many and historic disabilities. After much pondering, Buxton had made up *his* mind, very much to his credit, considering his Evangelical convictions and strongly Protestant entourage. He faced the almost certain effect of this determination upon his constituents at Weymouth with characteristic downrightness.

"Here I am waiting for the Catholic debate. . . . I am going to secure my own election next Parliament by voting for the Roman Catholics to-night. . . ."

Again a little later, in a letter in which he announced that he proposed to spend his forty-third birthday with Wilberforce, he says:

". . . during this session nothing has been thought of but the Catholic question!"

So engrossed was Parliament with this matter that no time could be found for pressing on the Mauritius campaign, although Sir Robert Farquhar, the ex-governor on whom Buxton had allowed the chief responsibility to fall, demanded a full investigation. The matter was also hindered by a series of irrelevant misfortunes, the bad health of the veteran Macaulay, and of Brougham, and one must wonder if the shocking state of the river Thames, outside the windows of the House, and no longer capable of disposing of the mass of sewerage draining out of a rapidly expanding London, may not have had an unexpectedly serious effect in retarding the progress of Emancipation. Buxton read his physician's opinion that he could not attend to the matter without endangering his life.

However, that influence we call chance in human affairs was impartial, and while such unpredictable accident may have held back the tide of human progress, other equally precarious ones helped it on. Twiss, the new Under-Secretary for the Colonies, was a far more sympathetic character than Wilmot Horton had been. Also the Commissioners appointed to investigate the matter of illegal Mauritius slave-trading, seem somehow to have triumphed over the dogged opposition with which they had been met, and produced a report which appeared to establish the case that Buxton had made out. Even then, the actual suppression of the trade so deeply entrenched was no simple matter. Byam, the police commissary, had been hounded from the island. General Hall, one of the more enlightened governors, had suffered much from opposition to his attempts to enforce the law. When Buxton induced Jeremie, ex-Chief Justice of St. Lucia, who had lost his post through his Emancipation opinions, to accept the post of *Procureur-Général* at Mauritius, the reply was: "Nothing shall induce me to go to a slave colony again . . . I have suffered enough!" "Why, it signifies very little whether you are killed or not, but it signifies very much if the right man goes to the Mauritius, or not, at this juncture," was Buxton's implacable reply. Actually, Jeremie went, and was compelled to seek refuge on a warship, and was finally recalled to this country in 1835.

Meanwhile, the dowager Lady Buxton had died at Bellfield, and while resigning himself to the loss of one who had had so ample a share of human existence, and used it so well, Buxton was full of gratitude for the continued health of his five surviving children. Alas, he spoke too soon. Shortly after, his second son, Harry, was found to be in a desperate condition. Again no explanation is offered by the *Memoirs* of why so fortunate a youngster should sink under some disease, vaguely called "consumption." The greatest comfort the sorrowing father received was a letter from the Reverend Charles Simeon, commending the state of the boy's mind, and he had to content himself with writing affectionate letters from the coaching halt at Newmarket, from London, or other places to which his busy life called him. The boy lingered until November, and is buried in the parish church of Overstrand, where the visitor to-day can read the touching verses of the heartbroken father:

"Full of bright promise, youthful, courteous, brave;
Grace in the form, mind beaming from the eye:
All that a Mother's fondest wish could crave,
Were lent awhile, and here they lie.

Here lies the wreck, the spirit wings her flight—
The ransomed spirit, to the realms above;
Ranges unfettered through the fields of light;
Rests in the bosom of eternal love;

Beholds the unnumbered host of angel powers,
Who, round Jehovah's throne, their anthems sing,
And joins the kindred band, those lovely flow'rs,
Cut down, and withered in their early spring.

Scenes by no tear disturb'd, no sin defil'd,
Scenes nor by heart conceiv'd, nor tongue confess'd,
Unveil'd to thee, dear spirit of our child;—
And we are comforted, for thou art bless'd."

One thing might have comforted the sorrowing parents. The "ruined" chancel in which they laid their child, is now repaired and in regular use. They were spared, it appears, any suspicion that the disease was curable. It says much for his courage that Buxton did not allow this severe blow to blunt his determination or diminish his zeal in the work of liberation. In writing to Dr. Philip about the position in South Africa, and giving news of the dying boy, he ended with the words:

"I have 100, perhaps 150, petitions waiting for me in London, but I do not leave home at present. When another election arrives, and if we have a change of Ministry, which may come soon, the subject will be more thought of than it has been. I must go to my afflicted wife."

The obviously molten state, not only of the short-lived Ministries which preceded the Reform Bill, but of the whole of the ancient system of representation, in spite of Wellington's declaration that it was as good as it could be, may have been the basis of Buxton's optimism, but there was another factor more patent to us than it can have been to him . . . the inevitably stupid nature of malice. Had the slave-owners, or the representatives of the bond holders, among whom there must have been at least some intelligent and humane men, only pursued, and made public a policy of what is now called "appeasement" they might easily have averted the attention of a legislature and representation that had more engrossing subjects nearer home for debate and action. But they seem to have been bewitched by their own shortsightedness. Instead of making even perfunctory promises to the home government, and cajoling the slaves with some show of indulgence, they flouted the not very vigorous suggestions made them, and appeared to be determined to "take it out" of the slaves. Even so, they took the course which common sense might have told them was bound to arouse the maximum adverse feeling in the home country. We have seen how the Anglican Church, somewhat naturally considering its position and prestige, was, at this date, before the general Evangelical movement had time to reach the then remote overseas possessions, more concerned with the white planter and official, and left the negro and mulatto to the dissenting bodies, who, from their nature and history, were bound to be democratic in feeling. The planters, with fatal wrongheadedness, recommenced the policy of persecution of the attenders of small Baptist and Wesleyan meetings that were doing their humble work among the slaves. Now the character of the British, always a puzzle to our neighbours, can be seen here again in its bewildering variety. For while the tough sporting type was just being weaned from its grosser field sports, just beginning to recognise self-imposed rules of fair play, and was inclined to say that it was a shame to beat the feeble and helpless (the case of Governor Haynau and Barclay Perkins' draymen comes to the mind), the other sort of Englishman, descendant of Bunyan and Cromwell, was also lifting up his voice in biblical denunciation. The planters found themselves at once qualified as "no sportsmen" and also as "persecutors of the prophets." Buxton saw this and declared:

"Proceed then, faster and faster; you are doing our work; you are accelerating the, downfall of slavery. A few more such triumphs, a few more such speaking testimonies of the merits of your system, and the people of England with one heart will abhor it, and with one voice dissolve it."

He never blinked for a moment the root cause which made slavery an abhorrent thing, in the ancient writings that form our Old Testament, in the gradual development of our own island social system—the ownership of one human body by another, producing forced labour, inferiority of status, and thus all the evils on which human progress has turned its back.

While the feeble and plainly doomed Ministry endeavoured to keep its balance between foreign affairs and domestic economic upheaval, between urgent representative reform and a clearly dying King, events now moved together, with what must then have seemed an awful impact. Indeed in many a history of the time, Daniel O'Connell and Louis-Philippe loom larger than Buxton and the slaves. Yet the real heart of the country was with him, the discontents of Ireland and France remote and often thought of as deserved.

In May, 1830, the Freemasons' Hall was packed as never before. The great lawyers, Brougham, Denman and Lushington were there in impressive array. The newly prospering, largely dissenting business and professional class, that cared as little for the troubles of slave-owners in far-off islands as for land-owners in the shires, crammed the building, beneath the Presidency of the veteran Wilberforce, who made his last appearance before such a gathering. They knew him. He was rich, but dissociated from the old feudal landed class. He too, was a dissenter, he was one of the four Members for Yorkshire, then an impressive position to hold. Buxton spoke first, and was seconded by the Lord Milton of that day. But even he was not sufficiently advanced for the spirit which had taken hold of the meeting, the members of which knew two things well—the missionaries they supported and had sent out were being ill-treated, and women were still being flogged. These facts struck against their newly gained sense of value for money, and also against their new "Victorian prudery." Buxton made this latter point at his last speech on the eve of Parliament being prorogued, and Brougham was able to pass by a handsome majority a motion for ultimate abolition. But it was no moment for any constructive legislation such as the complete case required. The King died in July, and it was clear that the forthcoming election would produce a heavy shifting of opinion toward what would now be called the left. Both parties were committed to moving in the direction of Emancipation, but the change of personalities, almost of tone, from the reign of George IV to the short, democratic in feeling, almost "interim" reign of William IV, was accentuated by the July Revolution in Paris, where absolutism, that had died so hard in both countries during the eighteenth century, was receiving its last blow. Indeed there was a certain similarity between Philippe-Égalité, and the Sailor King on our side of the Channel, with his unbrella and top hat, his disjointed personal conversation with his subjects. These subjects were increasingly of the type we have noticed at the monster meeting in London, and one scarcely less impressive was held in Edinburgh. Petitions poured in from every side, and Mathieson notices how the suppression of exhibitions of public feeling that had been enforced for a generation, not without some show of necessity during the Napoleonic Wars, was now breaking down. There could be no mistaking the tone of the new Parliament. Wellington had to give way to Grey, and Brougham was elevated to the Woolsack, although there always clung to him a certain unpopularity that often haunts brilliantly able men from the north of this island, who have, perhaps, made slower-thinking people do and say things that they knew they ought not, too often to be forgiven. His relations with Buxton are never quite clear. The latter knew and acknowledged his unparalleled abilities, but still felt bound to put his own deeply sincere point of view, and most of all when Brougham had gone to the Upper House.

Thus we find by April, having offered to leave the matter in the hands of the government, without effect, and conscious perhaps that not even his cherished campaign could compete with the burning question of Reform, Buxton told the cabinet he would move for "the extinction of slavery." He did so, and the result, as might be expected, was that while the government did not adopt his resolution, the tone of the new Order in Council, which the Colonies were going to be told to adopt or forfeit the right to participate in the financial assistance they so badly needed, was an advance, if small, on any official step hitherto taken. It may have been that the 500 petitions he was able to present to the government were at this moment opportune, for the first battle for Reform had been lost, and public opinion outside the House was important. Buxton's main theme, however, was still the disparity in the population figures between the free and the enslaved negro, and there was no denying it. So obvious was the turnover of opinion that, according to the *Memoirs*, O'Connell said to Buxton in the House after his speech, "I see land!"

But here, the exigencies of Reform again interrupted him, and he had to seek Weymouth and re-election.

We find him next entertaining a distinguished party at the brewery, on beef-steak cooked on the furnace, Grey ("careworn but cordial"), Brougham stopping the visit to the machinery to give a lecture on the steam engine, the Duke of Richmond, the Marquis of Cleveland, five Lords, including Shaftesbury, Howick, the under-secretary, who was so doughty a supporter of Emancipation, if not always on the same lines as Buxton, and Durham, destined to be known in connection with quite a different field of overseas legislation. To these were added the family group of Gurneys, Hanbury and others, while Lushington and Spring Rice perhaps represented the Evangelical Anglican, and the enlightened administrative circles. It was rather significant, among other things, as being one of the occasions that mark the progress of wealthy Quaker business men and the younger generation, who were to make their mark in the reformed Parliament, to the point at which they mixed on social terms with the older class of landed Whig grandee. The Spanish legitimist, General Alava, was present, but Talleyrand was prevented, it seems odd now to think, by the news of the election of Leopold as King of the Belgians.

What was the small talk of such a party ? We get a glimpse in a letter of J. J. Gurney. The fate of the Court of Chancery, the heresies of Paley which had prevented George III from making him a bishop, the story of a stage coach-man who swore at one of his horses when it stumbled and fell, in the words: "Come hup, you boroughmongering rascal," (rather a daring joke in the midst of the great Reform battle.) The party seems to have drunk "The King" and "The memory of George III," and went on to inspect the horses. Lord Grey deprecated hints about the possibility of Slavery legislation in the new Parliament, but made inquiries as to draymen's wages, and concluded that the substitutes they hired were as well paid as curates. He also told Gurney that he "entered Parliament at the age of two and twenty," and had been forty-five years a senator. "I am much too old for it. I would have refused the under-taking, if I could have done so consistently with my duty." He wound up with a Latin quotation from Erasmus, to explain why the Bishop of Norwich could not accept the see of Dublin. We laugh at the old Whigs to-day, but when we think of what they were and what they did, are we justified in doing so ?

The session was occupied with the well-known second battle for the Reform Bill and all its momentous consequences. With what relief did Buxton and Hoare seek their homes on the Norfolk coast:

"S. Hoare goes away to-day. Shooting has been good medicine for him; he came down with very gloomy views on the state of public affairs."

Buxton himself was either reassured, or possibly so immersed in Emancipation projects that he does not seem to have gauged accurately the trend of domestic opinion that Sam Hoare had perceived more clearly. He was soon disillusioned. One morning, at breakfast, his frightened servants came to tell him that a party of rioters were passing along the lane of quiet Northrepps, to break up a threshing machine on a farm. Characteristically, he went out at once to meet them with his children hanging on his arms, faced the rioters and made them a short speech on the folly of risking the gallows for such a project. This seems to have been ineffective, so he fearlessly confronted their leader, who was armed with a long pole, to which had been bound what is called a "reap hook" in Norfolk, and is actually a small sickle for hedge trimming. Buxton seized it, and, after a short struggle, his great physical strength prevailed, and he disarmed the man, and then another. After that the mob dispersed, and returned to their cottages. How far his bodily prowess, how far the prestige of a good landlord and well-liked local personality contributed to this end, it is now hard to judge. But a similar story is told about the other Norfolk figure, even a larger land-owner, and more gigantic bodily presence, Thomas William Coke, Earl of Leicester, as we think of him. He actually collared his adversary, flung him into a coach, and drove him to gaol. This is another side of the Whig character that must not be lost sight of. These men of the Reform Bill had no doubt of their obligation to lead and even master public opinion, nor any scruple about the means they employed, personal violence among others.

Nor was the spirit of the time confined to rough Norfolk labourers. We find Buxton writing in January, 1832, to a nephew who had been concerned in what we should call a school strike. He told the boy that, while he did not think any the worse of him for joining in these "insurrectionary movements," he must not be misled into thinking that anything but the system was wrong, and ended with a pretty homily on sparing his mother's feelings.

He was not destined, however, to escape so lightly from the agitations of Reform. His old college friend North had been divided from him by opposite opinions on the measure, and his efforts against it had hastened, if not caused, his death. Buxton wrote to the widow a letter which showed that party divisions made no gaps in his friendships, and recalled that only a year had passed since he had lost the son who was named after his dead friend.

While these scenes were being enacted at home, a parallel spirit of unrest and repression came to a bloody clash in the island of Jamaica. In certain ways the "insurrection" resembled that which had taken place nearly nine years earlier in Demerara. Those who have written on the subject always assert that the planters, or their agents, took no pains to conceal from the slaves the march of public opinion in the home country, and the gradually increasing pressure of the very moderate legislation directed against them, or their lack of intelligence in accepting a well-guarded and compensated scheme of emancipation. When no effect was produced the negroes concluded that something was being withheld, that manumission and other rights granted by Parliament were not being allowed by their masters and local officials. They may have been encouraged in this view by the missionaries who tended them, and this recalls the case of Missionary Smith.

But there were novel factors in the Jamaican outbreak. The relatively large number of half-caste, mulatto, and otherwise mixed racial types, were now siding with the negro against the European. They even ran a paper which discussed the means of, and progress towards, Emancipation. And beyond all this, there was the world-wide spirit of revolt. Human history was at one of the points at which the current, often sluggish and smooth, began to run swift and broken.

Finally, from some little-known, and possibly irrelevant incident, a rash word, some slight interference, the seething discontent boiled over. During the last week of 1832, parties of negroes refused to work, and burned stores and warehouses; the intervention of the military was bungled. Mathieson says that less than a score of white men lost their lives, by murder, arson, and the armed suppression of the "revolt." Soon the slaves were flocking back to work, but not before four hundred had been killed in the one-sided fighting, and a hundred sentenced to death and shot or hung, while as many were flogged. A score of Baptist and Wesleyan Chapels were damaged or demolished, the preachers misused or driven away. Only in the town of Kingston itself was the disproportion of white to coloured elements of the population too great to allow such excesses. The Governor, Lord Belmore, appears to have been unable to keep order, though he did protest, at the cost of extreme personal unpopularity.

At home, the Government was firmer, and took a stand on the mildly coercive measures contained in the Order in Council. The planters or their representatives had one more card to play, and that was to move their sympathisers in the Lords to ask for a Select Committee to inquire into the actual condition and treatment of the slaves. This was lent colour by the fact that many of the islands had indeed suffered great hardship through a hurricane about a year previously, though Jamaica escaped. Buxton considered that it was a device for postponing Emancipation, and he took the bold course of demanding a Select Committee to draw up a plan for the extinction of slavery. This clashed with the incidents of the great Reform drama of May, 1832, when even the greatest champions of Emancipation tried to induce him to forgo this motion. It was the moment at which the Reform Bill had again been defeated in the Lords, and Grey had resigned, but on Wellington failing to find a Ministry, Grey had to be recalled. In many eye-witness accounts of the scene we are told how one friend after another came up or wrote to Buxton to dissuade him from persisting in his Motion until Reform was carried. But he refused, at the cost of great personal anxiety, and his motion was overridden by an amendment confining the operation of his Committee to the resolutions of 1823, which he had tried to avoid. He had also the satisfaction of knowing that his persistence had not damaged the prospects of the Reform Bill, which passed under circumstances with which we are familiar, and received the Royal assent on 7th June.

Thus ends a further chapter in Buxton's life. His struggle for Emancipation was carried on with a startling disregard of the other tremendous events that were taking place around it. He was willing to risk delaying the passing of Reform, by giving a handle to the opposition by the intrusion of a motion in which the great bulk of the public were not deeply interested. But he was proved right, and once Reform was passed, the real obstacle to Emancipation, namely the constituent elements of the Commons, and the overriding prestige of the Lords, was removed.

In fact, the real nineteenth century, not merely that denoted by the Calendar, had come in; Buxton had been born under George III, had been in Parliament under the Regent, afterwards George IV, and William IV. Irrelevant as those names may seem (though Gloucester was his friend) they stand for a certain state of society, of the gradual education of public opinion. From the passing of the Reform Bill, although Victoria was still a girl, we are in the age to which she was to give her name, an age that could not brook legal slavery, that was to set a new fashion in pity for, and action on behalf of, the oppressed. Under these favourable auspices came Buxton's triumph and its consequences.

CHAPTER V

THE NEW AGE. 1832—1837

PERHAPS NO LARGE IMPERSONAL MOVEMENT SUCH AS THE PASSING OF THE REFORM Bill marks so clearly what was happening to England as does the death of Wilberforce. It was somehow a symbol of the great change in the nature of our political life. Up to approximately this point, a small number of quite exceptional men, endowed with vision far in advance of their time, a Beckett or a Burleigh, a Coke or a Hampden, had been guided or been overridden by authority vested in the Crown, with more or less effective support from the knights and burgesses in Parliament assembled. Under Walpole and Pitt the process had been confirmed and implemented, until, in 1833, the Royal power had become a decisive instrument in the hands of a Prime Minister. But when we look more closely, it is astonishing to see how few were their backers, and how vaguely such support represented any widely held opinion in the mass of this nation.

From 1833 the great vague discontent that had so often led to bloodshed began to find its expression in parliamentary majorities. The Chartist movement was perhaps the last visible sign that the Reformed Parliament was not even yet an adequate vehicle for realisation of the aspirations of that large section of the nation which was beginning to be called "the people." The Slavery movement, more fortunate, did find legislative and administrative fulfilment, And afterwards, matters of parallel gravity no longer relied on the impulsion of some individual or quite remarkable group, but flowed from the sedulous listening of the elected Member of the House of Commons to the dim rumour in his constituency.

Wilberforce was a member for Yorkshire, but it would be difficult to trace his lifelong advocacy of Emancipation to any articulate desire in the Yorkshire of the eighteenth century to free the plantation workers overseas. So Buxton himself must have felt, for he wrote to Zachary Macaulay, a few days after the first anniversary of Reform: "The happy, peaceful removal of dear Mr. Wilberforce must have been sudden at last. On Saturday was his funeral. We were a long time in the Abbey, standing near the grave, before the funeral came in—the coffin followed by a large, unarranged, but very serious troop of men, including the Royal Dukes, many bishops, the members of Government, many peers, and crowds of M.P.s of all sorts of parties.

"I can never forget the scene, as I stood on the steps of Lord Mansfield's monument—the open grave, and the remarkable group around it. Especially did I observe the Duke of Wellington's aged countenance, feeling how soon, probably, the same scene would be enacted for him.

"The coffin of Wilberforce is placed between those of Pitt and Canning. He had all the distinction man could give, yet it seemed a feeble tribute to one who had obtained something so infinitely beyond. . . . Everyone of any note, I think, except Mr. O'Connell, was there—your son, of course."

So passed one of the giants, if such a term can be applied to the diminutive figure of eighteenth century elegance. In another letter, Buxton describes his old leader, during his last days, reclining on a sofa, his feet wrapped in flannel, alert as ever. It was perhaps fitting that the old leader should live on to know that his cherished project was on the eve of realisation, and then slip peacefully away. There is fitness, too, in the figure of the aged Duke of Wellington, standing by the graveside, though Buxton was sadly out in his prognostications. Wellington was destined to outlive him by some years, and to be one of the principal figures at the opening of the Great Exhibition of 1851, the real hall-mark of the Victorian Era. But he was right enough in taking that stiff military figure for one of the portents of the past. Wellington could not understand Emancipation any more than the Repeal of the Corn Laws. And Buxton was also right in the homage he paid to the dead and the living. Wilberforce was the last reformer who was also a macaroni, one of the first Evangelicals to be powerful in Parliament. Buxton himself was not deeply concerned with outward appearances, or relied on his magnificent stature to carry off any occasion demanding them. He was fortunate in drawing his inspiration from a source outside Parliament, in becoming, as it were, one of the conduits of the spirit of a new time, into the time-honoured chamber that still, to-day, is quite inexplicable to strangers.

He was right, again, in seeing in Wellington one of those semi-political military figures of caryatid dimensions, the like of which was not to appear again until our own day, and then as a Prime Minister of military experience, father then of a soldier turned politician.

So the new age opened, and Buxton's good fortune in seeing through the mere political expedient of the hour, would, had we shared it, have saved us many a disillusionment in the nineteen-thirties.

The Reform Bill was a great wave-crest of progress. Buxton never misjudged the strong undertow that such a departure must cause. He was justified by events, and by his insistence in season and out of season, all through the critical weeks while the question of the passage of Reform by the creation of hundreds of new peers hung in the balance. So much so that members of the Government as well as his own friends, spent much time and paper in trying to dissuade him. He ,was right. The new Parliament was faced with the fact that it did not by its novel composition remove as many old causes of discontent as it created new ones, and the real, if not very well organised, or deeply supported, Chartist movement, showed as much. Ireland too, was full of trouble, and had he not clung so tenaciously to his belief in total and immediate Emancipation, there is no saying how much further delay might not have ensued. As it was, the march of events was stately, if continuous.

Buxton had, at this important moment, two sources of invaluable support. One was the Baptist Missionary, Knibb, who had been hunted out of Jamaica, his chapel demolished, his very life in danger. Mathieson observes, "Much as the planters detested Knibb, they would have done better in their own interest to tolerate him in Jamaica," and quotes Hinton's *Memoirs of Wm. Knibb.* "They had flung the firebrand from their hearths and it had fallen on the powder magazine." In other words, partly from indomitable character, partly perhaps from the treatment he had received, on Knibb's arrival in this country, he only waited to learn that Reform had passed, to override the scruples of the more sedentary of the Baptists, as to joining in a political agitation threatening them with a nation-wide campaign. Such was Buxton's ally among the populace outside Parliament.

Just as important, and far more subtle, was the help he received from within the administration. Extraordinary as it may seem, the century that had been dominated by Walpole and Pitt and a host of far less commanding figures, with all the corrupt and dishonest machinery of pocket boroughs and packed majorities, had produced that unique phenomenon, the English civil servant, whose like is not even now to be found in the world. Among them, at this very juncture, were the younger Stephen, the author of *England Enslaved* and one of the long family line that has graced our literature as much as our public service, and "Van Artevelde" Taylor, dramatist and critic in his spare time.

Both had won their posts, not by political opinions or even literary graces, but by sheer hard work and capacity for minute recording and précis writing in their special jobs. Both were staunch Emancipationists, and could back their strong private opinions by some direct knowledge of West Indian conditions and the ability to compose memoranda on which their chiefs in Parliament could rely.

Thus Buxton now found himself with an Emancipation Party, in the electorate, which produced monster petitions, held vociferous meetings, and could not fail to bring pressure to bear on Members of Parliament; and also with the sort of unseen brief-writer behind the Ministers who would have to sponsor the government measure of complete or partial Emancipation. Affairs had now moved far enough for this to be the crucial point. Taylor, according to Mathieson, produced, first of all, a scheme by which the slave, given his freedom for two days a week, against a compensation payment to his owner, could with the product purchase another day, and so on, until the entire week's

The Anti-Slavery Convention, London, June, 1840.

From a picture by Benjamin R. Haydon.

HEAD OF THOMAS FOWELL BUXTON.

From the picture of the Anti-Slavery Convention.

working time belonged to him. This ingenious device, however, did not recommend itself to the Ministers who had to expound it, and it was shelved in favour of another by which £15,000,000 compensation was to be given to the owners against their right of property in the slave, who was to be kept on the plantation where he was needed by vagrancy legislation and a tax on other land. This was perhaps the germ of the idea of a large lump sum payment as compensation. This scheme, however, pleased no one except Stephen, who drafted it, and the notion of Freedom qualified by labour under indenture now came to the fore.

By this time, that is early in 1833, three things were firmly established. The first, and most important, was that however lengthy might be the process, and cautious the procedure, the government were going to compel Emancipation. The second was that some large measure of money compensation would be offered the planters, and the third, that, by some means or another, the negro must be obliged to work.

This sounds simple and obvious at a distance of a century, but perhaps no generation can appreciate better than that of the nineteen forties, how complicated in fact were the issues, how bitter the feelings aroused. On the one hand stood the out-and-out Abolitionists, fired with the extravagant emotions of a decade when the furies of the French Revolution, which half the adult population remen.bered as contemporary events, looked like being re-enacted in France, and spreading to all the countries in Europe, including, some may have hoped, Great Britain. This section, or wing, with its own periodical and funds, its own methods of propaganda, shared the premises of the Anti-Slavery Society, and contained the hundred per cent Abolitionists, who abused Buxton for not going fast and far enough. Next to them was the solid body of the Anti-Slavery Society, with its Royal and noble patrons, its considerable prestige and achievement. In the centre was the government, based on the reformed House of Commons, overloaded with business, and like all executive bodies constitutionally incapable of taking the airy view that any change was for the better. On the other hand, those very men, Althorpe and Goderich, Grey and Howick, perhaps even Peel, and old Wellington, knew that Slavery was doomed as it had existed since time immemorial, and had been perpetuated in the West Indies on account of conditions only comparable to those of Feudal England with its serfs, of five hundred years earlier, They were just beginning, some of them, to call themselves Conservatives, but they were too experienced, and we may concede, too humane and sport-loving to put themselves in the futile position of defending Slavery. The thing had become against the rules. One could no more countenance it than one could countenance the shooting of a sitting bird, or the chasing of a stag in the wrong season. But they had in that very Parliament, though diminished in numbers and influence, a West Indian Party, most of whose members had never seen the West Indian estates they owned, or had mortgaged, or merely represented. Behind them, again, not only thousands of miles away in space and time, but centuries behind in progress, were the British possessions overseas, in most of which European-born men could not work as they would in their normal environment, and had been forced by climates as much as by custom already three centuries old, to compel simple aboriginal negroes, transported thither from Africa, to work for them. Under such conditions had grown up all the complicated and artificial relationships which gave Europeans who lived in the West Indies a distinct point of view not unlike that of the citizen of the southern United States, and placed next them members of a mixed brown race that was neither white nor black, but had slowly moved over from siding with the former, to siding against them. Amid this wide and shifting propaganda, Buxton had consistently stood just on the left or progressive side of the government, through whom he had always from the outset proposed to act. He had brought pressure to bear upon a great variety of Prime Ministers and Colonial Secretaries. He had always insisted on a government measure, passed over the heads of the Colonial legislatures, to oblige them to emancipate the negro from bodily ownership by his Master. But his own words speak for him. "The government have to-night taken the slave question into their own hands, promising to settle it 'in a safe and satisfactory manner.' This delights me, and now I scorn those critics who maintain that the children of Ham ought to be flogged by all good Christians."

His indomitable optimism, in and out of season, here again, ran a little ahead of the facts. He may well have felt, looking back as he did, by this time, over ten solid years of continual agitation in the House of Commons, and out of it, that the time for the realisation of his hopes was drawing near. He was perhaps justifiably disgusted when there was no mention of Emancipation in the King's Speech at the opening of Parliament. For some weeks he was in constant communication with members of the government, particularly with Lord Althorpe and Stanley the new Colonial Secretary. In the end he was still so lacking of any solid assurance of the government's intentions, that he stated in the most positive manner that he would introduce a motion himself on the first available day, 19th March. After an anxious interview with Althorpe, during the discussion of the Irish Coercion Bill, he expressed his determination, and the Minister is reported to have said: "Well, if you won't yield, we must."

When Buxton rose in the House, however, the Government spokesman asked him to desist. He was induced to do so, upon extracting from the government a promise that they would prepare a plan for the complete and immediate abolition of Slavery, and name a date for introducing it. He was met by a formal declaration from Lord Althorpe, that the government measure should be introduced on 23rd April. They kept their word, except that, owing to the exigencies of parliamentary procedure, the date had to be further postponed until 14th May, 1833. The new Colonial Secretary framed his measure, and popular support was increased by a pamphlet in which a young Quaker, Whiteley, narrated his experiences during a visit to the plantation islands, which had a certain value as a "horror" story, for propaganda purposes.

So at length he came to the momentous day. It was Wednesday, 24th July, 1833, and the full ten years had rolled by, and at last the British Government submitted its plan to the searching debate of the Committee of the whole House, after considerable preliminary skirmishing over its first and second reading. Buxton moved for the Committee stage and complained that, after all the futile attempts to induce the legislatures of the islands to move, so much was left still in their dilatory hands. He urged the West Indian planters to take the compensation (which had now grown to twenty millions) while they could get it, for he produced some startling figures which seemed to show that, while the negro cost over £200 to rear and train, only one in three of them became an effective workman, and that when he did, he only made a profit of five shillings a year for his master. Thus, by actuarial tables, the capitalised value of the whole slave population would be £4,800,000, and the planters were well out of the business at £20,000,000. He went on to attack the system of apprenticeship, and drew a scathing parallel between the bill and the legislation already in effective operation in Cape Province. "Hope and fear, the inducement of reward and the compulsion of want," he declared were the only known means of making men work willingly, and complained that the bill gave the negro neither hope nor wages. It was characteristic of him that he said he knew his own incompetence to argue with the ability and eloquence of the Colonial Secretary, but if he knew anything at all of common sense, this was one of its plainest dictates. He warned the government against trifling with the matter, lest the half-awakened, half-reassured negro proceed to lengths beside which the riots of Jamaica in 1832 would be insignificant, and cited the terrible events in St. Domingo in 1794. This had long been on his mind, and we know that he had always feared that at the last moment, the negroes, knowing that some move toward Emancipation was going on, would resort to those acts of violence that had occurred in Demerara as well as in Jamaica. His expression in private had been: "The gun is cocked and on the shoulder!" He did not repeat this homely East Anglian phrase in the House, but he had so obviously the support of a large number of the Members, and, in the background, an even larger majority outside in the nation, that "Mr. Secretary Stanley" opened his case for the bill in an almost apologetic tone and, while complimenting Buxton, protested that the government measure was not being fairly treated. He went on to detail its provisions. Slavery was to be abolished on and from the 1st August, 1834, giving the Colonial legislatures just time to act. "He would ask the Hon, Gentleman, or the most sanguine of his supporters, whether four of five years ago they could have believed, in their fondest expectations, that it would be enacted by a British Parliament . . . that the term 'slavery' should be blotted out not only from our Statute Book, but out of all Colonial Statute Books."

He then detailed the scheme for the twelve year apprenticeship, under which the planter was to be assured of the labour of the freed negro, and the calculations on which the £20,000,000 had been based and by what means it was to be paid. He left adjustments, both of period and method, open. The negro was to have one fourth of his time free.

Stanley evidently felt sufficient confidence in his argument, for he turned abruptly on a Mr. Fryer who interjected "Why should we pay anything?" and invoked the laws of England, in the matter of depriving any of the King's subjects of his property, whatever its nature.

He then dealt with the limitations of punishment, the institution of a special magistracy to control the delinquent negro, the necessity of a labour force in some form, the difficulty of fixing wages, and finally deprecated any reference to possible insurrection as bordering on incitement. He sat down, asking Buxton to consider the measure with more favour, and to exert himself to point out its real advantages.

Macaulay followed, on the whole favourable to the bill, but determined to let off squibs at papism, lotteries, Mahometans, the Established Church, Hessians and Amazons. He was, in fact, a "regular old anti" as we might say to-day, but he somehow derived a good opinion of the bill from all his negatives. Lord Sandon also supported the motion with some qualifications and Lord Howick had his doubts about apprenticeship. Lord Althorpe intervened to justify the monetary provisions, but O'Connell would have none of it, and stood out for total abolition with no compensation. Bernal also, who had often taken part in debates on the subject, was full of doubt, but

Buxton was allowed the last word on the natural excitement caused among negroes by the news of the very measure they were discussing. Even after his moving appeal, the Committee motion was passed by only seven votes in a House of over three hundred members.

The debate was resumed in the morning and exhibited wide varieties of opinion, ranging from a demand for an immediate reduction of the term of apprenticeship, to the strongest opposition to any compensation whatever. Lushington was concerned with the legal anomaly by which the child of a freed slave, and even an adult who had escaped from the island, might revert to slave status on revisiting the land of his birth. He carried his amendment by the government adopting it, and Members went on to tackle the length of apprenticeship. As one reads the debate to-day, one can only sympathise with Mr. Buckingham who declared "how inextricable were the embarrassments that were sure to surround those who set out on a wrong principle." The fact was that Buxton was right in standing out for the stark fact of immediate and total Emancipation. The wrong had been done when the slave, or his ancestor, had been shipped overseas. He was now producing more sugar than could be conveniently consumed, at a sacrifice which no one was anxious to perpetuate. Hence this long wrangle as to how the old iniquity was to be undone. It is odd to find that, as Buxton criticised and rather reluctantly voted for clause after clause of what was bound to be, in any case, a compromise between high moral purpose, and the hard facts of economics and industry, outside the House he was being increasingly criticised. While he himself had clung tenaciously to the necessity for strictly legal action, moving step by step by parliamentary legislation, however tardy or ill-advised he thought some of the clauses, the left wing of the Emancipation Party amid the general public, which he had created and fostered, had moved ahead of him. It was, by the time the bill had reached the committee stage, a nice question as to whether he was the more abused by the West Indian planter, or by the more extreme members of the "Agency" Committee, such as the Bristol Quaker, Sturge.

The lengths to which some of the more extreme reformers were prepared to go can hardly be appreciated by those who have not seen an obscure work published in 1854, which consists of letters written by George Stephen, dedicated to Brougham, but addressed to Mrs. Beecher Stowe, giving some inside information as to the "Agency" or extreme left wing of the Anti-Slavery movement. From this we learn how Cropper and others, among whom were the members of the Stephen family most concerned with the cause, met as a separate Anti-Slavery group, and put up a fund to run more vivacious propaganda than the main Emancipationist body, with which Buxton moved, would sanction. They got together a band of "Agents" (or "Agitators" would be a plainer word) to tour the country, hold meetings, and six of them, names unknown to fame, were paid. The West India houses in London sent their clerks to break up meetings, but the agents worked so hard that the affiliated or branch Anti-Slavery societies were increased by 200 in a single twelve months, to 1,300 in all. Stephen relates with glee how, finding pro-slavery "slogans" chalked on walls, he rushed to the nearest printers, and gave an order for a large number of posters of a violently opposite tenor, and had them posted over every West Indian scribbled placard. He had an "army of bill stickers," amazed Buxton, and coolly took the bill to Samuel Gurney, the banker, who seems to have been the treasurer to the "legitimate" or main body of the Anti-Slavery Society. That mirror of probity was naturally disconcerted by this demand for entirely unauthorised expenditure and what occurred is related with evident relish by Stephen to Mrs. Beecher Stowe. It was characteristic:

"The language of the placards excited Lord Grey's displeasure, and somebody came to the printer's, alleging that his lordship sent him to demand the author's name. They might as well have inquired for Junius; they would have got nothing from a single man in the office, had they put them all to the torture. So the fun went on, and I presume Lord Grey remonstrated with Buxton, for he was very sore about them, and told me he should repudiate them at an Anti-Slavery meeting at Devonshire House, where I, too, was asked to attend. But I was determined to be even with him.

" 'And now, my friends,' he began, 'about these placards. I cannot qualify my language in speaking of them; we are not reduced to such disgraceful weapons as these; our weapons are reason, principle, duty; I will not stoop to arm myself from the armoury of the incendiary,' etc., and a great deal more to the like purpose. After an hour or so my turn came, and to Buxton's amazement, for he fully expected me to vindicate them, I took my cue from him, and adopted the same vein, only in much more inflated style.

" 'I go much further than my honourable friend; I denounce not only the placards but the author, too. I wish I could discover him. I would hold him up to your abhorrence; but he dare not intrude here; he dare not exhibit his incendiary features in such a peaceful, right-principled assembly as this! he dare not face the withering indignation of my honourable friend,' and here I turned towards Buxton, and looked him full in the face. It was too much even for Buxton's gravity: he burst into fits of laughter, and the meeting consisting chiefly of young Friends, had been laughing heartily at every pause, and adding loud applause to their laughter, in defiance of repeated mementos from Mr. S. Gurney, the chairman, that such expressions of sympathy were forbidden by their rules; for there was not one in the room who did not know as well as myself that I was the offender. 'You have fairly done me,' said Buxton, after the meeting.

"But the joke did not end here. Shortly after the bill came in; it amounted to £500, and I sent it to a very rigid member of the Society who was on their 'Committee of Sufferings.' He called on me.

(Samuel Gurney is evidently intended).

" 'Friend Stephen, what am I to do with this ?'

" 'Pay it, to be sure.'

" 'I will show it to the Committee of Sufferings if thou wishest it, but they will not pay it.'

" 'Well, I won't, at all events.'

" 'I tell thee, friend Stephen, that they will not mix themselves up with such violence and wrong.'

" 'Neither will I. I will have nothing to do with it.' "

" 'But the man must be paid ?'

" 'To be sure he must, and you must pay it.'

"And he left me, taking the bill with him: he called again in a few days.

" 'Friend Stephen, I told thee right: the committee will have nothing to say to thy placards or thy bill; they entirely disapprove of such violent things.'

" 'Very well; 'tis all one to me.'

"I cared nothing about it, for the Agency committee, I knew very well, would settle the account at once, only I was loth to throw the burthen on them, as they wanted all they could muster for the work of the elections. In a day or two after, however, my friend on the Committee of Sufferings called again.

" 'Friend Stephen, here is a cheque for £500, for thou art put to heavy expenses in this matter. We want no account of it, friend; use it as thou wilt, but, remember, we want no account of it.'

"So the printers and the bill stickers were paid by me; not by the Quakers, you will understand; I paid them out of my own pocket, as I was bound to do, but somehow or other I was not a farthing out of pocket, nevertheless. I am quite sure that in any honest cause, if a Quaker could only reconcile it to conscience to carry arms, there is not a corps in our army, or yours, that could match them. Sebastopol and Cronstadt, too, would have fallen two months since, before an army of Quakers, if they could only be persuaded, now and then, to carry a Minie rifle.

"I remain, my dear Madam,
"Yours very faithfully,
"George Stephen."

However, Buxton held on his course, cheered, one cannot help thinking, by such incidents as the arrival, during one of the earlier motions on the bill, of a monster petition from the Females of Great Britain, of such dimensions that he had to ask the Speaker for assistance to bring it as far as the table, which eventually was accomplished by the aid of three other Members.

How prudent his line of conduct really was, can be gauged by the fact that Stanley, who had his own troubles and responsibilities in the background, and could neither afford to let the government be beaten on any material point, nor yet to allow the debate to drag out to an indefinite length, threatened to drop the measure. This gave Buxton the opportunity of summoning to breakfast the more irreconcilable of the advanced section, Pringle, Cropper, Sturge, Moorsom, and George Stephen, and to make them a speech expressing his determination to give no pledge to oppose the compensation clause in the bill, on which they short-sightedly proposed to try to induce him to defeat the measure, with unforeseeable consequences. So the debate moved forward at the majestic pace expected of the deliberations of a British Parliament; by Monday, 29th July, the tenth clause had been reached despite a delay owing to Mr. Wilks's desiring to know what provision the government intended to make for moral and religious instruction. On this clause Buxton moved an amendment safeguarding the freed negro's (or apprentice's) right not to be moved from one Colony to another without a declaration by him before two J.P.s, and carried it.

Stanley himself proposed an amendment to clause 12, limiting employment of apprentices to 45 hours weekly and, with Buxton's support, carried even the contumacious O'Connell with him. Next day the raising of the compensation to £20,000,000 was ratified in spite of the same Irishman in opposition. Two days were devoted to this, and while Peel supported it on technical grounds of procedure, O'Connell was so obstructive that Stanley told him:

"The hon. and learned Member was in the habit of making assertions which, so often as they were refuted, he made again and again, till by force of repetition he believed them to be true."

Stanley also had to run the gauntlet of Cobbett's bullying, but the Committee passed the clause by a majority of 152. Buxton tried to get half the grant held up to make quite sure that, having received the money, the planters did, in fact, free the slaves. This time he had O'Connell with him, and it may be that the irritation the latter caused by his abuse of Lord Sandon, whose patience was obviously exhausted, helped to provide the majority against the amendment. So the House turned from the Emancipation of the Slaves to that of the Jews. The clause was passed on 2nd August. By the 5th of the month clause 5 had been reached, that which laid down the apprenticeship. Buxton's part in this was to try to safeguard the apprentice's provision of food, so that any short-weight issued to him would be a cause for the breaking of his indentures; this he had to withdraw. He then tried to ensure the freedom of children born, or under 6 years of age, after the passing of the bill. This was lost, but on the striking out of the 53rd clause, apparently redundant, Buxton brought up the question of the Chapels that had been destroyed. This was relegated to the care of the Colonial legislatures.

So, through the broiling days, with the Thames stinking to heaven outside the windows of the old House of Commons, the bill toiled on. By August 7th, after losing clauses for the rebuilding of demolished chapels out of local rates, and that for spending £25,000 on religious and moral instruction, Buxton and Wilks secured the Free Sunday for the apprentices.

Thus on Wednesday, 7th August, the bill passed the third reading.

On the 12th we find it undergoing its second reading in the Lords, prefaced by old Wellington producing a petition from Jamaica against it. He could not secure a hearing for this and the bill went forward with support from the new Lord Ripon (Goderich had been given an earldom), and Buxton's neighbour Suffield, of Gunton Park. On the 14th the Upper House went into Committee, Wellington again leading the opposition. Brougham from the Woolsack, enjoyed a dig at the Duke of Cumberland who opposed the measure as one "illustrious by courtesy of the House," which caused a mild sensation. He was, irrelevant as it may seem, only illustrating the freedom of the negro, as a British subject, to sit in the House of Commons if duly elected. After this slight breeze, other clauses were passed one by one, and by the 15th, the Report stage was reached. On the 20th the bill passed the Lords. Wilberforce had been dead just three weeks.

On the 28th it received the Royal assent.

Althorpe said (according to the *Memoirs*) that Buxton and Lushington wielded a power too great for any individuals in that House of Commons, and this may have been true. But they had behind them the accumulated weight of ten years of hard work, and considerable sacrifice, the power of a large measure of the new public opinion, and of that eventual logic of things which in our day has brought about the downfall of tyrannies beside which the narrow-mindedness of the West Indian planter looks like benevolent parental care. Wellington, says the same authority, told Lord Suffield that he saw what influence moved him, and that it was useless to fight the bill, as the more reactionary members of the Upper House were prepared to do.

Somehow, as we read the various accounts of the closing stages, there creeps in a sense of anti-climax. Was it because ten years is too long for sustained human interest ? Was it that the end had been in sight so long, or because the actual enactment fell so far short of the vision of the negro as a happy peasant on the Swiss model, which Buxton evidently entertained ? At first, of course, there were well-earned congratulations exchanged between Northrepps and Gunton, as the two landowners bowed their acknowledgments for mutual support in Lords and Commons respectively. There were others between Buxton and the veteran leaders of the anti-slavery cause, Macaulay the elder, and Clarkson, one of the earliest advocates of Emancipation. The measure was highly praised in the King's speech at the opening of the new Parliament.

As these felicitations died down, those who had backed the legislative enactment through good and evil report began to look forward with anticipation to the working of the bill. The date on which the negro, if he did not become very much freer except in words, at least changed his legal status, had been fixed eventually at 1st August, 1834, eleven months after Royal assent.

The portents were favourable. The disturbances some had feared as a result of Emancipation, and Buxton thought more probable if the negroes were baulked of it, did not take place. The wildest differences of opinion have been recorded as to the actual results of the passing of the measure, nor is this wonderful when we reflect on the difference actually existing between conditions in so large an island as Jamaica, and so small a one as St. Kitts. Miss Martineau, quoted with caution by Mathieson, drew an idyllic picture of ex-masters and emancipated apprentices fraternising in the chapels the latter attended. We may hope it was true in places. One thing seems certain, there was no wholesale rioting, very little drunkenness or disorder.

However, we get confirmation from Mrs. Geldart's *Man in Earnest*, which relates how Buxton received a large mail from the Colonies which he carried out to read amid the peace and freshness and bird song of the Northrepps woods, in order, says Mrs. Geldart, to have "no other witness of his emotions than the Eye that seeth in secret." The place where this occurred can still be seen, in the grounds of Northrepps Hall. The letters, from whichever of his correspondents they may have come, spoke of the churches and chapels of the islands "thrown open, and the slaves crowded in to await the hour of midnight. When the hour drew nigh, they fell on their knees and listened for the stroke of the clock; and when twelve sounded from the church tower they sprang to their feet, for they were all free—all free. No confusion, no intoxication, no bloodshed, and on the following Monday they all returned to their work— to work as free men, and thenceforward to be paid for their labour."

The first part of the last sentence is supported from several sources. The rest is not by any means a full account of what many of the negroes felt.

It was, in fact, the old story, familiar to anyone who tries to improve almost any department of our human lot. There comes a point, in all education, at which the boy who cannot swim has to trust himself out of his depth. Generally he will manage to flounder ashore. He thinks this a wonderful achievement, and only gradually realises how much he has yet to learn. If he really wants to he learns it.

So the negroes were by no means free in any sense that we lend to the word, were still obliged to work for a portion of the week at least, for no wages, or rather for wages which instead of being paid to them were allocated to a purpose they could neither participate in nor control, the compensation of the owners, who, having lost the right to coerce them by personal violence, had to have recourse to statutory enactment. This, as often happens, was so difficult to bring into play that in some cases, at least, masters were glad to adopt the most miscellaneous variety of plans for inducing the "apprentices" to work for actual money wages, "task work" not unlike bribery, to do what they were bound to do by law. In fact, what seemed a simple matter of justice and right to Buxton, at Northrepps, or facing his critcs in the House, became, in the widely differing circumstances of the islands and mainland settlements of the Caribbean, a complicated task of adjustment, often decided by purely local conditions. Mathieson surveying it, found while some Colonies, Trinidad, and parts of the mainland had already adopted the "Spanish system" of manumission, Antigua and Bermuda decided to short-circuit the period of apprenticeship altogether with results which, at least temporarily inconvenient, were in no sense disastrous. In St. Kitts on the other hand, martial law had to be proclaimed. In Barbadoes, local opinion was unfavourable to apprenticeship, on economic grounds, and the smaller islands of the group gave "little trouble." Tobago, which had a relatively good record for a long while previous to the Emancipation movement, showed the complexity of the issue by the fact that, when the scheme was implemented, it was found that the negro had actually less time at his disposition than he had formerly had as a slave.

The most important example on account of size and population was Jamaica. Here, while the general reception of the new state seems to have been good, there were bad patches, flogging, and endless wrangles in the Assembly.

Two main facts appeared to create a paradox. The negro was unwilling to work with the regularity and energy of a European, and had to be lured on, now that he could only be forced by a cumbersome process. Yet the figures quoted seem to show that the output of sugar rose substantially, immediately and for years after the adoption of the bill, and the Colonial Secretary admired the prosperity of the islands.

This then was the result of Buxton's unremitting labours, and those of his associates. On the one hand, Sturge, Stephen, and others of the extreme "Agency" type of reformers would not hear of the bill in any form, and we learn that it was years before Sturge, who eventually visited the West Indies, could say an approving word for what had been done. On the other hand, the opposition of planters, or mainly of their representatives, and of certain sections of minor official and trading interests, died down, neither completely nor uniformly, but in very marked contrast to the bloodthirsty threats with which they had withstood the passage of the bill, and the acts of violence and libellous abuse they had visited upon its promoters in Britain, and the humble ministers and friends of the slaves on the spot.

Naturally, it was for some time impossible to see how so novel and widespread a scheme would work. There is a certain sense of pause, falling appropriately in the period between the passage of the bill, in August, 1833, and its date of enforcement in August, 1834. We became aware again of the quiet, almost Jane Austen country life that lay behind the feverish activity and daily soul-searching of Buxton's London life. The Hoares were losing their eldest son, one more mystery in the healthy country-bred families of the Norfolk coast. We get a glimpse of the scene in the *Memoirs*. Buxton wrote to his brother-in-law: "A century hence it will signify nothing whether at this time he was stronger or weaker in body; but it will then and for ever after be a matter of the greatest moment that he had a certain and just hope of eternal life through Christ." A few sentences further on, we get an account of an adventurous ride along the sands to Weybourne, the village next west of Sheringham, during which he saw eleven vessels ashore in the great gale of 1st September, 1833, that uprooted so many trees that parts of the grounds of Northrepps were inaccessible except in daylight. He recognised a Weymouth vessel among the victims, and records that all lives were saved. The letter ends, characteristically:

"I have, I hope, arranged that some birds shall be slain for you to-morrow, but I must be excused at present, I am in no great mind for shooting."

There was a historic social meeting with the Nathaniel Rothschilds and family, who were just emerging from the humble status of foreign money-lenders, against whom the "security" laws of the date operated, into that of something like Whig grandees. The talk was mostly "shop," broking and banking and good advice. The girls were handsome, and the son already a great horse-fancier, but had lost the Arab mare he had obtained from the "Emperor of Morocco." Possibly nowhere else is it related of Nathaniel Rothschild that he used to give a guinea to a chance beggar in the street, for the fun of seeing the man take to his heels, under the impression that the gift was an error, and that he would be made to return it.

We get a glimpse of the family circle from the following extract from an Album:

AN EVENING AT NORTHREPPS HALL, OCTOBER, 1838

Says Charles,[1] "Who comes, Mamma, to-night?"
"The cottage ladies, dear." "That's right. . . ."
The smaller folks all stand apart
To see the Giant[2] striding past—
He marches on and there he stands,
By horses' measure, twenty hands
At least in height—compared to us,
Goliath as to David was.
No books for pleasure then he seeks,
But lays him down—the sofa creaks—
Miss Gurney comes, and brings a book,
All idle works are then forsook:
For what? Because this great man deigns
To read of death and bear the pains
Of negroes, slaves, poor helpless men.
"They have no mind," some say—What then?
They know what's pain, nor only so,
But daily meet with what they know.
But to return—Miss Gurney reads
A sentence—Says Mrs. B. "Who feeds
The stork when Charles is out?" "My dear,
We're reading what should draw a tear,
Of starving men, not birds. Go on,
Miss Gurney, we shall ne'er have done."
Miss Gurney reads—'Twas not for long
The ladies held their slipp'ry tongues.
They talk, they whisper.—"I will go,"
Says Mr. B. "You chatter so."
That silenced them, for to appear
To wish him gone they greatly fear.
He sleeps—but lest we should mistake
His sleep, and carelessly should wake

---

[1] Author of the *Memoirs*.   [2] The Liberator himself.

His pleasant doze, he tells us plain
By snoring o'er and o'er again.
At length the tea-time comes, and he
Is sleeping most complacently.
"Come! Come!" says Mrs. B. "My dear,
Wake, wake! 'tis time, the tea is here."
"I'm wide awake, my dear, I am."
"I'm not quite sure of that. Hem! Hem!"
He sleeps again—His tea gets cold.
Poor Esther knows that he will scold
To find it so. At length a cry,
Which she does hear most joyfully
Of "Spectacles"—a boy—a boy—
"What are you made for—to employ."
His tea is cold—his temper's hot.
"You've put no water in the pot."
The tea is almost done, when lo!
In come the Hoares—"How do." "How do,"
Pass quickly round. "You're very late,
We've just done tea—we could not wait."
The evening's spent in merry talk.
The Hoares go home—some ride—some walk,
The cottage ladies disappear,
The supper comes with ginger beer.
When all sufficiently are fed,
They leave the room and go to bed.
Thus ends an ev'ning at the Hall.
I've mentioned many great and small,
Some well—some ill—but all I've served
Just as their character deserved.

There were visits to the new shoot at Trimingham, where Moscow, the
Newfoundland dog, was allowed in the dining-room during the repast. The
sheep were to be sold, and Anna Gurney would take Buxton to see Mr. Lear,
where there was a "craniologist" who spent an hour examining his head,
"and told me strange news of myself, some hitting the mark, and others far from
it." He had discovered a mysterious Lady Mico who had left a large sum of
money, under restrictions which had resulted in tying it up for the benefit
of white slaves in Barbadoes. In view of what had now happened to all such,
he was able, with the assistance of Lushington, Macaulay and others, to get
this dormant sum allocated to the education of negroes. The money, placed
in the hands of competent Trustees, was made available by legal processes of
which doubtless Lushington knew the intricacies, for territories embracing
the more neglected West India islands, and even Mauritius and the Seychelles.
The Archdeacon of the Bahamas seems (in his earlier capacity as "the Rev.
J. M. Trew") to have been one of the administrators, and under the scheme
500 teachers were trained, for service amid the newly enfranchised. A century
later, one of his descendants found a flourishing training college, whose pupils
still honoured the name of Buxton.

Buxton's domestic circle, so often and bitterly afflicted, was now enlarged
by the marriage of his eldest daughter to the Member of Parliament for St.

Andrews, Andrew Johnston. The girl had been his principal secretary (many letters quoted are addressed to her), the occasion was utilised to make Buxton a present of plate, commemorating the achievement of Emancipation.

Hardly had Buxton seen the triumph of the cause he had upheld in the West Indies, than he turned his glance to a similar, but by no means identical problem. We have seen that he had already noticed the condition to which white immigration had reduced the aboriginal tribes of South Africa, then called Cape Province. Here, we must remember, the problem was not one of legal slavery, but of economic dislocation. There is nothing to show for how many centuries the dark-skinned native of immense regions south of the tropical valleys of equatorial Africa had led their sparse and primitive life, without imagining any other state of being.

Now it was, and is, clear that no artificial system for keeping the immense extent of the African continent free from European contact can be made permanent. It is equally certain that not the most altruistic and highly sensitised classes of European society will provide the bulk of the immigration. It will be the adventurous, the dissatisfied, even the grasping and, above all, the strongly independent types that will take the daring step of transferring themselves to a new, "savage," unsophisticated domicile. That, in fact, we know was what happened. The Dutch, with a proportion of French, British, and mixed settlers, were in many cases, refugees from religious persecution, with all the stern severity of character that might be expected of them, and these had gathered to themselves every variety of Western European who had good, or at least urgent, reasons for making a fresh start in a new world. Pioneer "Trekkers" who had risked everything to establish their right to some Calvinistic or Lutheran variety of Protestantism, thousands of miles from Europe, were not especially prone to toleration, or likely to regard the dark-skinned native as an equal; in fact, in his attitude towards the native the early settler was also influenced by the fact that the intitial step had been taken by a Dutch trading company, to whose members the "Hottentot" was a lazy and obstructive owner of the means of life, not to mention the means of profit. But contrary to West Indian conditions, these sturdy and determined colonists, who gradually ousted the "Hottentot," were met with a more virile black race from the north. There was nothing like the physical constriction of island life, and the now nearly extinct pure Hottentot, and the remaining Kaffir, were just as sparsely nomadic as the European settler. Faced with enormous distances and forbidding conditions of drought, the tendency seems to have been to conscript any coloured man, wandering "poor white" of various degrees of racial impurity, and even to import a certain number of slaves, for the purpose of doing the drudgery which is the curse of primitive communities.

This made no difference to Buxton. They might have been east-end wage-earners, or unfortunates caught in the prison system of the period. They happened to be a sort of dark African, different from that on whose behalf he had just won a signal legislative victory at the head of a new body of enlightened opinion. He felt no more need to go to South Africa to see what the Boer or the Bantu looked like, than he did to go to Jamaica to survey at first hand the members of the Gladstone family which owned plantations, or the imported slaves that he had now converted into indentured apprentices. Here were souls to be saved by the method of making the downtrodden into industrious, independent peasants.

It did not dawn on him all at once. As late as 10th May, 1828, Jane Philip, wife of the "Wilberforce of Africa" wrote to her husband, about the "May Meetings" of Exeter Hall. After mentioning the "neat speech" of the Duke of Gloucester, who presided, she said: "I was very pleased with Mr. Denman, Sir James Macintosh, and Mr. Buxton. I like his, Mr. B.'s, face very much (though I wish he would stir himself a little on behalf of the Hottentots) . . ."

As we have seen, she had not long to wait.   In less than two months, although, as the *Memoirs* point out, he was deeply engaged by what he may have felt was the more crying evil of the evasion of the Slave Trading Prohibition in Mauritius, Buxton found time to move the Act known as the 50th Ordinance, that is described as the Magna Charta of the Hottentots. It had been ratified shortly after, and the position seems to have been that the Cape Province executive of those days had almost simultaneously rectified the legal status to which the Hottentot had been relegated, and gave them, in the words of Philip, "the power of bringing their labour to a fair market."

It is curious to note how the line of progress laid down by Dr. Philip, on behalf of the primitive inhabitants of South Africa, who were being ousted from their natural habitats partly by European immigration, and partly by migration of more war-like coloured races, coincides with that which, thousands of miles away, was being slowly worked out for that other section of the African aborigines, which had been transported to the West Indies. It must make us feel that Buxton and incidentally Philip were right. The only eventual cure for slavery is the raising not merely of the legal but of the economic prestige of primitive man.

The scene of the experiment in this realistic kind of liberation, for the Hottentot, was the Kat River Settlement mentioned earlier. Buxton himself became so engrossed in his main West Indian scene of activity that it was only from time to time that we find him in correspondence with Philip, and inquiring into the Kat River project. After what seemed a conclusive victory, Dr. Philip embarked on the long voyage back to his scene of operations, and it was not until September, 1829, that he was able to observe on the spot the results of the legislation passed in London. He found a bitter campaign being waged which, ostensibly the result of a rumour that the more or less enfranchised Hottentot was about to make a general attack on the white settlers, was really an attempt to evade settling the Hottentot on the land, as the ideal "peasant" of Buxton's hopes, and force him to become the cheap labour force the European farmer required. In fact, allowing for the difference of scene and condition, it was a movement towards a kind of indentured labour hardly distinguishable in its main characteristics from the apprenticeship which had resulted from Buxton's West Indian campaign. Two purely local features had close parallels in the West Indies. One was that not even the Hottentot was capable of making what would be, to the colonial view, an intelligent use of his liberty, the other that such successful experiment as was then found possible, as at Kat River, Theopolis, and other "Institutions," was on far too small a scale to solve the problem of a race dispersed over thousands of miles of undeveloped continent, whose very emptiness was an invitation to European exploitation.

When this related problem re-emerges as a subject for Buxton's attention, Emancipation in the West Indies was an accomplished fact. But in South Africa local opinion had taken a reactionary turn, and a demand was arising, partly natural, partly propagandist, on behalf of supporters of colour-bar sentiment, for a "Vagrancy Act" which should tie the ineffective, hereditarily nomad Hottentot to some definite domicile, where he would have to work for whatever wages he was offered, or perish. The alternative was something like English poor law public assistance of the period. Macmillan says: "The Vagrant Law was a commonplace attempt of reactionary or merely ignorant employers to get State sanction for a policy that would secure a plentiful supply of cheap, subservient and exploitable labour. Buxton had already laid it down, with that instinct for some simple general principle that had served so well in the West Indian field:

"(1st) The natives have a right to their own lands.
(2nd) That, as our settlements must be attended by some evils to them, it is our duty to give them compensation for those evils by imparting the truths of Christianity and the arts of civilised life."

Once again, the main struggle was to bring the wide variety of local conditions, racial sentiment and individual outlook into the compass of so simple a framework. Largely owing to his personal influence with the Ministers who had succeeded those upon whom he had worked so hard and so long in the interest of the West Indian negro, the South African Vagrancy Act was forestalled. But this was only part of the picture. On the vague and remote borders of the already immense Cape Province of those days, lay immensity greater still, and from far away, irrational, inexplicable, migratory movements were bringing into clash with the primitive Hottentot and Bushman, as well as with Dutch and English settlers, a far more difficult race, the "Caffres," to-day written Kaffirs, and spoken of by Macmillan at least as undistinguishable from "Bantu." The Bushman was doomed to extinction, the Hottentot to absorption, but the Kaffir persists, and at the date of the Buxton-Philip action on behalf of the Hottentot there was flaring up the Sixth "Kaffir" War.

Buxton moved an address to the King in July, 1834, on the subject of the "commando" raids of armed European colonists into the border districts, confusingly called "Kaffirland," where this nomad, but fierce and persistent, people played much the same part as the Scottish clans, over whose border forays Sir Walter Scott has thrown so romantic a glamour. The facts seem to have been that the Kaffirs were accused of cattle thieving, and probably did take, or drive off, any beasts pastured by European settlers on the remoter grounds from which Kaffir and European alike had driven the Hottentot. So serious were the combats resulting that British troops were sometimes called to the aid of the armed Boer Commandos familiar to us from the South African War of 1899, and perpetuated in the term used for shock reconnaissance troops to-day. The information which filtered through from Dr. Philip on the one hand and by the office sources to which Buxton had access on the other, did not take long to rouse his crusading spirit, and it seems almost a providential coincidence that during these years, 1834 and 1835, there seems to have been a slight pause in the urgency of the cause in the West Indies, as those islands and districts assimilated the great change that the act of 1833 had inaugurated.

After having assisted in preventing the "Vagrant Act," a proposal not unlike our own Plantagenet "Statute of Labourers" ("an insidious measure" he called it), we find him accepting the challenge the new call flung down:

"I shall devote myself to three great subjects now on my hands:
(1st) The completion of Emancipation, for much remains to be done.
(2nd) The abolition of the Spanish and Portuguese slave-trade.
(3rd) The just treatment of the Aborigines."

There followed a prayer, but how human a creature he was is shown by the next entry in his "Commonplace book" on 18th January, Northrepps Hall:

"Late yesterday evening, I returned to this sweet home, having for the seventh time been elected, and having had my prayers answered; I have been, I thankfully acknowledge, guided and directed. May it please thee, thou prayer-hearing God, to make my being in Parliament conducive to the spread of thy name among the heathen, and to the interests of humanity, justice, freedom, and real religion."

The concrete result of this animation of the spirit was characteristically far from visionary. It issued in the setting up, at his instance largely, of a parliamentary committee of inquiry into the Kaffir War, and the whole question of the treatment of primitive races on the borders of the territories occupied by Europeans.

The curious duality of mind, incomprehensible to most people born outside these islands, is further illustrated by the next letter which begins: "I went to the city to the Alliance, to the Anti-Slavery Society, to the Aborigines' Committee, and to the meeting at Lushington's about Mauritius . . ." and in the same breath: "We had a pleasant journey down to Coggeshall where Edward, Edmund, Abraham Plastow and myself took a walk of an hour and a half, and very interesting it was to me and Abraham recounting old events. It is strange that, having hardly been at Coggeshall since I was a boy, of all the numbers of persons associated in my recollection only my Uncle and Abraham remain my seniors."

Turning from these country rambles of his boyhood, he amassed the facts of South African Policy, and wrote to Lord Glenelg, the new Colonial Secretary, that he considered certain facts established, and that they demanded a decision: "That you may be guided to a righteous deed and that you may stand between the oppressor and his prey, is my heartfelt desire and prayer."

The facts he tabulated were:

"(1)   That the colonists, or at least some of them, have long been actuated by an eager desire to get possession of the Kaffir territory.

(2)   That the Commando system is the real cause of the War.

(3)   That facts are stated relative to the death of Hintza, which, if true, throw a deep reflection on the colonial authorities, and which demand a close inquiry."

How forgotten and superseded are these early attempts at a just and working settlement! Who could have foreseen that within half a century the whole of the Kaffir territory involved would have been opened up, not merely to European influence, but to a new kind of industrial development, that the Commando System, with its irresponsible local Militia carrying out the will of the white settler on the spot, would have given way to one of the most celebrated police organisations in the world, and that searchers would look in vain for the name of Hintza, save in Buxton's *Memoirs*, or the files of the London Missionary Society?

But at that time bright hopes were possible. As a result of Buxton's influence, Governor D'Urban's proclamation, expelling the Kaffir chiefs from the border district then called, "the Province of Queen Adelaide," was rescinded. Not that they were guiltless of cattle-raiding, but that they and the local Commandos acted as perpetual counter-irritants to each other, as Philip, better acquainted with conditions on the spot, knew. Under Glenelg's impetus, received from Buxton, D'Urban gave way and accepted the chiefs as British subjects.

It must have seemed to Buxton, looking always rather to the principle, more clearly than to Philip, living on the spot, that a new era had been inaugurated. We can still find dim traces of it on the modern map. Not only are the counties labelled, "Albany" and "Beaufort" (though "Adelaide" now only indicates a small township), but Lord Charles Somerset, the Governor, and Andries Stockenstrom have their memorial in administrative divisions named after them. The latter is perhaps the most typical example of the best in what we now know to be a passing phase of the slavery question in South Africa. Declaring himself "a frontier Boer" this enlightened man of strong local sympathies, found himself "Landdrost" (would "Prefect" be the nearest equivalent?) of one of those disturbed districts, where the rather immature authority of "Cape Province" merged into even less settled land, on which the European colonist fought for the ill-defined grazing rights of the illimitable veldt, and they both held down the feebler Hottentot and disappearing Bushman. He seems to have been the prime mover in the Kat River Settlement, possibly the most successful, certainly the most often mentioned of the various attempts to set up and stabilise what corresponded fairly closely to the "reservations" allocated to the Red-skin by the administration of the United States.

Why did such well-meant efforts fail ? This is important on account of the light it throws on the final chapter of Buxton's effort to translate the negative side of Emancipation into a positive one of settlement of black peasants on their own land.

No one reason will account for it, and this itself may have misled Buxton. On the Kat River, under Stockenstrom, at Bethelsdorp (founded by the Dutch Batavian Government) Theopolis (an offshoot) at Pacaltsdorp and Glendendal which seem to have been sponsored by the Colonial Government of the day, at stations of the London Missionary Society and "Caledon Institution," various classes and tribes, now only names, were accommodated with land and resources. Some authorities say that the project was all along hopeless, that the Hottentot, and more certainly the Bushman, was incapable of becoming a law-abiding and industrious small holder. Some blame local administration or conditions. Even more positive are the statements that the facilities available were always too sparse to cure the malaise of a continent. Most striking of all are the statements quoted by Macmillan to the effect that the Great Trek which created the Boer Republics and so much of South African history, was mainly undertaken because the Dutch-dominated mixture of colonial settlers would not submit, on biblical grounds, to the black native being raised to equal status with themselves. If the British Government aided its Colonial representatives to put the black man on a level with themselves, then they would move on to some place where the curse of Ham still operated. Only the disillusioned will ask how far this was a religious conviction, and how far it was an instinctive demand for the necessary labour to perform the daunting drudgery inseparable from early colonial life. The whole question has been remodelled by modern industrial development.

How far was Buxton misinformed, or left in ignorance, and how far did his indomitable optimism, natural to a man of great physical courage, mislead him ? It is now impossible to tell. The subject of South Africa just fades out from the *Memoirs*. When Philip, in 1836, brought to this country "Tzatzoe the Caffre chief," Stoffles, a Hottentot, and a Mr. Read with his Kaffir wife, and half-

breed son, they dined with their Liberator at Northrepps. Queerly bedizened
in a sort of burlesque uniform, their remarks about the peaceful, sober and
prosperous appearance of England of 1836, their childlike gratitude to Buxton,
their demand for infant schools, were laboriously translated from native dialect
into Dutch, and so into English.   After dinner all three sang a hymn, in Dutch,
then Tzatzoe and Read a Kaffir song, then Stoffles a Hottentot war song.

"They could eat no more, but laughed heartily."

On leaving, they made speeches of thanks, and Buxton bade them, "be
firm to their God and Saviour, for that was the only path to peace, to happiness
and to Heaven." What did it mean to them? We cannot tell. We can only
see across one hundred and five years of British overseas history, crowded
with names and faces, then unknown and unguessed at, independent Boers,
enigmatic Rhodes, Chartered Company servants, British soldiers, gold
prospectors, great modern industrial cities, there, in the drawing-room at
Northrepps, dark-skinned men, dressed in gold lace and their own fuzzy hair,
gorging, chattering, laughing, singing and departing with a Christian's blessing.
It all fits in somewhere but God alone knows where.

After that no further reference occurs to the Slavery Question in South
Africa as such, except that, just as Buxton embarked upon his final statement on
the world question, as distinct from localised phases of it, which we know as
"The Slave Trade and its Remedy," there is a brief note that "the Kat River
Hottentots, Caffres, West Indian negroes are all doing beautifully."

Evidently he was satisfied, and was turning, as ever, to the generalised
question. When we come to the African Civilisation Society, when he began
to accept the title of the "Friend of Africa" he was not thinking of the detail
of which side of the Kat River was the more appropriate for the demarcation
of native reserves. A new and positive project was forming in his mind, and
so far as it was to be localised, it was a thousand miles from "Cape Province,"
in equatorial West Africa, at the mouth of the Niger. It may have been that
his attention was deflected into this channel by his investigations of the secret
slave trade still carried on from this district. It was in removing the means
from the hinterland of the Gold Coast, that his energies found their final outlet.
The scheme was a failure, as we shall see, but once again, it was the detail in
the remote jungle that eluded him. There was nothing wrong with his basic
idea.

CHAPTER VI

FULFILMENT. 1837—1846

WE NOW COME TO THE FINAL PHASE OF BUXTON'S LIFE. IT CONTAINED
disappointments over certain specific projects. It contained also the inevitable,
the one unavoidable tragedy of all human lives. It records the gradual decline
of his powers and death. It apparently shows how that which had been to him
a personal preoccupation broadened out from the confines of his individual
life and became a matter of national habit of thought, instead of the policy
of a political party. For this last decade during which Buxton lived and worked
on our earth saw the blossoming of a new spirit, latent in human progress,
nursed and fostered by Buxton and his associates, how consciously it is now
hard to determine. It did not reach its completion during his lifetime, nor

H

perhaps for some five years after, if we accept the view now commonly held that the Great Exhibition of 1851 marks the establishment of what we now speak of as the Era of Victoria. But it was well advanced before he closed his eyes, and in no small measure was the distinctive character it lent to the rest of the century due to him, and the relatively small band which he led, and which in turn influenced a much larger section of opinion in a new time.

Much has been written these twenty years past about the Victorian Age. It is usual to stress the accidental nature of this classification, that the Queen understood little the currents of thought that moved her subjects so deeply, and led them to play so conspicuous a part in rapid developments, and would have sympathised even less, if she had understood. Or the chance that she lived far longer than the average and retained her faculties is held to be the mere freak of Providence which it may be. But study of Buxton's last years seems to show that those who became "Victorians" in 1837, were influenced by some of the girl Queen's qualities. The older men who had mainly opposed Buxton's efforts, it is charitable to hope through the sheer incapacity of age, would never have behaved as they did to any male Prince, however young. Wellington and Melbourne adopted an avuncular, almost an elderly admirer's attitude towards the unknown and, they doubtless felt, unformed young creature who was destined to become a Queen Empress. And, what is far more striking, the clash between her early marriage and monumental domesticity, and the Court atmosphere that had survived up to her advent, made up the national scene in which Buxton had to work. Moreover, her young husband came forward as an active supporter, as we shall see, of the African Society, which was, perhaps, Buxton's most constructive effort, to a degree no previous sovereign or consort had done, and was a far more effective figure than the former Prince Regent or the Duke of Gloucester, both of whom had lent some measure of support to his campaigns.

So that we cannot be wrong in feeling that the cause of Emancipation gained by the brusque transition from the eighteenth century character of the eighteen-thirties to the Age of Victoria, and justly, since it was Buxton and his associates who had contributed so much to forming the opinions which, under her ægis, became characteristic. It is, therefore, all part of a sustained and successful effort, that the actual reign of Victoria began when Parliament had already reformed itself, and legal emancipation of slaves in British Overseas possessions was already an accomplished fact. Aberdeen, destined to play a significant part as a Victorian Prime Minister, had sent Buxton encouraging accounts of the improving conditions in the West Indies, and from other sources came pictures of schools being opened, of the young married negro women forsaking the fields to tend their own homes, as marriage according to European rites became more practicable. Friendly Societies were being established and the Church was directing its massive resources towards the elevating work that had been hitherto so largely in the hands of small dissenting missions.

Either the feeling that these promising results justified an abridgement of the period of apprenticeship, which he had never liked, or his experience of the reactions of ex-slave owners in South Africa, prompted Buxton, during the last year of William IV, to move for a Committee of Inquiry into the extent to which the conditions of the gift of £20,000,000 compensation to the ex-owners of slaves were being carried out.

The means by which this was computed can be seen by the following copies of forms in use:

(1) *Form of Claim:*

| Name of Estate or Domicile of Slaves Plantation Philadelphia | GUIANA Return of the number of Slaves and Estimated value thereof in each class in possession of Walfert Katz on 1st day of August, 1834. | No. 378 |

Total number of slaves . . . one hundred and eighty-seven.

DIVISIONS	No.	CLASSES	MALE, FEMALE NUMBER	VALUE IN STERLING £
Predial attached	1	Headpeople	9	2,070
	2	Tradesmen	7	1,260
	3	Inferior tradesmen	2	200
	4	Field labourers	107	18,146
	5	Inferior field labourers ..	36	3,420
Predial unattached	1	Head people	—	—
	2	Tradesmen	—	—
	3	Inferior tradesmen	—	—
	4	Field labourers	—	—
	5	Inferior field labourers ..	—	—
Non-Predial ..	1	Head Tradesmen	—	—
	2	Inferior tradesmen	—	—
	3	Headpeople employ	—	—
	4	Inferior people of the same description	—	—
	5	Head domestic servants ..	—	—
	6	Inferior Children under six years of age, 1st August, 1834 ..	20	1,000
		Aged, diseased, non-effective ..	6	180
			187	26,276

(2) *Form of Award:*

ADJUDICATION AND AWARD

| Jamaica ⎫ Hanover ⎭ | No. of Claim 31 | Office of Commissioners of Compensation 12th December, 1836 |

We undersigned Commissioners of Compensation appointed under the Act of the 3rd William 4 Cap. 72 do Adjudicate and Award upon the above claim that the sum of three hundred and twenty-seven pounds nineteen shillings and twopence is due and payable as compensation money in respect of the slaves in the said claim mentioned and that Mary Spence the Claimant in the above claim mentioned was entitled to and possessed of the said slaves for and during the term of her natural life with remainder to William Spence Herm his Heirs and Assigns under and by virtue of the will of William Spence, late of the parish of Hanover and Island of Jamaica Esq. being date, etc., appointment of Trustees.

He was also concerned in the Committee to inquire into the treatment of Aborigines. So full was he of these projects that he was obliged to take periods of rest with his new son-in-law, Johnston, in Scotland. He had hardly amassed the information on which the reports of these Committees were based, than he found himself listening to the "sweetness of voice" and admiring "the most exquisite grace of manner" in which the young Queen delivered her first address to the Houses of Parliament, surrounded by her chief officers of state, to a man relics of the eighteenth century. It was but twenty-two years, almost to a day, since Waterloo, and he felt prophetically, that it was the opening of a new time. The type of man who had been entrusted with the Governorship of Jamaica, Lord Sligo, on the one hand, the vigorous preaching of the rising lights of the Evangelical Church and dissenting bodies on the other, were in tune with his own convictions. He actually prefaced the Queen's dissolution of the last Parliament of her predecessor by moving for an inquiry into East Indian Slavery. It must have been his last Parliamentary act, for at the succeeding election at Weymouth, he was defeated, after representing the borough for twenty years.

It is said that his defeat had nothing to do with his opinions on Slavery. The "Reform" that had so changed the House of Commons had hardly yet penetrated to such ancient boroughs as Weymouth and Melcombe Regis. The tiny electorate was outrageously corrupt, and when Buxton characteristically refused to "open" (i.e. subsidise) the public houses and "lend" (i.e. give) £1,000 to the electors, it was seen that his cause was lost. Even eighty years later many an elector who was canvassed for his vote in such boroughs still replied: "What is it worth ?"

How little personal antagonism or reasoned opposition there was against him can be seen by the fact that his late constituents gave him a piece of plate. The children collected the money for this presentation, and this may lead us to reflect again on how few were the effective voters behind Buxton's Parliamentary effort, and how much he must have relied on less directly articulate opinion, which could only make itself heard by petition and other even less immediate means. It must be a striking thought to many readers to-day that the majority in the Weymouth constituency that Buxton represented for twenty years was composed of a small proportion of the adult males, enfranchised on the oddest pretexts, such as "freemanship." The fate of one of them, at least, is recorded in the *Memoirs*, which tell how an aged naval officer, whose last act was to vote for Buxton, expired on returning home, while his wife was helping him into bed, at the age of ninety-two.

It is refreshing, after this tale of defeat, a cardinal example of the ingratitude of the political life, to find Buxton turning with such relief to the homely life of Northrepps. Within a few months of this turmoil he was telling his brother, that he was taking the shooting season easily that year, having purchased a pony. "He is a wonder . . . quiet as a lamb, and strong enough to carry, and sometimes does carry, Mr. Hoare and myself together, eats bread and cheese, drinks beer, is a particularly good judge of porter, and prefers ours." To his other brother he recounts how, "I have shot execrably all the year . . . so employed a Holt carpenter to hew me a stock according to my own fancy, out of the trunk of a tree. . . . I shall send you a basket tonight, as a proof that my log of a gun stock can do execution." He adds that this weapon served as a luncheon table, in the coverts. "I shall, I trust, take the conceit out of the young men with it!" He adds that since Parliament closed he had ridden 500 miles and walked 1,500. (This must have been chiefly through his own coverts, as he shot over them.) He now had time to look about him, and seems, at first, not to have favoured the shortening of the apprenticeship term of twelve years in the West Indies, but contact with Sturge and other irreconcilables converted him during the winter, and by the spring of 1838 we find him, no longer a member of the House, as busy as ever with his associates, Glenelg, Lushington, and other stalwarts of the anti-slavery cause.

So the alternating currents of his life swung back, and the close season had hardly settled upon the Northrepps shoot before he was up in London, realising, perhaps for the first time, what his defeat at Weymouth had meant, just as the sufferer from a wound or injury may at first fail to feel the soreness which will soon overtake him. The occasion was a motion by Sir George Strickland in the Commons, for the Abolition of the new Apprenticeship system, before half its contemplated term had run. The matter seems to have been complicated by the opinion of many devoted opponents of slavery, that under the new conditions of manumission, of the purchase of freedom even from apprenticeship by the new type of piecework jobber that some negroes had become, and the prevailing prosperity of the islands, the Colonial Assemblies might have been induced to grant a waiver of the remaining years of the semi-bondage that had yet to be worked off. Buxton had to sit as a spectator, in the House in which he had been a dominating figure, and listen to speeches which traduced his motives and attacked his efforts. Among the spectators, it is odd to notice, was a promising young member named Gladstone who produced what must have been the forerunner of some of his budget speeches of half a century later. Mathieson says he misused the figures he quoted about the export trade of the West Indies. Even the rising, or risen, Parliamentary figures such as Grey and Lord John Russell held Buxton up as a supporter of apprenticeship, until he had great difficulty in controlling himself, and vented his feelings in what must have been a pungent letter to the latter. The motion was lost by 64 votes only. But this defeat was not in vain. By May, Eardley Wilmot produced yet another motion and carried it by three votes. The conclusion of the apprenticeship period was moved forward from August 1844 to 1838. Sturge and the Quakers (among whom Buxton for the moment included himself, in the account he gave his sister) applauded so loudly that they offended against the proper procedure of the House. "We strangers were all turned out for rioting! I am right pleased!" he says.

He now settled upon the final step towards the complete uprooting and prevention of slavery. He had found that the success which had crowned his efforts in the West Indies, South Africa and the Pacific Islands, so that there no longer existed any legal state of slavery under the Union Jack, was being circumvented by the lack of support given to British Government measures by the legislative bodies of Spain, Portugal and Brazil, so that a very large trade (he arrived at a figure of 150,000 captive negroes, shipped from West Africa per annum) was feeding the plantations of Cuba and Brazil. The attitude of so native an Englishman as Buxton now strikes us with a kind of wonder. He assumed that the British Navy was in charge of the seas, and certainly spoke as if a right of search existed or could be argued, so that one of his first demands was that the West African Squadron should be increased and a base established at Fernando Po. There can be no doubt of the horrors of the trade, in which human beings were treated as we should never allow animals to be, to-day. But perhaps one reason why Buxton went further than his immediate demand for an increased naval patrol was that some limit existed to the powers of even British Naval officers. Those of us who were children in the nineties, can remember a number of story books and serials in the *Boy's Own Paper*, in which the British sailing Man-o'-War pursued the infamous Slaver into the jungle-lined creeks of the Caribbean and the "Slave Coast." This reflects a certain tradition which had persisted at least for half a century, into a world which had forgotten its origin, and possibly accounts for the easy contempt still rife, for the "dago" (diego ?) nations, now as complete an anachronism as the sailing Man-o'-War.

As early as 1837 Buxton must have seen that something more than ocean patrol was needed, for while staying at Earlham in that year, he seems to have roused one of his sons (who perhaps were already used to the insomnia with which his work afflicted him) who records: ". . . sitting down on my bedside" the narrative runs, (he) told me that he had been lying awake the whole night, reflecting on the slave trade, and that he believed he had hit upon the true remedy for that portentous evil." This remedy was "the deliverance of Africa . . . by calling out her own resources."

He embarked upon this final effort in spite of the natural inevitable changes in the personalities around him. Old Zachary Macaulay died just before the abolition of apprenticeship. The loss of this veteran figure, a survivor from the days of Wilberforce, was a bad blow. It was somewhat compensated by a coming together of the Buxton party with that of Sturge, the Bristol Quaker, and the irreconcilables; one wonders how far this was facilitated by the loss of the seat at Weymouth. Another change was the introduction of the name of Palmerston among the familiar ones in the seats of authority, Greys, Stephens, Stanley and Spring Rice. We may doubt how far Palmerston was deeply afflicted by the sufferings of the negro, and how far he was pleased to have a chance of demonstrating that the Royal Navy could shoot up anyone, anywhere, on almost any occasion. Buxton, however, held on his way, accumulating, with the help of his son-in-law, Johnston, a formidable mass of statistics and details with which he hoped to force ministers to act energetically. All that had ever been true of the bestial cruelty of the original slave trade was still no exaggeration when applied to its lingering relics that had survived the Abolition of 1807 which had withdrawn British Shipping from any share in it, and the Emancipation of 1833 which had removed the whole market that the British Overseas possessions had once constituted. It is now difficult, perhaps impossible, to recover the sense of desperate urgency and deep emotion with which Buxton collated the sickening tale of the crowded decks of the slaver, the dead chained to the living, the complete neglect, not only of elementary sanitary measures, but even of necessary food and water, until the proportion of living human cargo landed in some South or Central American port was but one in three. Those who want to realise what moved him so profoundly should turn up the pages of some adventure story, such as *Tom Cringle's Log*, and grasp that the lurid passages are no flight of the imagination, but realistic accounts of what the British Navy hunted down no longer than a hundred years ago.

"The real remedy, the true ransom for Africa will be found," he declared, "in her fertile soil."

He went beyond the usual vision of the negro as the "happy peasant" which he and other reformers had always shared. He now seems to have contemplated a considerable degree of industrial and mercantile activity. Gold, iron and copper are enumerated among the minerals susceptible of exploitation, rice, wheat, coffee and sugar among the foodstuffs, hemp, indigo and cotton, among the fibres, mahogany, ebony and dyewoods, and, he added, little knowing how prophetically, "the oil palm, besides caoutchouc and other gums."

He stated that the natives were ready and eager for intercourse with Europeans. He does not seem to have expected much difficulty in training the West Coast and Central African tribesman for the agricultural or industrial life. He assumed that the average negro would pass willingly and thankfully from his precarious subsistence, agricultural or nomad life, straight to something like an idealised crofter state of society, with districts where industry of the type of the organised plantation production of the West Indies might be set up. He derived his estimates from a wide selection of authorities, of which Fulk Greville, Mungo Park and De Caille are perhaps the best known. But he did foresee, if he did not rightly appreciate, what was to prove the outstanding difficulty. He wrote to the Rev. Hugh Stowell, "The climate of Africa presents an obstacle to European agents being employed in the work to any extent, and we must look to the natives themselves to be agents in this great enterprise. This is no new scheme, for you will observe that it has been tried in various quarters of the globe with considerable success."

The circulation of the statement he had collated appears to have been the basis of his publication, *The Slave Trade and its Remedy*. In September, 1838, he was summoned to an interview with Lord Glenelg, the friendly Colonial Secretary in Lord Melbourne's Government. Apparently the Premier himself had spared some time from his courtship of his young sovereign to make himself acquainted with the subject, and the Cabinet met to consider it, though it is not clear if Melbourne was shown the proofs, or any advance copy of the book, which was certainly not at that date available to the public, or a resumé of the material on which it was based.

By December the Cabinet had been discussing what are called in a letter Buxton wrote from London, "my nine propositions." Indeed the main framework, on which he proposed to extinguish all trace of the Slave Trade, and set up an entirely new social and economic scheme in Africa, is variously arranged, and could be made to come to nine points, but those which are most important and were enumerated by him for the meeting at which the African Society was to be privately launched by its small inner band of founders, before it made its appeal to the general public, are elsewhere listed as:

"The deliverance of Africa by calling forth her own resources: In order to do this we must:

(1) Impede the Traffic (i.e. the Slave Trade to America).

(2) Establish Commerce.

(3) Teach cultivation.

(4) Impart education.

"To accomplish the first, we must increase and concentrate our Squadron, and make treaties with coast and inland chiefs.

"To accomplish the second, we must settle factories and send out trading ships.

"To accomplish the third, we must obtain by treaty lands for cultivation, and set on foot a company.

"To accomplish the fourth, we must revive African institutions, look out for Black agents, etc.

"What then is actually to be done now by Government?

"Increase the Squadron; obtain Fernando Po; prepare and instruct embassies (or authorise governors) to form treaties; including prevention of slave traffic, arrangements for trade; grants of land.

"By us: form a trading company; revive the African Institution."

This was in April, 1839, and by the end of July the Society made its public appeal. Characteristically Buxton took a certain almost saturnine pleasure in mixing the most incongruous elements of the then much more rigidly separated elements of English social circles. He noted that: "It was a glorious meeting. . . . Whig, Tory, and Radical, Dissenter, Low Church, High Church, tip-top High Church, or Oxfordism, all united." The heterogeneous members of this mixture did not always enjoy meeting one another, but Buxton's enthusiasm swept them along. He was fortunate in the fact that on the retirement of Lord Glenelg, who had been so accessible to Emancipation, the Secretaryship was filled by the almost equally friendly Lord Normanby. The conclusions arrived at by the meeting were embodied in two separate societies, one of a missionary, educational and religious character, one a commercial venture. The whole project was laid before the new Colonial Secretary, who announced to a deputation embracing three Lords, the Bishop of London, Dr. Lushington, and members of the Acland and Inglis families, that the Government proposed to send a frigate and two steamers to the Niger. Sir Edward Parry, the Comptroller of Steam Machinery, was to prepare these vessels, which were to sail in November.

Here we come to one of those extraordinary sidelights on Buxton's life that render our appreciation of it so complicated. We have just arrived at the point at which Emancipation, as he had conducted it, is falling into a recognisable place as part of the, to us, recent Victorian scene. But as we embark on an examination of the practical outcome of Buxton's life work, we find ourselves confronted with the Niger expedition, and at once the whole matter is clothed again in almost medieval mystery.

Why the Niger? There is no explanation in the *Memoirs*, and when we turn to the works on the subject, the fantastic limitations of the "modern" philanthropic industrial England of Victoria, in which Buxton seems a national and typical figure, become obvious. According to Mathieson, the unhealthy coast from Senegal down to the Cameroons, dotted with the early attempts of Iberian colonisation, had always had an attraction for those who wished to make Africa something more than a reservoir of cheap slave labour. It seems obvious to us to-day, that north of this lengthy tropical coast, or the small coastal strip alone accessible to the means of the eighteenth and early nineteenth century, warlike tribes and desert conditions made no establishment possible. Southward we come to greater distances, even less certain possibilities, But as for any deliberate and logical choice, we find that as late as 1816, the Admiralty supposed that the Congo was identical with the Niger, and many of the best informed and most enlightened people, including Buxton, held in 1840 that the climate of such places as Sierra Leone, and Fernando Po was "salubrious." Clearly, knowledge and reason had little to do with the choice, which for some unexplained cause, trade winds or probable river facilities, the weakness of the Portuguese, or the relative nearness to South America, had made this large little-known district the scene of experiments since the very birth of the Emancipation movement.

When Granville Sharp first established that mere landing on our island shores gave an enslaved negro his freedom, the outcome was that a small party of blacks thus liberated, were transported to Sierra Leone to start a free settlement that possibly gave Buxton his first idea. It was about as successful as the republic of Liberia is to-day. Again, the choice may have been influenced by the fact that British Naval Forces were by this date patrolling from Gambia to below the Congo and were centred on Sierra Leone, where tough old Zachary Macaulay had survived his term of governorship very well, and better than most. But possibly the strongest reason was the idea present throughout the long controversy, that the African Negro who was the raw material of the Slave Trade, could be made into something like the Bavarian or Dutch small farmer. Since many of the slaveship cargoes were filled up around the Bights of Benin and Biafra, the attempt at conversion of raw Africa into a civilised Europe-like continent must be made here, and the Niger was by far the most usable waterway to the interior. It is quite astonishing that after half a century, not only of theorising but of actual experiment, so little should have been known, or realised, of the actual possibilities of the scheme, and it may be here that Buxton's lofty vision, which had kept his campaigns so clean of mere expediency, did him ill service. Even so, it is inexcusable that those whose business it was to deal in facts seem to have done nothing to disillusion him, and apparently no moral was drawn either from the very meagre success of the earlier "African Institution" in turning Sierra Leone into a prosperous market town, or from the sinister casualty rate, some fifteen per cent, among the crews of the British men-of-war which were successful enough in chasing and capturing the horrible, stinking, floating hells in which hundreds of helpless primitive Africans were packed literally like sardines. Nor does any one of the promoters of the scheme seem to have been warned by the ill-fitting, if high-principled, procedure, under which British frigates hunted down the slave ships, only to see the wretched victims flung, manacled, to be devoured by sharks, or set afloat in tubs to impede pursuit, or at least to convoy the "prize" during weeks of insufficient food and water, to the "adjudication" court at the Naval Base at Sierra Leone. That equivocally named spot had seen five governors and several acting governors between 1825 and 1835, which we may think was ominous enough. It now seems as if the righteous desire to stop instantly a hideous loss of life, not to mention a considerable expenditure of energy and health of British naval personnel and a substantial cost to the nation, which undertook all these burdens with very half-hearted support from other countries, blinded Buxton to the difficulties of any positive policy. In any case he received no warning from those who knew something of conditions on the West African coast, and his powerful influence hurried the Government into giving official sanction and support to the project of the Niger Expedition. Sixty thousand pounds was voted by Parliament, and the ponderous machinery of Government subsidy and private philanthropy got laboriously under way. So slowly indeed did things work that Buxton finished his book, working all day and far into the night, with seven secretaries, and when finally the result was safely in his bag, he crossed to the continent where Mrs. Buxton had preceded him, and there is a note from Montreuil (then one of the first posting stages after Calais) to the effect that he had been sleeping almost continuously in the coach to catch up the nights' rest he had lost.

We now see a rare and unexpected side of his character, that of the English-man of property and leisure, enjoying the continental tour which, part of every gentleman's education in the eighteenth century, as we know by the diary of his relative Hudson Gurney, had been forbidden to all such by the Napoleonic Wars. He was accompanied by the lame Miss Gurney from the Cottage at Northrepps, and his second son, destined to be his biographer. They crossed the Mt. Cenis by the diligence road amid a snowstorm so severe as to be dangerous, but the only thing which impressed a sportsman of Buxton's calibre was the sight of a wolf, from which he promised himself a type of sport prohibited to English country gentlemen since the day of King John. Spink, the Cottage coachman, took what is to-day called "a poor view" of the precipice within a foot of two of his off hind wheel, as the cross traffic from Italy squeezed past. However, a finer spell intervened, they descended the southern slope amid scenes of beauty such as only the Alps can provide, and which called out all the sport-loving boy that Buxton fundamentally was. By December they were in Rome seeing the sights, and Buxton had an agreeable interview with the Pope, and highly approved of the strongly worded Bull in which his Holiness castigated the traffickers in human flesh, much to the fury of the Portuguese ambassador of the day. But the important thing was that Boar hunting had begun, and mounted on a "jackass," attended by Spink on another, Buxton ploughed through the forest of myrtle, wild lavender and arbutus, towards Monte Sacro and Soracte, quoting Horace, and doing great execution, one boar of eight years weighing 400 lb.

In Christmas week he turned to wild-fowling in the Numician lake near Orta. He took Virgil for his guide, but was sufficiently conscious of the passage of time to compare St. Peter's favourably with the Friends' Meeting House at Plaistow, for architecture, though he gave the palm to Plaistow for real religion.

So to woodcock and snipe shooting in the Macarasi, where Spink was attacked by robbers who infested the district, but gave a good account of himself without bloodshed. It may have been this incident that turned Buxton's mind to the prison system, or it may be that he was as incapable of leaving the subject of the oppressed as he was of forsaking his favourite field sports, and between the two, he was pulled one way or the other.

He found the Roman prisons "very clean (to be sure, they knew we were coming, and it must be remembered throughout we were never able to take them by surprise), the rooms are lofty and the air always fresh and good." He found, however, what he considered a great lack of classification, murderers and common assault cases herded together. No inspection and no regular work were provided, except that felons on long service worked in the public streets. There seems to have been no regular gaol delivery, and some cases had been under arrest untried for a year. There was no school, but regular prayers once a day, and one Mass on Sunday. There were no chains and no solitary confine-ment.

These particulars, taken from the letter to Sam Hoare, reprinted in the *Memoirs*, give a fair idea of the mature conclusions to which Buxton had come after a third of a century of service in the cause of every type of unfortunate, and his preoccupation with negro slavery must not blind us to the fact that reform of the penal system and prevention of unemployment, those inter-related curses of the civilised state, had been the first of his efforts, those on which he was, so to speak, trained, and to which most of his relatives had devoted time and money and something of genius. He passed on, at the end of January, to the civil hospitals with their staffs of 260 attendants, and 90 physicians and surgeons, and madhouse attached, and also an orphanage where "We saw one curious plan. Anybody who wants a wife may order one at this shop." However, the establishment was in charge of an Abbess. We get a glimpse of the scope and standards of the English colony in the Rome of those days. "I must tell you about the dinner party at Lord Shrewsbury's yesterday. Except myself, and I think one more, there was no one who had not some mark of nobility on his coat. There were three ambassadors, some English noblemen, and about half-a-dozen princes—twenty-four in all." Among this company he met the young Duc de Bordeaux, pretender to the throne of France, and liked him extremely, as he did other exalted Roman families, who in Holy Week went to wash the feet of the patients in the Hospital. His next social engagement took him into Bonapartist circles, not to Louis Napoleon, but to the Prince of Musignano, "Bonaparte's nephew and heir."

He went later to the San Michele asylum for orphans, and old men and women; annexed was a female prison, in which, out of 280 prisoners, only 30 could read. An even larger establishment at Civita Vecchia, "contains 1364 desperate-looking criminals." This one, however, was not on the same lavish (if antique) scale. Here in a heavily vaulted room, roughly twenty feet by thirty, murderers and bandits were chained to their platforms. Apparently an armed guard was thought necessary. In the worst compartment the "incorrigibles" guilty of many stabbings, mouldered in the dark and damp, enlightened by a weekly sermon from Capuchin monks. The most conspicuous inmate was one Gasparoni, something of a Robin Hood, who replied to Buxton's inquiry as to how many people he had murdered—"I cannot exactly recollect, somewhere about sixty!" but the Mayor added that this was about a quarter of the number. The man seems to have been almost exactly a forerunner of Capone, in organising ability and ruthlessness. The methods he employed, as described to Buxton, were almost the same as the New York and Chicago racketeering methods, kidnapping of children to enforce payment of ransom, crucifixion of spies, and maintenance of a secret service. Gasparoni practised a devout Catholicism, but told the Mayor that his first act if he escaped would be to cut the throat of every priest, but not apparently on a Friday. This strict observance seems to have arisen from the fact that, when at length the Government had made his position untenable by the offer of a reward of 3,000 crowns for his head, by seizing all his relatives and friends and starving out his "intelligence" agents, he was betrayed by a priest, who induced him to surrender on a promise of pardon and pension.

Even this character was not apparently condemned to capital punishment, but was incarcerated with his whole band. When Buxton asked which was his lieutenant, he replied: "My gun only was my lieutenant, that never failed to obey me!" He employed his long leisure in making caps, of which Buxton bought three, and told him that it was intended to have his likeness taken for a particular purpose, though the painter would not be able to come for some time.

"No matter!" was the reply, "let him suit himself, he will always find me at home!"

Amid all this interlude of gangster film mingled with elements of Italian opera, Buxton had but one thought, the reform of the Italian prison system. He had strongly urged on Prince Borghese the importance of founding a prison discipline society and was received with smiles and bows. When, however, Buxton's observations were embodied in a report and presented to prominent Italians for signature and transmission to the Government, nothing short of consternation prevailed in the circles in which the party had been so hospitably received.

"What ?" one of them exclaimed, his hair standing on end, "Am I to concur in telling my Government the plain truth ? Am I in the plainest manner to expose the errors and evils of their system ? There is not a Roman subject in the whole state who dares with the most cautious circumlocution to hint a fiftieth part of what Mr. Buxton states to them of their mistakes. He speaks as plainly as if he was speaking to his brother! I see how it is : Mr. Buxton thinks he is in England, and he has no notion that there is any harm in telling the Government that they ought all to be hanged. But we live under a different sky. Speaking plain truth to the authorities is quite an unheard-of thing at Rome." Later Buxton learned that the permission for him to visit the prisons had been given in the terms, "show him everything but with due caution."

As the spring advanced he was attacked by serious trouble in the respiratory passages, to which no name is given in the *Memoirs*, but which was sufficiently severe to interfere with his sleep, so that the ladies of the party took it in turns to read to him during the night, and he accepted it as a warning to put his affairs in order. Thus he missed participation in the great quail hunt and much pleasant scenery, and one can hardly help wondering how far his visits to the Italian gaols may have given him some infection.

A minor excitement was the difference of opinion between the British and Neapolitan Governments on some obscure question connected with the sulphur trade, but on the arrival of the Mediterranean Squadron from Malta the danger, whatever it amounted to, subsided.

By April the party had reached Naples, which he found "singularly like Weymouth," and, recovering from his illness, we may think largely owing to the care of his wife and sister, who had forcibly prevented him from writing, he became interested in the newly unveiled wonders of Herculaneum and Pompeii. He was much struck by the fact that "the world wanted and possessed in those days almost everything to which we now attach value." He seems to have been shown (fossil ?) foodstuffs, "Mrs. Diomed's garment, at least a piece of it ; the ornaments that were found upon her head, the ring on her finger, and the key her hand still kept hold of ; there was the helmet of the faithful sentinel who was found at his post, and the iron to which the legs of the prisoners were still fixed ; there were the appurtenances which belonged to a very fine lady, rouge among the rest."

He visited the Sibyls' cavern, Avernus and Puteol, and next Pompeii, where he was conducted along the Via Consularis, and saw the skeletons, the remains of food, of trades in progress, and pathetic efforts to escape.

So he made his way home, via Marseilles, Lyons, Paris, hoping to see the Duc de Broglie about the Slave Trade, and thus leaving Havre de Grace in May, "famously well, no headache, no cough, no cramp, no nothing. I am in capital spirits, hoping that I am going to see my children's children, and peace upon Africa."

He was but in time to prepare for the culminating, and alas, the final triumph of his career.

On the Ist June, there met possibly the most distinguished gathering that Exeter Hall had ever seen. "At eleven o'clock the Prince Consort entered the hall, which was already crowded with an audience of the highest respectability." This meant the Duke of Norfolk, two Marquises, six Earls, thirteen Barons, seven Bishops, and M. Guizot.

The meeting was opened by the Prince Consort, and Buxton was the first speaker and he made what was, to that generation, a novel point, that the suppression of the iniquitous trade was "a road to glory more noble, more illustrious, purer and grander than the battles of Waterloo and Trafalgar."

He was followed by a remarkable list of speakers, Archdeacon Wilberforce, son of the man from whom the leadership of Emancipation had been handed on to him, Sir Robert Peel, two of the Bishops, his associates Murray and Lushington, his relatives, Sam Gurney and The Reverend J. N. Cunningham. The meeting was not without its incidents, as when the entrance of O'Connell provoked "clamours for a speech from that gentleman." Negligible and semi-comic as this may sound it was a portent. The march of time, the stream of events had loosened and was disintegrating the social fabric amid which Buxton's campaigns had been waged. Chartism, Ireland, Free Trade were becoming the major issues in early Victorian England, the lead was passing from the country gentleman of Buxton's sort to the manufacturing families such as Peel's, and to the professional politician such as the Irish demagogue. But at the moment it was a portent only. As we can see by the "platform" at this vital and typical meeting, territorial land-owning grouped around the represent-ative of the Crown dominated any progressive movement. Nor was there any doubt as to the principal figure in so distinguished a gathering. Shortly after this meeting Buxton received an intimation that the Queen desired to confer a baronetcy upon him, which, after ascertaining that it was not a step initiated by any of his friends in high places, he accepted. This meeting, and the act of recognition that followed, mark the zenith of his Emancipation career, the late fruit of toil, endeavour and sacrifice. Before we pass on to the actual expedition intended to carry into effect his mature plans for final prevention of slavery in any form throughout the world, which was destined to elude him during his remaining years, it may be as well to place on record what his ultimate objective was. This can be learned from notes, apparently the basis of a manifesto which seems to bear marks of his personal editorship, and which is still kept in the archives of the Anti-Slavery and Aborigines' Protection Society, and may well be regarded as Buxton's last word. It runs as follows:

SOCIETY FOR THE EXTINCTION OF THE SLAVE TRADE AND
FOR THE CIVILISATION OF AFRICA

12, Parliament Street

Instituted June, 1839.
President : His Royal Highness Prince Albert, K.G.

PRESENT STATE OF AFRICA

Upwards of 30 years, and more than 15 millions of money have been consumed in fruitless attempts to put down the Slave Trade yet it has doubled in this period. The annual loss of life caused by the Trade has risen from 17 to 23 per cent. 170,000 Africans are computed to be annually reduced to Slavery, 330,000 more annually to perish, and the total annual loss to Africa to amount to 500,000 persons (T.F.B. African Slave Trade and Remedy). Africa, immensely rich in natural resources—teeming with inhabitants—anxious for European Manufactures and instruction—still remains under the desolating influence of the Slave Trade, an uncultivated desert, degraded by superstition and deluged with blood.

Sir T. F. Buxton's Plan—

Sir T. F. Buxton emphatically declares that, next to Christianity (the great and only effectual cure) the "deliverance of Africa" is to be sought in "calling out her own resources." Partly this duty devolves on Government, in enforcing the Treaties already made for the suppression of the Trades, obtaining other and more efficient Treaties with Native Chiefs as well as with European and other powers; and promoting and protecting the legitimate efforts of individuals engaged in the same object.

Another part devolved on individuals, which he proposes to divide between two associations, namely, first, a Benevolent Society to watch over and befriend the interests of Africa; and secondly, a Company which shall cultivate the fortunes of her soil. The object of the one to be charity, of the other legitimate gain; distinct, therefore, in their purposes, and separate in their management, yet both accordant in principle, and conducing to the same benevolent end.

Objects of this Society

The present Society, adopting the benevolent and pacific portion of Sir Fowell Buxton's scheme, proposes to accomplish the following objects, by agents and other suitable means:

(1) To make the Africans acquainted with the inexhaustible riches of their own soil, and sedulously to direct their attention to its cultivation on a system of free labour. To convince them, moreover, of the immeasurable superiority of Agriculture and innocent commerce, even in point of profit, over the Slave Trade, which excludes them.

(2) To instruct the natives in Agriculture and practical science; to cultivate small portions of land as models for their imitation, distribute agricultural instruments, seeds, plants, etc., introduce local and other improvements, and suggest and facilitate with means of beneficially exchanging the produce of Africa for the manufacture of Europe.

(3) To examine the principal languages of Africa and reduce them, where advisable, to a written form.

(4) To investigate the diseases, climate and local peculiarities of Africa for the benefit as well of natives as of foreign residents and travellers; to send out medicines and practitioners and thus to separate the practice of Medicine from the horrid superstitions now connected with it.

(5) To co-operate by every means in its power with the Government Expedition to the Niger, to report its progress, assist its operations—circulate the valuable information it may communicate, and generally to keep alive the interest of Great Britain in the suppression of the Slave Trade and the Welfare of Africa.

Expense

Means like these, on an adequate scale, will, of course, require numerous agencies, both at home and abroad, and perhaps further expeditions into the interior of Africa. These must occasion considerable expense; yet if the result be in a good degree commensurate with the design, even a large outlay will be abundantly repaid.

Let it be remembered, then, that Africa has imperative claims on the sympathy of the whole civilised world; that it presents a field of labour to the Christian philanthropist, the man of science, and the lawful merchant, that this Society, in fine, under God's blessing, and with the sanction of a benevolent Government aims to prepare the path, and to facilitate the success of each of these classes of labourers; and this may be said to consecrate its own efforts— to peace, to liberty, and to God.

Mr. Trew, Secretary

A Subscription of One Guinea and upwards per annum constitutes an Annual Member.

A donation of ten guineas and upwards constitutes a Life Subscription, and donations of a smaller amount will be thankfully received.

Subscriptions and Donations received by the Treasurer, J. Gurney Hoare, Esq., Barnett Hoare & Co., 62, Lombard Street, Barclay Bevan & Co., 54, Lombard Street, Messrs. Coutts & Co., 59, Strand; Messrs Drummonds, Charing Cross; Hanbury Taylor & Co., 60, Lombard Street, Hankeys, 7, Fenchurch Street; Messrs. Hoares, 37, Fleet Street; Messrs. Williams Deacon & Co., 20, Birchin Lane, and by the Secretary, Rev. J. M. Trew, 15, Parliament Street.

Recently published:
The African Slave Trade and its Remedy
by Sir T. Fowell Buxton, Bt.   Murray, Albemarle Street.

Just published:
An abridgement of the above, with an explanatory preface and appendix

Recently published:
Proceedings of the First Public Meeting of the Society for the Extinction of the Slave Trade, and for the Civilisation of Africa,
held at Exeter Hall on Monday, 1st June, 1840.
H.R.H. in the chair.

*   *   *   *   *

Shortly will be published by subscription price One Guinea
—A series of picturesque views on the River Quorra, the Niger of the Ancients,
by Commander William Allen, R.N.

*   *   *   *   *

After much delay, three iron steamers were built, launched, manned and commissioned:
Captain Henry Dundas Trotter commanded the *Albert*.
Commander William Allen the *Wilberforce*.
Commander Bird Allen the *Soudan*.

These together with Captain William Cook were empowered by the Government to make treaties with native chiefs for the abolition of the Slave Trade. They took with them Dr. Vögel, a botanist, Mr. Roscher, a mineralogist, Dr. Stanger, a geologist, and Mr. Fraser of the Zoological Society, a naturalist. A draftsman and a seedsman were added, while the Church Missionary Society was represented by The Rev. Frederick Schön and Mr. Samuel Crowther, with power to recommend the establishment of missions.

But, above all, Buxton himself was intent on the establishment of an agricultual settlement, by a new body called, "The Agricultural Association, owning land on the Niger banks, which it as hoped would gradually oust the Slave Trade by healthy competition, while making the native a self-respecting small farmer." An influential committee, among whose members Buxton's relatives were conspicuous, put up a fund of £4,000, and Buxton himself worked to the verge of a breakdown to get the expedition launched.

"I am like my old horse, John Bull," he told Lushington, "he does well enough for a lady to take a canter in the park, but give him a brush along the road or a burst across the fields, and he's done up for a month!"

However, he persevered, but from that moment everything went wrong.

As we look at it from this distance, it may well seem that Buxton had simply fulfilled his particular task, and that, in the general scheme of human affairs, it was the moment for him to have retired and allowed new men and new methods to carry on where he left off. Nothing of the sort, of course, would he have contemplated, and the result was that his immense personal influence, and the basic principles on which he had acted, now reacted against him. The lofty vision that had enabled him to brush aside much irrelevant detail now served him ill. Confronted with the climate of the Niger, he was deceived. Probably he believed Zachary Macaulay, who had survived residence there, that Sierra Leone and Fernando Po and the neighbouring districts were "salubrious." He had so often been told that this, that, and the other couldn't be done, on account of climate, or personal inclination, or tradition. But there are also signs that a new sort of person growing up in England resented his immense prestige, and disagreed with his methods. The Agricultural Association had a bad Press, and though loyal friends worked hard to organise meetings in its favour all over the country, a storm of abuse and misrepresentation broke over it; Chartists broke up the Norwich meeting, at Liverpool a practical shipowner had already embarked on a rival scheme. Perhaps the sponsorship of the Prince Consort was an ill omen, for already that early popularity Albert had enjoyed was waning, and his projects were going unaccountably wrong, and when he accompanied Buxton to bid God-speed to the Emancipation Fleet, where it lay moored in the Thames, a serious accident was only avoided by the most narrow margin. Perhaps the date (1st April) might have warned the superstitious. As it was, the Royal Party, with its attendant Ansons and Keppels, were involved in a collision, and from laughing about using the "life-saving" apparatus (a buoy with a phosphorus beacon) came very near to swimming for their lives. However, they escaped, and a fortnight later the expedition sailed, with its plucky crew of volunteer ratings and marines, working for double pay, its elaborate devices for "purifying the air" by passing it through chambers containing chloride of lime, its adjustable "centre board" type of keels and rudder footing to permit of river navigation.

Buxton had no doubts. His own personal courage served him ill. He had already said, months before: "What are miseries and mail coaches as compared with the vision, all sunshine, of a people, thousands, and hundreds of thousands, springing from bondage to liberty, from stripes and howling, to wages and singing, from being things to being men, from blindness to the Gospel. I feel very thankful, and am a happy man this night."

It was almost the last time. For, while his health declined, and his projects became entangled with the insistent demands of what proved to be the economic revolution of Free Trade, the three little ships, weeks and weeks behind schedule, handicapped by every freak of weather and mishap to their grotesque "scientific" machinery, staggered out to the sinister Niger, carrying Buxton's blessing, his quotations from Cowper and the 121st Psalm, his indomitable courage that might, in an earlier age, have made him a martyr or legendary hero.

The expedition, in fact, was not eight weeks late, but just fifty years too soon. In the nineties, Lugard (whose surgeon was Dr. Guy N. Mottram) with immense difficulty, shivering with fever and often abandoned by uncomprehending natives, carried out what might have been the ultimate project of Buxton's expedition. In 1841 there was nothing before such an attempt but plucky failure.

On the 20th August, 1841, while Buxton was recuperating with deer-stalking in Caithness, the three little ships entered the Nun branch of the river, observed the evidences of considerable local agriculture and trade and reached Aboh, where the chief Obi came on board in his scarlet uniform and scarlet trousers, and was treated to "some experiments with Smee's galvanic battery."

"The objects of the Expedition as well as each article of the treaty were then fully explained to him by an intelligent interpreter from Sierra Leone." He "formally concluded" it. This dark potentate, while by no means easy to convince, made the pertinent remark that, "if he abolished the Slave Trade, his people must have something to live by!" As he possessed twenty war canoes, armed with swivels and muskets, this could hardly be gainsaid, and the Commissioners in their ships, reinforced by a sailing schooner, left him with every feeling of confidence in his desire for legitimate commerce, and the settlement of missionaries.

The next journey was to Iddah (Ida on modern maps) where, although cultivation, including that of cotton, was considerable, and fine mountains were visible in the distance, the foreshore was low and swampy, and should have warned more experienced explorers. Although delighted with the scenery and prospects, those officers who went ashore, received an "unpleasant impression" of the inhabitants, while the Attah of Eggarah, in whose territory lay this town of 7,000 souls, was found, "much less intelligent and civilised than Obi." A treaty was also concluded here, and he appears to have signed it, in some unspecified way. Next come the ominous words: "On 4th September, fever of a most malignant character broke out on the *Albert*, and almost simultaneously on the other vessels."

With great courage, short-handed, and impeded by the nature of the channel, the ships pushed on to the point at which the Niger receives a stream, then called the Tchadda, as it was supposed to originate in Lake Chad, but is now known to be the Benue. While the highest hopes were entertained that, now the delta was passed, the climate would prove more propitious and the signs of regular agriculture were visible on all sides, the town of Adda was found to have been destroyed by the fierce, slave-trading Fulatahs.

Nothing daunted, the commissioners surveyed, and seem to have marked out and occupied the strip of land near Mount Palteh, which had been ceded

I

by the Attah for the model farm, that was the main object of the expedition. Not only foodstuffs, tropical grains, plantains and yams were being cultivated, cotton was grown, and "Mr. Schön observed a mallam or priest wearing a silk robe of native manufacture. The Commissioners felt that if a sufficiently protected trading station could be built at that point, fifty million people would be dependent on it." So far, the object of the Expedition had been attained and everything promised a favourable termination to the mission.

Out of the strip of territory, quoted by Mathieson as sixteen miles by four, 400 acres were leased for five years, at a penny per acre, to a coloured lessee who had travelled with the expedition, and he was left with two white, and several local assistants, and some stores, landed with difficulty, and the sailing schooner. The spot seems to have been where Lokoja is now marked.

By now the state of the personnel was such that, after discussion, the *Soudan* was sent down stream with the sick. The Commander, Lieutenant Fishbourne, the sole member of the ship's company able to stand, had to work her single-handed for the last few miles, and had H.M.S. *Dolphin* not met her, there is no telling if he would have reached Fernando Po. The *Wilberforce* was obliged to follow two days later, and finally the *Albert*, heading for Rabba, struggled as far as Eggah. At Gori, on the way, they found a flourishing market for cloth and iron tools and primitive milling was going on. Captain Trotter, finding some slaves in a canoe, held a formal trial, and liberated them, with the consent, so it is alleged, of the owner, and the son of the Attah who represented his father. At Budda, which the natives said had been a slave market, the proclamation against the trade had been made according to the treaty. At Eggah itself, however, slave traders said that the King of the Fulatahs at Rabba must give permission if the trade was to be stopped.

Here, 320 miles from the sea, the heroic leaders of the expedition, still believing that had they continued to Rabba they might have made some permanent settlement with the most powerful tribe yet encountered, were obliged to turn back. The geologist, Stanger, "having learned how to manage the engines from a scientific treatise on board" had to keep them going, while Dr. MacWilliam, besides tending the sufferers, worked the ship with the only white sailor remaining erect. Thus they reached Lokoja where Carr and his white assistants at the farm were equally ill, and had to be taken on board, the natives being left with the schooner. They had then appeared to have enlisted native help.

At Abo they obtained food and fuel, and a little further were thankful to see a British steamer, ploughing its way up stream to their assistance. It was the *Ethiope* of Liverpool, in which a Mr. Jamieson, none other than the great critic of Buxton's plan, had tried to penetrate the Niger country ten years previously. It was not a moment too soon. Such was the state of the *Albert's* company, that the *Ethiope's* men had to be put in charge to get her as far as Fernando Po, and eventually Ascension. Even then, true to British Naval traditions, and the fervour of Missionary enterprise, the only discussion was, how best to make another attempt.

"One of the officers," Schön reported, "is apparently dying; many are still suffering, and others, though free from fever, are in such a state of debility that they will not be able to do duty for a considerable time. . . . Nothing I have hitherto seen or felt can be compared with our present condition. . . . Yet, there was not one of those whom I attended in their sickness, and at their death, but who knew perfectly well that the climate of Africa was dangerous in the extreme . . . no expression of disappointment or regret did I ever hear; on the contrary they appeared in general to derive no small consolation from the conscious purity of their motives, and the goodness of the cause in which they had voluntarily embarked."

The matter was decided for them. The Expedition was recalled, with the proviso that one vessel should try to communicate with the model farm. Lieutenant Webb took the *Wilberforce* and seven volunteers, but chiefly manned by blacks, who, it was observed, did not suffer from fever. He reached Lokoja, though Carr, who had attempted to return with native canoes, was never seen again.

At the settlement, it was found that the Africans had reverted to a state in which they had committed all sorts of crimes, and were using whips to coerce the natives hired to work for them. Obi had turned hostile and the Attah had recommenced slave trading. The order for recall originated with the Government, which had supplied the ships, and released the naval personnel from their normal duties. Of the 145 white personnel, forty-three died of fever, and six from accident, which is about the same proportion as that suffered by Jamieson's Liverpool Expedition, nearly ten years earlier. Nine pounds of public money, paid for the "settlement," had to be written off, as the Commissioners found that a native chief's signature was not honoured by himself or anyone else at a short distance, a short time away from that at which he received his "present." It is now difficult to assess how far Buxton's heart was "broken," to use the conventional phrase, by sheer disappointment, just when his most cherished dreams seemed about to be realised, or how far the health he had willingly squandered on the negro cause would in any case have declined as he approached his sixtieth year. As the melancholy despatches trailed home in the sailing ships of that day, the *Memoirs* tell us, "He rarely spoke of the Expedition—to Captain Bird Allen's death he could scarcely allude at all; but his grave demeanour, his worn, pale face, the abstraction of his manner, the intense fervour of his supplications that God would 'pity poor Africa'—these showed too well the poignancy of his feelings."

"The blow, however, is tremendous," he wrote to his son. "There is no comfort to be found under it, save in the assurance that it is the will and the work of our merciful God."

The spring of 1842, while Lieutenant Webb was making the last journey to the Model Farm, was spent in such negotiations with the Government as might ensure an occasional visit to the spot, and it is evident that Buxton had the sympathy of ministers. He continued, however, to lose strength, and was unable to attend the midsummer meeting of the African Civilisation Society. Perhaps it was just as well, for although Lord John Russell, two Bishops, and an imposing array of titled and influential people made a strong platform, it was impossible to represent the Niger Expedition as having firmly established the kind of agricultural colony Buxton had in mind, and which might have proved a factor in eliminating the Slave Trade. He received every kind of assurance of support from his many friends and co-workers, even a donation of £500 with an offer of personal leadership of a new expedition from a Captain Bosanquet. The Committee of the Society, however, did not feel able to shoulder the responsibility of a renewed effort, and in January, 1843, he went to London to wind up the Society. "I feel as if I were going to attend the funeral of an old and dear friend," he wrote.

Then came, as sometimes comes at the end of a stormy and disappointing day, a gleam of sunshine.

He bought some land at Runton, a mile or two west of Cromer, along the same line of low, gravelly hills on which Northrepps stands, and here he devoted himself to planting what are to-day some of the most beautiful woods anywhere, naming the enclosures by the names of the places in Africa so dear to his heart. "Niger," "Fernando Po," and others. So far was he from despair, that when a friend said to him:

"Your plantations will some day be the pride of the country if England stands!"

"England stand!" he replied. "I will never believe that any country will fall which has abolished slavery as England has done!"

He was able to tell his son-in-law Johnston: "I am getting decidedly stronger and feel more like myself!" In fact he was happily reverting from the harassed Member of Parliament to the country gentleman he had been born and essentially was. Perhaps that was, after all, his natural role. He would never have admitted it, but the change of key, not only in the *Memoirs*, but in all the minor periodicals and reminiscences dealing with his life, directly the narration turns upon his rural pursuits, is unmistakable. What, for instance, has Sir George Stephen to say when, for a moment, he abandons the theme of African Slavery on which he was writing to Mrs. Beecher Stowe, in 1854: "In rapidity of perception Mr. Buxton excelled most men . . . he was, though charitably liberal, rarely deceived in his estimate of men. Largeness in every respect was his characteristic. . . . In stature gigantic; far exceeding the ordinary height of men; but he was also æsthetically large. . . . He appeared out of his element in trifles that to the average man seemed great. . . . The only matters of the kind in which he appeared to me to take personal interest were the points of a horse, or the make of a gun. . . .

"An instance of his playful self-indulgence in this way is worth mentioning: When he wanted to see me, he generally asked me to call on him, on my way to the City. On one of these occasions, being pressed for time, he ordered his horse, and we rode along the New Road together; we were arrested in our conversation by a gentleman passing us at a rapid pace, mounted on one of the handsomest ponies I ever saw. Mr. Buxton had but a glance of it, when turning to me he exclaimed: 'After him, Stephen, I must have that pony,' and we both put spurs to our horses in full chase. We were well mounted— Buxton was seldom otherwise—but the noise of our pursuit set the little animal on its mettle, and away we flew up Pentonville Hill with a dust and clatter that John Gilpin could not have rivalled, for the pony was clearly the master so far as his rider was concerned; it was a glorious burst; At Islington, I succeeded in overtaking him; I knew the horseman by sight, and told Mr. Buxton of my acquaintance with him, on which he dropt behind. 'The rascal may know me too; so strike a bargain without me, but get me a trial.'

" 'What's your figure, Sir?' I began.

" 'Figure, Sir,' replied the rider, without once looking at me, but chafing and panting ten times worse than his little elephant, 'a pretty figure you have made of me by your insolence;' and then, looking at me for the first time, driven almost to rage by my uncontrollable laughter, it proved to be no dealer, but an old acquaintance, though his Mackintosh cloak had been flying about him in a way that prevented immediate recognition.

" 'What the deuce do you mean by your folly ?   Can't you let a man ride along in peace ?'

" 'Impossible, on such a trotter as yours; I want him, so state your price.'

" 'Fifty guineas.'

" 'Pshaw, you are joking.'

" 'Not one farthing less, I gave it only last week, and were he not too much for me, you should not have him for a hundred.'

"By this time Mr. Buxton had joined us.

" 'Is all right ?'

" 'Yes, but I have said nothing about trial.   I will mount him for you!'

" 'Indeed you shan't.   I'll mount him myself!'

" 'You! why, you'll break his back!'

" 'He would carry us both for that matter,' and without further colloquy he exchanged horses with the owner, and inhumanly, as I told him, deposited his twenty stone of humanity on the back of a pony under thirteen hands, amidst the jeers and jokes of a crowd whom our dealing had gathered round. He was quite right in his judgment; the little animated castle trotted away with him as if he had been a feather-weight, though his long limbs nearly touched the ground, and his towering height almost concealed the animal from view. There was a ludicrous congruity, however, between horse and rider, for each was in his way a well-built tower of strength.   In ten minutes the trial was over. 'He will do exactly for Priscilla!' and going into the nearest shop he wrote a cheque for fifty guineas on the spot.   He did me the honour of naming his purchase after me."

The devoted Secretary of his later years, Nixon, whose task can never have been a light one, illumined as it was by bursts of great generosity, and frank admission of error on the part of his exacting master, also records the following anecdote that Buxton used to relate:

"Poor old Abraham was the finest horse I ever had in my life.   At the time when George IV was very unpopular, I was riding through St. James' Park, just as the King passed, surrounded by an immense mob.   The shouts and groans and yellings were terrific, and there I was wedged in among the multitude, in the midst of noises which might have frightened the most courageous animal. But my noble-spirited horse pricked up his ears, distended his nostrils, curved his neck, and stood immovable.   The next day came the Marquis of —— to endeavour to buy my horse.   I said I did not wish to sell him, that he was a great favourite of mine and perfectly suited to my purpose.   Nothing daunted, the Marquis held his ground, made me first one offer and then another, and at last told me that he was not endeavouring to buy the horse for himself, but was authorised to go as far as £500 for a friend.   This offer I still refused, when as a last resource, 'The fact, is, Mr. Buxton' said he, 'it is the King who has sent me to buy your horse, and I hope you will not refuse to sell to His Majesty.'   This took me rather aback, but I had made up my mind, so with very many apologies and regrets, and in the politest manner possible, I maintained my ground, and thus the matter ended.   What I meant, though I did not think it exactly civil to say so, was: 'You may tell His Majesty that I'm happy to hear he's so fond of a good horse, but so am I, and having got one, I mean to keep him!' "

He was indulgent to the begging-letter-writers with whom he was plagued. ". . . send him another sovereign; and as this is the seventh time he has promised never to apply to me again . . . I'll see his neck stretched before I send him another halfpenny! . . . not to put it too sharp," were his parting instructions. Nixon adds: "I hardly ever saw such affection towards little children . . . he could hardly make up his mind to turn them out, when they came to him in his study, without a present of sweetmeats or cakes, which he used often to hoard up for them!"

From time to time as the eighteen-forties wore on, he rallied, and it is hard to disconnect these happier periods with the outdoor life of Northrepps, and the life-giving air of the bluebell and bracken covered slopes of the Norfolk coast, or watching the village cricket team disporting itself. When the intervals of bodily weakness intervened he went to Bath at doctor's orders, but his spirits fell, though not so far as to rob him of his keen interest in the later phases of the anti-slavery campaign, which the Government of Sir Robert Peel was conducting by an increased vigilance of patrol of naval vessels off the slave coast, and a system of sugar duties designed to prevent influx of Brazilian and Cuban slave-grown sugar into this country. Both the Prince Consort and the Prime Minister wrote to him as to an equal, but he was, perhaps fortunately, prevented from taking an active part in the final debates on the methods of making formal, legal slavery impossible on earth. For one arm, and to some extent his memory were already affected by what must have been a stroke. However, his second son was the marry the fifth daughter of Samuel Gurney, and this gave him evident pleasure and confidence in the future. But his mainstay was that evangelical faith which he had learnt in childhood, of which he was one of the principal exponents in his generation, and which sustained him in his last moments. So, gradually failing, he passed some days in intermittent torpor and sleep, and on the 19th February, 1845, with his family gathered about him, in his home at Northrepps, he relinquished the gun and the whip that had laid low so many birds and subdued so many horses, and also the care of those dark-skinned remote millions of whom he had never seen half a dozen, but upon whose fate he, probably more than Clarkson, who first called attention to it, and Wilberforce who was their first parliamentary champion, had more effect than any other single individual.

At least, so the liberated negroes thought. For they came in thousands, in the parishes of the West Indian islands, the Veldt, and the African coast to bring to the Missionaries whom he had befriended, and whose status he had done so much to establish, their small gifts to add to the fund which the Prince Consort headed, and the results of which are to be seen to-day, in the memorial statue in the North Transept of Westminster Abbey, and the bust in the Cathedral of Sierra Leone. And for those of us who need convincing by monuments in stone that should be proof tangible enough. The inscription in the Abbey is as follows:

To the Memory of
SIR THOMAS FOWELL BUXTON, Bart.
Born 1 April, 1786, died 19 February, 1845.
Endued with a vigorous and capacious mind
Of dauntless courage and untiring energy,
He was early led by the love of God
To devote his powers to the good of man.

In Parliament he laboured
For the improvement of Prison Discipline
For the amendment of the Criminal Code,
For the suppression of Suttee in India,
For the Liberation of the Hottentots in South Africa,
and, above all,
For the emancipation of eight hundred thousand slaves
in the British Dominions.
In this last Righteous Enterprise
After ten years of arduous conflict,
A final Victory was given
To him and his co-adjutors,
"By the Good Hand of our God"
On the memorable 1st of August, 1834.

The energies of his mind were afterwards concentrated
on a great attempt
to extinguish the Slave Trade in Africa,
By the substitution of Agriculture and Commerce
And by the civilising influence of the Gospel.

Exhausted in mind and body
"He fell asleep"
Reposing in Faith on His Redeemer,
In the 59th year of his age.

This Monument is erected
By his Friends and fellow-labourers
At home and abroad
Assisted by the grateful contributions
Of many thousands of the African race.

But is there not something more ? What actually did Buxton do that goes deeper into the sum of human existence than the most elaborate monument that can be erected ?

Surely his real achievement was in setting an example that has been closely followed by British policy ever since, and in confirming a principle held to-day more completely and securely in his country than in any other save possibly the United States of America. It is not easy to find a single word to convey what it was, and it had so little "publicity value" that we may be astonished when we read contemporary history or biography to see how little his work is mentioned. It was overshadowed by the World War of his day, and the resounding domestic developments which immediately followed, and which stretched far beyond the end of his life.

He was an exponent of that devolution from above, carried out by public debate and representative majority vote which is so utterly unlike anything that happens in other countries. We have only to compare the change he wrought in the condition of negroes in the West Indies and the methods he employed to achieve it with the parallel process in neighbouring Hayti, or to read the horror which his notions of prison reform evoked in the Italy he visited.

His is the natural avenue of a privileged member of society sure of his place in the universe and his position in the world.   Himself a member of the owning and directing classes, he attacked the outmoded system from within, by parliamentary means.   He was trained from his early association with the Gurneys to substitute education and occupation for repression and tyranny, in the prison, the workship and finally, the plantation.   What practical wisdom and attention to detail he lavished on his projects becomes obvious to anyone who has stood in his study at Northrepps and seen the great maps of the "White N'gorra" and "Black N'gorra" in their cases on the wall.   It was not his fault that the sciences which have enabled others, a century later, to extinguish tropical diseases, were so little developed, nor that the knowledge of the geography of the district in which his great experiment was tried, was so little known.   How near the centre of his native tradition he stood, can be seen to-day, when the words, "liberation" and "liberator" appear every day in our newspapers.   It is therefore appropriate that by such a title he should be known.

THE END

INDEX